The Castle Lectures in Ethics

THE MORAL ECONOMY

WHY GOOD INCENTIVES
ARE NO SUBSTITUTE
FOR GOOD CITIZENS

SAMUEL BOWLES

Yale

UNIVERSITY PRESS

New Haven and London

Yale University Press books may be purchased in quantity for educa-
tional, business, or promotional use. For information, please e-mail
sales.press@yale.edu (U.S. office) or sales@yaleup.co.uk (U.K. office).

Set in Gotham and Adobe Garamond type by Newgen North America.
Printed in the United States of America.

ISBN 978-0-300-16380-3 (hardback : alk. paper)
Library of Congress Control Number: 2015956890

A catalogue record for this book is available from the British Library.

This paper meets the requirements of ANSI/NISO Z39.48-1992
(Permanence of Paper).
10 9 8 7 6 5 4 3 2 1

Parts of this book were given as the Castle Lectures in Yale's Program in Ethics, Politics, and Economics, delivered by Samuel Bowles at Yale University in 2010.

The Castle Lectures were endowed by Mr. John K. Castle. They honor his ancestor the Reverend James Pierpont, one of Yale's original founders. Given by established public figures, Castle Lectures are intended to promote reflection on the moral foundations of society and government and to enhance understanding of ethical issues facing individuals in our complex modern society.

To my teachers
Alexander Gerschenkron
&
Charles E. Lindblom

Political writers have established it as a maxim, that in contriving any system of government . . . every man ought to be supposed to be a *knave* and to have no other end, in all his actions, than his private interest. By this interest we must govern him, and, by means of it, make him, notwithstanding his insatiable avarice and ambition, cooperate to public good.

. . . It is, therefore, a just *political* maxim, that every man must be supposed a knave: Though at the same time, it appears somewhat strange, that a maxim should be true in *politics,* which is false in *fact.*

—David Hume, *Essays: Moral, Political, and Literary* (1742)

Contents

Preface

Any book in the making for almost thirty years is indebted to many helping hands. This one is based in part on my Castle Lectures at Yale University, where the critical commentary of Bryan Garsten, Phil Gorski, Laurie Santos, Steven Smith, and Chris Udry resulted in many improvements.

This is the second time that I have learned from Yale's social science faculty. The first was as a student in the precursor to the Ethics, Politics and Economics major, which sponsored my Castle lectures. My first debt, then, is to my mentor and inspiration in that program, Charles Lindblom, who pushed me to think analytically while trespassing the well-guarded boundaries of the academic disciplines. (The tradition that Lindblom championed at Yale is still evident in the disciplines of those who commented on my Castle Lectures: a historian, a psychologist, two political scientists, and an economist.) My subsequent study of economic history as a doctoral student with Alexander Gerschenkron at Harvard convinced me that the large questions about how societies might be better governed and how they evolve over time are worth asking and sometimes might have answers, though not necessarily the answers I was hoping for at the time.

During my work on this project since the late 1980s, my thinking on these issues has been shaped by the members of the September

Seminar past and present—Pranab Bardhan, Robert Brenner, Harry Brighouse, the late Gerald Cohen, Joshua Cohen, Jon Elster, Suresh Naidu, Philippe van Parijs, Adam Prezeworski, John Roemer, Rebecca Saxe, Seana Shiffrin, Hillel Steiner, Robert van der Veen, and Erik Olin Wright, and by the Santa Fe Institute Working Group on the Coevolution of Behavior and Institutions (since 1998)—Larry Blume, Robert Boyd, Herbert Gintis, and Peyton Young. Gintis' doctoral dissertation on how society shapes our preferences and my collaboration with him since has profoundly influenced my thinking on these issues.

Many of the ideas in the pages that follow were first tried out during the late 1990s in the Norms and Preferences Research Network headed by Robert Boyd and Gintis, whose members I thank, especially Colin Camerer, Martin Daly, Ernst Fehr, Simon Gaechter, Edward Glaeser, George Loewenstein, and the late Margo Wilson. For their comments on earlier drafts of this work and other contributions to the research, I would particularly like to thank (in addition to those already mentioned) Mahzarin Banaji, Yochai Benkler, Ragnhild Haugli Braaten, Juan Camilo Cardenas, Wendy Carlin, Ruth Grant, Joshua Greene, Jonathan Haidt, Kieran Healy, Bernd Irlenbusch, Rachel Kranton, Ugo Pagano, Elizabeth Phelps, Sandra Polanía-Reyes, Carlos Sickert Rodriguez, Daria Roithmayr, Paul Seabright, and, especially, Elisabeth Jean Wood.

My collaborators Sung-Ha Hwang and Sandra Polanía-Reyes are virtual coauthors of parts of the book; I am grateful to them for permission to use the results of our joint work. Chapter V draws upon work published in *Philosophy and Public Affairs* (2011), and I thank the journal for permission for its inclusion in this work. Chapters III and IV include material published jointly with Polanía-Reyes in the *Journal of Economic Literature* (2012).)

Susan Karr, Chiara Valentini, and, especially, Erica Benner helped me understand Niccolò Machiavelli, a figure who plays a leading and complicated role in the story I tell. Translations from the Italian of passages in Machiavelli's *Discourses* and *The Prince* are my own.

The Santa Fe Institute and the Certosa di Pontignano of the University of Siena have provided unsurpassed environments for research, reflection, and writing. Their staffs have made this research both enjoyable and possible, with particular thanks to Margaret Alexander, Joy Lecuyer, Barbara Kimbell, and Susan Macdonald of the Santa Fe Institute Library. I would also like to thank Nicole Villar Hernandez for assistance with the research, Davide Melcangi and Sai Madhurika Mamunuru, repectively, for creating the figures and the index, and the MacArthur Foundation, the Behavioral Sciences Program of the Santa Fe Institute, and the U.S. National Science Foundation for financial support. Finally, I am indebted to the late George Cowan and Adele Simmons for their abiding confidence in my research trajectory and for their support over the years.

In case you are wondering how such a little book could take so long to write, the short of it is that I had a lot to learn. Here is the story in brief. When I started working on the cultural effects of markets and incentives in the late 1980s, I found myself writing abstract models, which did not allow me to say anything about what had attracted me to the subject: the empirical challenges of designing better policies, institutions, and constitutions. I fell to doing models by default: available data were inadequate to test my hypotheses about people's ethical, intrinsic, and other noneconomic motivations and how they might be affected by the incentives, legal constraints, and the other instruments of public policy. There was even serious doubt—and not only among economists and biologists—whether such motives were common enough to warrant serious study.

This started to change during the 1990s. The Norms and Preferences Network (just mentioned) gave me the opportunity to conduct a series of behavioral experiments in cultures around the world (with Joseph Henrich and a large group of anthropologists and economists). I also avidly learned from the experiments of others (especially from Ernst Fehr, Simon Gaechter, Armin Falk, Urs Fischbacher and the Zurich school). The empirical outlines of what became Chapters III, IV, and V in this book were beginning to take shape.

Around the turn of the millennium, I took up what seemed to me the obvious next question: if, as the experiments appeared to show, people are more generous and civic minded than either economists or evolutionary biologists assumed, this posed a puzzle. Neither natural selection nor any of the then-prominent models of cultural evolution provided a ready answer to how this could have come about.

I began work on the archaeological, genetic, and ethnographic evidence relevant to the evolution of human social behavior. With Jung-Kyoo Choi, Astrid Hopfensitz, and Herbert Gintis, I developed models and computer simulations providing an account of the cultural and biological evolution of what Gintis and I called (in the title our 2011 book) *A Cooperative Species,* namely, humanity. The evidence made it clear that the experimental results were not anomalies: there are good genetic and cultural reasons to expect ethical and generous motives to be common in human populations.

It was time, then, to return to the challenge that had started me off and to see what implications this new empirical knowledge of human behavior might hold for the design of policies and institutions that would work well for people given to both self-interest and generosity, both moral action and amorality. And so I went back to work on the project I had set aside two decades earlier.

This short book is the result of that long journey.

The Problem with *Homo economicus*

Two and a half centuries ago, Jean-Jacques Rousseau invited readers of his *Social Contract* to consider "Laws as they might be" for "men as they are."[1] Aside from the gendered language, the phrase still resonates. We know that governing well requires an understanding of how people will respond to the laws, economic incentives, information, or moral appeals that make up a system of governance. And these responses will depend on the desires, objectives, habits, beliefs, and morals that motivate and constrain people's actions.

But what are we to understand by Rousseau's "men as they are"?

Enter economic man—*Homo economicus*. Among economists, jurists, and the policy makers influenced by their ideas, it is widely held today that in thinking about the design of public policy and legal systems, as well as about the organization of firms and other private organizations, we should assume that people—whether citizens, employees, business partners, or potential criminals—are entirely self-interested and amoral. Partly for this reason, material incentives are now deployed to motivate student learning, teacher effectiveness, weight loss, voting, smoking cessation, the switch from plastic grocery bags to reusable ones, fiduciary responsibility in financial management, and basic research. All are activities that, in the absence of economic incentives, might be motivated by intrinsic, ethical, or other noneconomic reasons.

Given this assumption's currency in legal, economic, and policy-making circles, it may seem odd that nobody really believes that people are entirely amoral and self-interested. Instead, the assumption has been advanced on grounds of prudence, not realism. Even Hume, at the end of the epigraph for this book, warns the reader that the maxim is "false in fact."

I hope to convince you that when it comes to designing laws, policies, and business organizations, it is anything but prudent to let *Homo economicus* be the behavioral model of the citizen, the employee, the student, or the borrower. There are two reasons. First, the policies that follow from this paradigm sometimes make the assumption of universal amoral selfishness more nearly true than it might otherwise be: people sometimes act in more self-interested ways in the presence of incentives than in their absence. Second, fines, rewards, and other material inducements often do not work very well. No matter how cleverly designed to harness the avarice of <u>knaves</u> (as Hume put it), incentives cannot alone provide the foundations of good governance.

If I am right, then an erosion of the ethical and other social motivations essential to good government could be an unintended cultural consequence of policies that economists have favored, including more extensive and better-defined private property rights, enhanced market competition, and the greater use of monetary incentives to guide individual behavior.

I show that these and other policies advocated as necessary to the functioning of a market economy may also promote self-interest and undermine the means by which a society sustains a robust civic culture of cooperative and generous citizens. They may even compromise the social norms essential to the workings of markets themselves. Included among the cultural casualties of this so-called crowding-out process are such workaday virtues as truthfully reporting one's assets and liabilities when seeking a loan, keeping one's word, and working hard even when nobody is looking. Markets and other economic institutions do not work well where these and other norms are absent or compromised. Even more than in the past, high-performance knowledge-based economies today require the cultural underpinnings of these and other social norms. Among these is the assurance that a handshake is indeed a handshake; where one doubts this, mutual gains from exchange may be limited by distrust.

.The paradoxical idea that policies considered necessary by economists for "perfecting" markets might make them work less well applies beyond markets. A people's civic-mindedness, their intrinsic desire to uphold social norms, may be squandered as a result of these policies, perhaps irreversibly, shrinking the space for better-designed policies in the future. Thus, while some economists imagined that in a distant past *Homo economicus* invented markets, it could have been the other way around: the proliferation of amoral self-interest might be one of the consequences of living in the kind of society that economists idealized.

The problem facing the policy maker or constitution writer is this: incentives and constraints are essential to any system of governance. But when designed as if "men as they are" resemble *Homo economicus,* incentives might backfire if they foster the very self-interest that they were designed to harness in the service of the public good. The problem would not arise if *Homo economicus* were indeed an accurate description of "men as they are." In that case there would be nothing to crowd out. But over the past two decades, behavioral experiments (as we see in chapters III, IV, and V) have provided hard evidence that ethical and other-regarding motives are common in virtually all human populations. The experiments show that these motives are sometimes crowded out by policies and incentives that appeal to material self-interest. Here is an example.

In Haifa, at six day care centers, a fine was imposed on parents who were late in picking up their children at the end of the day. It did not work. Parents responded to the fine by doubling the fraction of time they arrived late.[2] After twelve weeks, the fine was revoked, but the parents' enhanced tardiness persisted. (Their lateness, compared to that of a control group without the fine, is shown in figure 1.1.)

The counterproductive result of imposing these fines suggests a kind of negative synergy between economic incentives and moral behavior. Placing a price on lateness, as if putting it up for sale, seems

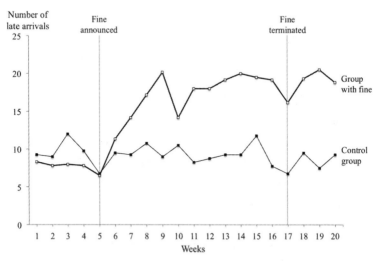

Figure 1.1. The effect of a fine for lateness in Haifa's day care centers (Data from Gneezy and Rustichini 2000.)

to have undermined the parents' sense of ethical obligation to avoid inconveniencing the teachers, leading them to think of lateness as just another commodity they could purchase.

I do not doubt that had the fine been sufficiently high, the parents would have responded differently. But putting a price on everything might not be a good idea, even if this could be done and the right prices could be found (both very large ifs, as we will see).

Even the sight of money and the discussion of coins (rather than nonmonetary objects), in a recent experiment, induced children to later behave in less prosocial ways and to be less helpful toward others in their ordinary interactions.[3]

In another study, kids less than two years old avidly helped an adult retrieve an out-of-reach object in the absence of rewards. But after they were rewarded with a toy for helping the adult, the helping rate fell off by 40 percent. Felix Warneken and Michael Tomasello, the authors of the study, conclude: "Children have an initial inclination to help, but extrinsic rewards may diminish it. Socialization practices can thus build on these tendencies, working in concert rather than in conflict with children's natural predisposition to act altruistically."[4]

This might be good advice for public policy too.

How should policy makers respond to the realization that while both economic incentives and ethical and other-regarding motives are necessary for effective policy, the former may diminish the latter? If both sources of motivation are taken into account, then policy makers may reasonably consider giving economic incentives a more limited role in their policy packages. If incentives undermine social values, yet incentives and social values are both needed, then it would seem to follow that one ought to make less use of incentives than one would in the absence of this crowding-out problem.

Similar reasoning might lead policy makers to restrict the role of markets in allocating resources, and to favor instead a larger role for governments or informal nonmarket organizations. Doing so would be consistent with Michael Sandel's main point in *What Money Can't Buy: The Moral Limits of Markets:* "Putting a price on every human activity erodes certain moral and civic goods worth caring about."[5] Sandel makes a convincing case for a public debate on "where markets serve the public good and where they don't belong." Debra Satz provides political reasons for this in *Why Some Things Should Not be For Sale,* advancing the view that restricting some markets is essential to sustaining the political equality that is fundamental to a democratic culture and political system.[6] My concern is less with the extent of markets (as opposed to governments or other systems of allocation) than with the sometimes problematic use of economic incentives, whether in markets, firms, or public policy. The evidence that incentives may crowd out ethical and generous motives is complementary to the reasoning of Sandel and Satz.

But a good case can also be made that incentives per se are not entirely to blame. Crowding out may reflect fundamental problems stemming from the relationship between the person implementing the incentive and its target. The incentives built into an employer's compensation and supervision policies, for example, may tell the employee that the employer is greedy or controlling, or does not trust the employee. Or the incentive may inadvertently convey the wrong message—such as, in Haifa, "It's okay to be late as long as you pay for it."

If this is the case, then the policy maker can do better than limit the role of incentives and markets. She may be able to turn crowding out on its head. In a new policy paradigm based on this reasoning, the conventional policy instruments—incentives and punishments—

might enhance rather than undermine the force of citizens' ethical or other-regarding motives, which in turn might contribute to the effectiveness of the legal constraints and material inducements. The idea that laws and morals might be synergistic goes back at least to Horace two millennia ago: "What is the point of dismal lamentations if guilt is not checked by punishment? What use are laws, vain as they are without morals?" (*Odes,* book 3, no. 24).[7] For Horace, both laws and morals, working in tandem, are essential to a well-ordered society.

I wish to advance here this policy paradigm of synergy between incentives and constraints, on the one hand, and ethical and other-regarding motivations, on the other. Before Horace, the ancient Athenian assembly devised the rudiments of such a paradigm. And I explain in the last chapter why things might have turned out quite differently in Haifa had its example been followed.

A new policy paradigm would be based on an empirically grounded view of "men as they are." Replacing *Homo economicus* would be a place to start. But a complementary part of such a paradigm would incorporate new evidence on cognitive processes that account for the actions we take. The work of Richard Thaler, Cass Sunstein, Daniel Kahneman, Amos Tversky, and others has made it clear that people are not nearly as farsighted, calculating, and consistent in their decision making as economists have generally assumed.[8] Instead, we are biased toward the status quo and inconsistent in choosing among alternatives occurring at different times in the future.

Even after being instructed in how to avoid these biases, we insist on making what economists consider computational mistakes. For example, in taking actions in an uncertain situation, people treat a positive probability that something may occur, *no matter how small,* as very different from knowing for sure that it will not happen.

Kahneman, a psychologist honored by economists as a Nobel laureate in their own discipline, concluded, "People are myopic in their decisions, may lack skill in predicting their future tastes, and can be led to erroneous choices by fallible memory and incorrect evaluation of past experiences."[9]

Economists, who have placed the act of choosing at the center of all human activity, have now discovered, in short, that people are not very good choosers.

Thaler, Sunstein, Kahneman, and others have drawn out the public-policy implications of the new evidence on cognitive processing. In part for this reason, in the pages that follow I am less concerned with how we make decisions than with what we value when we make decisions, how incentives and other aspects of public policy may shape what we value, and why this suggests there should be changes in how we make policy.

I will begin by explaining what the *Homo economicus*–based policy paradigm is and recounting the strange story of how its practitioners came to be either unaware or unconcerned that the policies it favored might crowd out ethical and other social motivations.

| |

A Constitution for Knaves

Having noticed a suspicious bunching of sick call-ins on Mondays and Fridays, the Boston fire commissioner on December 1, 2001, ended the fire department's policy of unlimited paid sick days. In its stead, he imposed a limit of fifteen sick days; firemen exceeding that limit would have their pay docked. Here is how the firemen responded: the number calling in sick on Christmas and New Year's Day increased tenfold over the previous year.

The fire commissioner retaliated by canceling the firemen's holiday bonus checks.[1] The firemen were unimpressed: during the next year, they claimed 13,431 sick days, up from 6,432 a year earlier.[2] Many firemen, apparently insulted by the new system, abused it or abandoned their previous ethic of serving the public even when injured or not feeling well.

I admit to having some sympathy for the commissioner. I once offered my teenage kids a price list for household chores as a way of topping up their modest weekly allowance. In response, they simply stopped doing the housework that they had once more or less happily done without incentives.

The commissioner's difficulties and my failed experiment in home economics are far from exceptional. As we have already seen, imposing explicit economic incentives and constraints to induce people to act in socially responsible ways is sometimes ineffective or even, as Boston's fire commissioner discovered, counterproductive. Is this a problem? My hunch is that a larger penalty would have worked. The firemen's massive sick call-ins on Christmas and New Year's Day do not mean they had lost interest in money. Had the fire commissioner imposed a heavier penalty, the firemen would surely have shaped up, even if their anger and distrust would, as a result, have eclipsed their sense of duty. Economic interest would have substituted for pride in serving the public.

• But these constraints and incentives may have limits. Heavy fines or more draconian punishments might have deterred phony call-ins, but would they have motivated the subtler and more immeasurable aspects of a fireman's professionalism and bravery? Even if extreme penalties could do the job, a liberal society might find them repugnant. Instead of letting penalties substitute for the firemen's sense of duty, the commissioner might have looked for policies that would affirm and enhance their civic pride.

Whether you think the firemen's response to the commissioner's incentives is a problem lines you up on one or the other side of some venerable and unresolved questions in the philosophy of governance. These are, roughly, whether a constitution for knaves could possibly work, and if so, would it be a good idea to govern according to one. I will begin addressing these questions by telling the remarkable story of how the constitution-for-knaves idea came about and the radical turn it took in the hands of the economists who transformed the market into a morality-free zone, beyond the reach of the ethical judgments we routinely make in the family, the polity, and the neighborhood.[3]

Machiavelli's Republic *- social custom (good)*

Political philosophers from Aristotle to Thomas Aquinas, Jean-Jacques Rousseau, and Edmund Burke recognized the cultivation of civic virtue not only as an indicator of good government but also as its essential foundation. "Legislators make the citizens good by inculcating habits in them," Aristotle wrote in the *Ethics*. "It is in this that a good constitution differs from a bad one."[4] A century earlier, Confucius had provided advice about how this might be done, and about the pitfalls to be avoided: "Guide them with government orders, regulate them with penalties, and the people will seek to evade the law and be without shame. Guide them with virtue, regulate them with ritual, and they will have a sense of shame and become upright."[5]

But through a twenty-first-century lens, reference to virtue and shame as the basis of a well-ordered society appears quaint, and to some even pernicious. Friedrich Hayek celebrated markets as "a social system which does not depend for its functioning on . . . all men becoming better than they now are, but which makes use of men in all their given variety and complexity, sometimes good and sometimes bad."[6] In the aftermath of the stock market crash of 1987, the *New York Times* headlined an editorial "Ban Greed? No: Harness It," which continued: "Perhaps the most important idea here is the need to distinguish between motive and consequence. Derivative securities attract the greedy the way raw meat attracts piranhas. But so what? Private greed can lead to public good. The sensible goal for securities regulation is to channel selfish behavior, not thwart it."[7] An economics Nobel laureate, James Buchanan, illustrated how this might work, describing a visit to a farm stand near his home in Blacksburg, Virginia: "I do not know the fruit salesman personally, and I have no particular interest in his well-being. He reciprocates this attitude. I do not know, and have no need to know, whether he is in the direst poverty, extremely wealthy, or somewhere in between . . . Yet the two of us are able to . . . transact exchanges efficiently because both parties agree on the property rights relevant to them."[8]

Jurists paralleled economists in this way of thinking. "If you want to know the law and nothing else," Oliver Wendell Holmes Jr. told students in 1897 (and every entering law school class since has been instructed in the same belief), "you must look at it as a bad man, who cares only for the material consequences which such knowledge enables him to predict, not as a good one who finds his reasons for conduct, whether inside the law or outside it in the vaguer sanctions of conscience . . . The duty to keep a contract at common law means a prediction that you must pay damages if you do not keep it—and nothing else."[9] Hayek attributed a similar but more nuanced view to Adam Smith: "There can be little doubt . . . that Smith's chief concern was not so much with what man might occasionally achieve when he was at his best, but that he should have as little opportunity as possible to do harm when he was at his worst."[10]

The long road from Aristotle's Legislator inculcating good habits in citizens to a system of economic governance and law for "bad men" began in the sixteenth century with Niccolò Machiavelli. Like Aristotle, he was concerned about social customs that would ward off what he termed "corruption," but he gave rather different advice, in a passage anticipating Hume's maxim on knaves (in the epigraph to this book) by more than two centuries: "Anyone who would found a republic and order its laws must assume that all men are wicked [and] . . . never act well except through necessity . . . It is said that hunger and poverty make them industrious, laws make them good."[11] Machiavelli's "laws make them good" might sound a bit like

Aristotle's Legislator "inculcating habits" in the public. But here, as with his "all men are wicked," Machiavelli uses "good" (*buoni*) and "wicked" (*rei*) to describe actions, not aspects of character.

The political philosopher Leo Strauss traced the genesis of this thinking among twentieth-century economists and others to the sixteenth-century Florentine: "Economism is Machiavellianism come of age."[12] But while the origins of what Strauss termed "economism" can indeed be found in his writings, Machiavelli, like Aristotle but unlike many modern economists, did not imagine that good governance was possible in a self-interested ("corrupt") citizenry: "Neither laws nor orders can be found that are enough to check a universal corruption. For as good customs have the need for laws to maintain themselves, so do laws have the need for good customs so as to be observed."[13]

For Machiavelli, laws have two functions: providing incentives and constraints to harness self-interest to public ends, and at the same time maintaining the good customs on which the effectiveness of the laws depends: "Good examples [of *virtù*] are born of good education [which is] born of good laws."[14] Machiavelli thus endorsed exactly the synergistic policy paradigm that I advance in the closing chapters, in which good laws and good customs are complements rather than substitutes.

Nonetheless for Machiavelli, government's task was preeminently to induce citizens motivated by the "natural and ordinary humors" to act as if they were good. Machiavelli makes clear, especially in *The Discourses on Livy,* that it is not the morality of its citizens that ensures that a republic will be well governed, but rather the capacity of a statesman to "order its laws."[15] Compared to Italy, he wrote, Spain and France were well governed; but this was a distinction deriving "not much from the goodness of the people, which is for the most part lacking, . . . but from the way that these kingdom are ordered." "France," he continued, was "a kingdom moderated more by laws than any that has been known in our times."[16]

The message was unmistakable: citizens of ordinary predispositions and desires could nonetheless be well governed if their behavior was "moderated . . . by laws." The new idea here was that the quality of the governance of a society was not any simple aggregate of the quality of its citizens. Good governance was less a matter of a society being composed of good citizens than of how social institutions ordered interactions among citizens.

Modern day physical scientists might rephrase Machiavelli to say that the quality of the governance of a society is an emergent property of the polity, that is, a property of the whole that cannot be directly inferred from the characteristics of the citizens making it up. To Machiavelli, good government, then, was an emergent property of a well-ordered society.

Two centuries later, a radical version of this idea was the key message of Bernard Mandeville's scandalous *The Fable of the Bees*. In it, the eccentric Dutch doctor turned Londoner held that for the maintaining of social order, virtue was dispensable, even pernicious. Mandeville's hive thrived on licentious greed and invidious competition. But when the bees turned virtuous, collapse and disorder ensued. (Mandeville could not have known that members of the genus *Apis,* among the most cooperative of all species, are genetically programmed not to compete.) Mandeville's insight that by dampening the demand for goods, the virtue of frugality might be a source of economic collapse is thought by some to be a precursor to the paradox of thrift, which is the foundation of Keynesian economics. The 1714 edition of his *Fable* announced in its subtitle that the work contained "several discourses to demonstrate that human frailties . . . may be turn'd to the advantage of civil society, and made to supply the place of moral virtues," with the result, wrote Mandeville, that "the worst of all the multitude did something for the common good."[17]

In case the reader might fail to decipher the lesson of the *Fable,* Mandeville explained in a prose commentary that: "Hunger, Thirst and Nakedness are the first Tyrants that force us to stir; afterwards our Pride, Sloth, Sensuality and Fickleness are the great Patrons that promote all Arts and Sciences, Trades, Handicrafts and Callings; while the great Taskmasters Necessity, Avarice, Envy and Ambition . . . keep the Members of the Society to their labour, and make them submit, most of them cheerfully, to the Drudgery of their Station; Kings and Princes not excepted."[18] To Mandeville, the benign consequences of what Machiavelli called the "ordinary humors" is not a natural fact about human society. Just as Machiavelli saw the foundation of good government in the human capacity to order the laws, for Mandeville it was "the dextrous Management of a skilfull Politician" that allowed the "Private Vices" to be "turned into Publick Benefits."[19]

* In contrast to the Aristotelian view that good laws make good citizens, Mandeville's *Fable* suggested that the right institutions might harness shabby motives to elevated ends. It was left to Adam Smith to explain how this improbable alchemy might be accomplished, and it comes in his famous description of the motivation of the businessman, the consumer, the farmer: "He intends only his own gain, and he is in this, as in many other cases, led by an invisible hand to promote an end which was no part of his intention. Nor is it always worse for the society that it was no part of it. By pursuing his own interest he frequently promotes that of the society more effectually than when he really intends to promote it."[20] Competitive markets and secure, well-defined property rights, Smith explained,

would order a society so that the invisible hand could do its magic: "It is not from the benevolence of the butcher, the brewer, or the baker that we expect our dinner, but from their regard to their own interest."[21]

Thus, under the right institutions, elevated consequences may follow from ordinary motives.

A Constitution for Knaves

Attention turned to the design of institutions that might accomplish this. In his *Essays: Moral, Political, and Literary* (1742), David Hume had recommended the following "maxim": "In contriving any system of government . . . every man ought to be supposed to be a *knave* and to have no other end, in all his actions, than private interest. By this interest we must govern him, and, by means of it, make him, notwithstanding his insatiable avarice and ambition, cooperate to public good."[22] In a similar spirit, for the design of public policy Jeremy Bentham offered his *"Duty and Interest* junction principle: Make it each man's *interest* to observe . . . that conduct which it is his *duty* to observe."[23] In his *Introduction to the Principles of Morals and Legislation,* the first text of what we now call public economics, Bentham laid out the public policy implications of Hume's maxim.

But while harnessing knaves was their leitmotif, these and other classical economists did not believe that economic actors and citizens were indeed amoral. Quite the contrary.

Hume pioneered the study of the evolution of social norms; and in the sentence immediately following the passage about knaves quoted above, he mused that it is "strange that a maxim should be true in politics which is false in fact," Smith, in his *Theory of Moral Sentiments,* held that "How selfish soever man may be supposed, there are evidently some principles in his nature that interest him in the fortunes of others, and render their happiness necessary to him, though he derives nothing from it except the pleasure of seeing it."[24] In practice, the policies advocated by the classical writers did not overlook appeals to ethical and other-regarding motives. Bentham, as we will see, believed that punishments should be "moral lessons."

The same tension between the assumption of unmitigated self-interest and the empirical reality of more complex and elevated human motivations did not seem to trouble the twentieth-century legal thinkers who took up the *Homo economicus* paradigm. Just a few lines before directing law students' attention to the "bad man," Holmes insisted that "the law is the witness and external deposit of our moral life."[25] Legal practice today, like the classical writers' policies, recognizes a broad range of social dispositions rather than simply the presumed bad man's self-interest. Market regulation, for example, combines fines for violations with requirements for public disclosure of the wrongs done, in order to shame the blameworthy.

Even Machiavelli introduced the idea of corrupt citizens, quoting a widespread expression of the time—"*It is said that* all men are wicked"—as a prudent assumption, not as evidence of a malign human nature. In his *Discourses,* Machiavelli rejected this assumption on empirical grounds: "Our reasonings are about those peoples where corruption is not very widespread and there is more of the good than of the rotten," adding, "Very rarely do men know how to be completely bad or completely good."[26] Aristotle had much worse things to say in this regard. "Most men are rather bad than good and the slaves of gain . . . as a rule men do wrong whenever they can."[27]

Thus the appeal of the constitution for knaves was not that citizens were in fact knaves. Rather, it was, first, that the pursuit of self-interest had come to be seen as a benign or at least harmless activity compared with other, more disruptive "passions," such as religious fervor or the pursuit of power; and second, that as an empirical matter the virtues alone provided an insufficient basis for good government on the scale of the national state.

In the Middle Ages, avarice was considered to be among the most mortal of the seven deadly sins, a view that became more widespread with the expansion of commercial activity after the twelfth century.[28] So it is surprising that self-interest would eventually be accepted as a respectable motive, and even more surprising that this change owed little to the rise of economics, at least at first. The year before Adam Smith wrote about how the self-interest of the butcher, the brewer, and the baker would put dinner on our table, James Boswell's Dr. Johnson gave *Homo economicus* a different endorsement: "There are few ways in which a man can be more innocently employed than in getting money."[29]

Smith's passage above is widely cited as one of his few references to the invisible hand. But it should be remembered too for advancing the new idea that motives other than self-interest could be pernicious: "By pursuing his own interest he frequently promotes that of the society more effectually than when he really intends to promote it."

It was the shadow of war and disorder that made self-interest an acceptable basis of good government. During the seventeenth century, wars accounted for a larger share of European mortality than in any century for which we have records, including what Raymond Aron called "the century of total war," recently ended. Writing after a decade of warfare between English parliamentarians and royalists, Hobbes (in 1651) sought to determine "the Passions that encline men to Peace" and found them in "Feare of Death; Desire of such things as are necessary to commodious living; and a Hope by their Industry to obtain them."[30] Knaves might be preferable to saints.

The second appeal of the constitution-for-knaves approach was more directly related to Machiavelli's work and to the practical turn in political theory that he advocated. "It seems more appropriate to go the reality of things rather than how we might imagine them," he wrote. "There are many imagined republics and principalities that have never been seen nor known to exist in reality."[31] A century and a half later, Baruch Spinoza opened his *Tractatus Politicus* with: "No men are . . . less fit to govern . . . than theorists or philosophers . . . [who] sing the praises of a human nature nowhere to be found, [who] . . . rail at the sort which actually exist [and] conceive of men not as they are but as they would like them to be."[32] A generation after Spinoza, Mandeville introduced his *Fable* with virtually identical language.

But it was more than realism about human motives that recommended the retreat from virtue as the sine qua non of good government. If the "others" with whom we would seek to govern were our kin, neighbors, or friends, then our concern for their well-being and our desire to avoid social sanction or retaliation for violating social norms might induce us to act in ways that would take account of their interests and contribute to good governance. But with the growth of cities and the consolidation of the nation-state, the metaphor of the polity as a family or even a lineage became untenable. The scope of governance had expanded too much. With the increasing size of nations and the reach of markets, individuals interacted not with a few dozen familiars but with hundreds of strangers, and indirectly with millions.

The new policy paradigm was a response to the concern that when large numbers of strangers interact, ethical and other-regarding motives would be an insufficient basis for good government, which therefore would need to adopt a system of constraints and incentives to supplement the civic virtues. It was the insufficiency of the civic virtues, not their absence or irrelevance, that worried Machiavelli. The classical economists who shaped the new policy paradigm knew that no economy or social system could function well in their absence. Even the scandalous Mandeville reassured his readers on this point: "I lay it down as a first Principle, that in all Societies, great or small it is the Duty of every Member of it to be good; that Virtue ought to be encouraged, Vice discountenanced, the Laws obey'd and the Transgressors punished."[33]

Similarly, the "natural liberty" that Smith endorsed was constrained by morality. His famous line "Every man . . . is left perfectly free to pursue his own interest in his own way" was conditioned in that very sentence by the proviso "as long as he does not violate the laws of justice." Justice, he explained, required "every member of the society [to be protected] from the injustice or oppression of every other member of it."[34] Mandeville expressed the very same idea memorably, comparing human proclivities to the unruly growth of an untended grapevine: "So Vice is beneficial found, when it's by justice lopt and bound."[35]

The classical economists were thus quite aware that what later came to be called *Homo economicus* was a simplification, one that differed from what they knew about human behavior, but one that would clarify, among other things, how policies that altered economic incentives would affect behavior. Here is John Stuart Mill, among the last of the classical economists, laying down boundaries and key assumptions of economics that remained with us until very recently: "[Political economy] does not treat of the whole of man's nature . . . It is concerned with him solely as a being who desires to possess wealth . . . It predicts only such . . . phenomena . . . as take place in consequence of the pursuit of wealth. It makes entire abstraction of every other human passion or motive."[36] He termed this "an arbitrary definition of man."

The advent of the neoclassical school of economics in the late nineteenth century did not change the status of self-interest as a handy but empirically false abstraction. F. Y. Edgeworth, a founder of the neoclassical paradigm, expressed this view in his *Mathematical Psychics:* "The first principle of economics is that every agent is actuated only by self-interest."[37] But in the same passage he recognized as a fact that "the happiness of others as compared by the agent with his own, neither counts for nothing, nor yet 'counts for one.'"

But like Mill, Edgeworth held that political economy could study the effects of incentives that appeal to the wealth-maximizing side of individuals without reference to the other motives that they both fully recognized but took to be beyond the purview of the discipline.

Separability of the Moral Sentiments and Material Interests

What the classical economists (and most economists since) missed is the possibility that moral and other prosocial behavior would be affected—perhaps adversely—by incentive-based policies designed to harness self-interest. "Why should it be," Kenneth Arrow asked in his review of Richard Titmuss's *The Gift Relationship: From Human Blood to Social Policy,* "that the creation of a market for blood would decrease the altruism embodied in giving blood?"[38] Until recently, most economists have been sure enough of the answer that they have not bothered to reply. But to Arrow it was "really an empirical question, not a matter of first principles."

To most economists, however, the unspoken first principle was that incentives and morals are additively separable, a term from mathematics meaning that the effects of variations in the one did not depend on the level of the other. When two things are additively separable, they are neither synergistic—each contributing positively to the effect of the other, like a duet being better than the separate parts—nor the opposite.

I return to this separability assumption in subsequent chapters. You have already seen where it can go wrong. The firemen's sense of duty toward the citizens of Boston was not separable from their self-interested regard for their own pay: a policy addressed to the latter appears to have diminished the former. The whole in this case was less than the sum of the parts. It is exactly this possibility that the self-interest-based policy paradigm overlooked.

Separability is hardly an everyday word, so it is worth pausing to consider an example. Amy Wrzesniewski, Barry Schwartz, and their coauthors studied the motives that led young men and women to attend the U.S. Army's academy at West Point.[39] They used questionnaires administered by the institution to nine annual cohorts of incoming cadets to assess whether an individual had sought admission for instrumental motives ("to get a better job," the "overall reputation of West Point" presumably being seen as a plus on one's résumé) or intrinsic motives ("desire to be an Army officer," "personal development"). They then followed the 11,320 cadets for a decade after graduation to see whether these motives for admission correlated with later success.

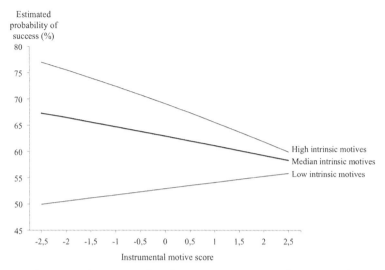

Figure 2.1. Instrumental and intrinsic motives as substitutes in the postgraduation performance of West Point cadets *The measure of success on the vertical axis is the estimated probability that a cadet will become a commissioned officer. Thus, each point on a particular line refers to the expected success probability for a cadet with the instrumental motivation score given by the horizontal axis and the intrinsic motivation score given by the label for the line. The instrumental motive score measures self-interested reasons for attending West Point. The intrinsic motive score measures the intrinsic motives mentioned in the text. High scores on this factor refer to those at the ninety-fifth percentile; low scores refer to those at the fifth percentile. (Data from Wrzesniewski et al. 2014.)*

Figure 2.1 presents reports of how instrumental motives were statistically associated with the probability of becoming a commissioned officer (one of the measures of success) for cadets with high intrinsic motives for attending West Point, median intrinsic motives, and low intrinsic motives. What do the data show?

First, notice that for those with a mean level of instrumental motives (the zero on the horizontal axis) having strong intrinsic motives is associated with a substantially increased likelihood of making commission (the line for high intrinsic motivation indicates greater success in becoming a commissioned officer). Second, for those with very low intrinsic motives (the bottom, upward-sloping line), stronger instrumental motives were also associated with an enhanced likelihood of making commission.

But the big news is the third observation: for cadets with median or high intrinsic motives (the two downward-sloping lines), having strong instrumental motives was associated with worse performance. Intrinsic and instrumental motives were not additively separable, they were substitutes: more of one diminished the positive effect of the other.

How might the military academy use this information to train officers? If it believed that its pool of potential recruits largely lacked intrinsic motives, it would take the bottom line in the figure as its guide. As a result, it would appeal to their instrumental motives, stressing the job opportunities in the armed forces and the value of West Point's reputation in getting jobs outside the military. But if it knew (correctly) that many cadets are highly idealistic young men and women wishing to serve their nation, it would be guided by the two downward sloping lines, and downplay the appeal to instrumental motives.

Economists have routinely either made the first assumption — that intrinsic motives are absent — or, if they recognized motives other than self-interest, assumed (for the most part unwittingly) that the two sets of motives were separable. But if they were really separable, all three lines in the figure would be upward rising and parallel.

The implicit assumption of separability has led economists to ignore two important possibilities: first, the use of incentives to harness self-interest to the public good might attenuate civic virtue or its motivational salience, and second, there might be conditions under which ethical and other-regarding concerns can jointly flourish and synergistically promote societal outcomes.

Markets as Morality-Free Zones

The broad (though for the most part implicit) acceptance of separability meant that assumptions about economic behavior did not have to be squared with facts and observations about human psychology. Since the late eighteenth century, economists, political theorists, and constitutional thinkers have embraced Hume's maxim and have taken *Homo economicus* as their working assumption about behavior. Partly for this reason, competitive markets, well-defined property rights, and efficient and (since the twentieth century) democratically accountable states are seen as the critical ingredients of governance. Good institutions displaced good citizens as the sine qua non of good government. In the economy, prices would do the work of morals.

From there, it was a short step to thinking that while ethical reasoning and concern for others should inform one's actions as a family member or citizen, the same did not go for shopping or making a living. Lewis Carroll's Alice had taken the economists' message to heart. When the Duchess exclaimed, "Oh, 'tis love, 'tis love makes the world go round," Alice whispered, "Somebody said that it's done by everyone minding their own business."[40]

How could people minding their own business take the place of love? This was the classical constitutional challenge posed by Bentham, Hume, Smith, and others, and it still constitutes the holy grail motivating policy design. The quest is to find laws and other public policies that will at once facilitate peoples' private pursuit of their own ends, yet also induce them to take adequate account of the effects of their actions on others.

In economic language, this can be done if each actor internalizes the entire costs and benefits of an action, including the effects on others, rather than taking account merely of one's private benefits and costs, that is, those that affect one's own profit or loss, pleasure or pain.

Deliberately taking account of the effects of one's actions on others is what it means to have other-regarding preferences. Variations on the golden rule and other ethical precepts are one way to pursue this objective (or as the Duchess put it, "love").

The other approach—"everyone minding their own business," as epitomized by Buchanan's indifference to his neighborhood fruit seller—relies on prices doing the work of morals. This could, in principle work if two conditions are met.

First, everything that matters to people when they decide what to do must have a price. This "everything has a price" requirement applies not only to goods (identical goods must have the same price), but also to any other aspects of a transaction, such as the noise nuisance effects of the goods' production on neighbors or its carbon emissions.

Second, taxes, subsidies, and other policies must affect prices in such a way that the price a buyer pays to acquire a good includes all the costs incurred by anyone as a result of its production and use, and the price a seller receives likewise includes all the benefits (to the buyer and to others) of making the good available. Prices must measure *all* the social costs and benefits of the good's production and distribution, rather than just the private costs to the buyer and seller. Call the second condition "the prices are right."

Under these conditions, "everyone minding their own business" means that simply by paying attention to prices, self-regarding people will implement (albeit unwittingly) the holy grail: they will take full account of the effects of their actions on others. This is exactly what Mandeville had in mind when he startled his readers with the claim that "the dextrous Management of a skilfull Politician" would allow the "Private Vices" to be "turned into Publick Benefits."

Smith went further than Mandeville. The remarkable idea behind his invisible hand is that under the right institutions, the "skilfull Politician" might not even be necessary: prices determined by market competition could do the job by themselves, entirely unaided by subsidies, taxes, or other government policies. Smith stressed that competition among buyers and among sellers was critical to this result, and he warned about the ways in which monopolies and cartels could thwart the invisible hand: "People in the same trade seldom meet together, even for merriment and diversion, but the conversation ends in a conspiracy against the public; or in some contrivance to raise prices."[41] Smith was also well aware of the many areas of policy, such as the provision of public education, that lay beyond the reach of the invisible hand.

Economists since then have stressed that the institutional conditions necessary for the invisible hand to work go beyond competition. For every good to have the right price, all economic interactions must be governed by what economists call complete contracts. This means that every aspect of an exchange—anything valued by either the exchanging parties or anyone else—has a price that is included in a contract governing the exchange. Complete contracts assign claims and liabilities in such a way that each actor "owns" all the benefits and costs resulting from his or her actions, including those conferred or imposed on others.

If contracts were complete, the equilibrium result of competition among self-interested individuals would ensure both that "everything has a price" and that "the prices are right." As a result, competitive markets would implement outcomes that are termed Pareto-efficient, meaning that there would not be another technically feasible outcome in which at least one individual would be made better off without anyone being made worse off.

Kenneth Arrow and Gerard Debreu demonstrated the above reasoning in what I term the "invisible hand theorem," and won a Nobel Prize for it. The axioms of this first fundamental theorem of welfare economics, as it is known to economists—notably, the assumption that contracts are complete—clarified the nature of an idealized world in which governmental intervention was not needed to address market failures, namely, situations in which uncoordinated exchanges or other economic activities resulted in Pareto-inefficient outcomes.

Less heralded, but more important for our purpose, is that in this world—as Hayek and Buchanan hinted—good governance does not seem to require virtue. The first fundamental theorem is true regardless of people's preferences, including entirely amoral and self-regarding ones.

Markets thus achieved a kind of moral extraterritoriality akin to the suspension of a host nation's sovereignty and laws accorded to foreign embassies. One could frown on or even chastise a neglectful parent or a citizen who transgressed laws when it served his purpose. But a selfish shopper? Or for that matter, a selfish banker? As long as everything has the right price, one's pursuit of self-interest in a market setting is constrained (by these right prices) to take appropriate account of the effect of one's actions on others. This is why Buchanan felt no shame in expressing his indifference to the well-being of his fruit seller.

The voluntary nature of transactions and the efficiency of the results (under the assumptions of the theorem) made competitive exchange a special domain in which one could suspend the normative standards commonly applied to relationships among citizens or family members. Generalizing Buchanan's indifference and designating the market a "moral free zone," the philosopher David Gauthier held that "morality arises from market failure. . . . Morality has no application to market interactions under the conditions of perfect competition."[42]

And so avarice, repackaged as self-interest, was tamed, transformed from a moral failing to just another kind of motive, like a taste for ice cream.

Economics for Knaves

But what if, unlike Buchanan and his fruit seller, two parties do not agree on the property rights relevant to an exchange? This happens when contracts are not complete and there are aspects of an exchange that are not priced: you breathe my secondhand smoke; farmer Jones's bees pollinate farmer Brown's apple trees. When Jones exchanges his honey for Brown's apples, he typically cannot also charge for the free pollination services provided by his bees. Their assistance to farmer Brown and countless other orchard owners nearby is a spillover (termed an "external economy" or simply an "externality"), that is, a direct effect between economic actors that is not priced or covered by (is "external" to) the contractual terms of the exchange. The bees' services are not included in the price Jones gets for his honey. As a result, the "everything has a price" and "the price is right" conditions do not hold, and Jones's private revenues from the sale of honey fall short of the total social benefits his farm produces (the bees' pollination services are not included). As a result, inefficiently little honey (and bee pollination services) will be produced.

Contracts are also incomplete (or nonexistent) in team production processes such as research and the provision of legal services, and in the voluntary provision of public goods such as neighborhood amenities or adherence to social norms. Public goods—such as radio broadcasts or ideas—are an extreme form of incomplete contracts because (by definition) they are both nonrival (my having more does not reduce the availability to you) and nonexcludable (the enjoyment of the public good cannot be restricted; if I have it, so can you).

In cases like farmer Jones's pollination of farmer Brown's bees, or the provision of public goods, unregulated market interactions among self-interested actors fail to implement efficient outcomes (too little pollination, too little of the public good). But this does not mean that self-interested competition in markets should be restricted; it means that public policy has to take on the task of getting the prices right.

In the early twentieth century, Alfred Marshall and Arthur Pigou spelled out the economic logic for nonetheless letting prices do the work of internalizing the effects of one's actions on others, even when markets fail. Where contracts were incomplete, they advocated taxes on industry for the environmental damage (external diseconomies) it imposed on others, and subsidies for a firm's worker-training activities, which benefit other firms when workers change jobs.

Farmer Jones would get a subsidy equal to the value of his bees' pollination service to Farmer Brown so that Jones's revenues (including the subsidy) would measure the full social benefits of his honey production. What came to be called optimal taxes and subsidies were those that recompensed an economic actor for the benefits his actions conferred on others and made him liable for the costs of his actions borne by others, when these benefits and costs would not otherwise be accounted for in the actor's private revenues and costs.

Green taxes that "make the polluter pay" for environmental spill-overs are an example. Where feasible, these optimal incentives would exactly implement Bentham's "duty and interest junction" principle: altering the material incentives under which the individual acts, in order to align self-interest with public objectives. The optimal taxes and subsidies advocated by Marshall, Pigou, and economists since then are thus a substitute for complete contracts, an effort to extend the reach of the invisible hand to cases in which its assumption is violated. Ideally, such taxes and subsidies can put a price on everything that matters and also get those prices right.

The resulting guide for the policy maker clarifies what is required to induce citizens to act if they were good, namely, the kinds of incentives and constraints that motivate a self-regarding individual to act as if he valued the effect of his actions on others in the same manner that those who are affected would evaluate them. The job description of the wise policy maker in this case is no longer that of Aristotle's Legislator, tasked with uplifting the population, but instead that of Machiavelli's republican, tasked with ordering the right laws to induce citizens to act *as if* they were good.

Bucolic examples like farmer Jones's bees and Brown's apple blossoms were staples for economists teaching about incomplete contracts. The textbook example of a public good was the lighthouse, whose light can be seen by all if it can be seen by anyone. But the problem of incomplete contracts is not some *curiosum* on the periphery of the economy. We will see that it is a ubiquitous characteristic of markets for labor, credit, information, and the other central arenas of the capitalist economy.

The fact that incomplete contracts are the rule and not the exception sets in train a series of implications for the use and limits of incentives, and it is worth pausing to consider why it is true.

Information about the amount and quality of the good or service provided in an exchange is very often either asymmetric, that is, not known to both parties, or nonverifiable, meaning that even if known to both, it cannot be used in the courts to enforce a contract. Where this is the case, some aspects of an exchange will not be in the contract: the contract is incomplete. As Emile Durkheim put it: "Not everything in the contract is contractual."[43] As a result, market failures are not confined to environmental spillovers, but occur in the everyday exchanges essential to a capitalist economy: labor markets and credit markets. It is impossible to write an enforceable employment contract that specifies that the employee will work hard and well. Credit contracts cannot be enforced if the borrower is broke.[44]

The labor- and credit-market examples share a common structure: a principal (the employer or the lender) wishes to induce an agent (the employee, the borrower) to act in a way beneficial to the principal but counter to the agent's interests (work hard, use the money borrowed in a way that maximizes the expected repayment, not the expected returns to the borrower). But because information about work effort or the use of the money is either not known to the principal or not admissible in court, the conflict of interest between the two cannot be resolved by specifying the terms of a complete and enforceable contract.

When contracts are incomplete, the de facto terms of the exchange are determined in large part by the strategic interaction between the parties, not by the courts. The outcome of this interaction depends on the bargaining power of the two parties and their social norms. The same problem arises when a farmer pays a share of his crop to the landowner. In all three cases, the agent (including the sharecropper) does not own the results of his or her actions: the lender takes the loss if the borrower cannot repay; the employer enjoys most of the benefits of the employee's hard work but likewise cannot recover back wages if the work has not been done.

Thus, in much of a modern capitalist economy, the complete-contracts assumption of the invisible hand theorem is violated. The great contribution of the mathematical representation of the workings of a market economy that allowed a proof of the "invisible hand theorem" was to clarify just what Adam Smith's idea really required. Here is how Arrow later described the contribution of his theorem: "There is by now a long and . . . imposing line of economists from Adam Smith to the present who have sought to show that a decentralized economy motivated by self-interest and guided by price signals would be compatible with a coherent disposition of economic resources that could be regarded in a well-defined sense as superior to a large class of possible alternative dispositions . . . It is important to know not only whether it *is* true but whether it *could be* true" (original emphasis).[45]

Thanks to Arrow and others, the conditions under which it "could be true"—not only competition but also complete contracts in everything that matters—are now known to be highly restrictive, showing how unlikely it is that a policy of thoroughgoing laissez-faire would implement an efficient outcome. I know from experience that writers of introductory economics textbooks struggle to find empirical examples of even a single market that approximates the model on which the theorem is based.

From Machiavelli to Mechanism Design

But maybe the kinds of optimal subsidies and taxes proposed by the Marshall-Pigou tradition can provide surrogates for the complete contracts missing from the credit, labor, and other markets. If so, prices could yet do the work of morals; the domain in which "people minding their own business" would be a good policy could be vastly expanded.

Many ingenious systems of incentives have been proposed to this end. There is even an academic field called mechanism design that exists for this purpose. A mechanism is simply a set of property rights, incentives, constraints, or other rules governing how people interact. But as we will see (in chapter VI), the assumptions required to make these clever mechanisms work are about as remote from real economies as the axioms on which the first fundamental theorem of welfare is based. Mechanism design has not yet devised incentives that make ethical and other-regarding motives redundant, nor is it likely to. Getting entirely self-regarding people reliably to act as if they cared about the effects of their actions on others has so far eluded jurists and policy makers. I explain why in chapter VI.

So it is no surprise that except on the whiteboards of economics classrooms, people try to avoid dealing with *Homo economicus.* Employers prefer to hire workers with a strong work ethic; banks prefer to lend to people whom they trust to conduct their business as proposed rather than to adopt self-interested but riskier projects. Again except on the whiteboard, everyone knows that "the contract itself is not sufficient," as Durkheim wrote a century ago; "regulation of the contract . . . is social in origin."[46] He was repeating the commonplace that handshakes matter; and where they do not, the economy underperforms.

In a paper explaining his invisible hand theorem, Arrow wrote: "In the absence of trust . . . opportunities for mutually beneficial cooperation would have to be forgone . . . Norms of social behavior, including ethical and moral codes [may be] . . . reactions of society to compensate for market failures."[47] In other words, because contracts are incomplete, morals must sometimes do the work of prices, rather than the other way around.

Arrow's point is that social norms and moral codes can attenuate market failures when they have the effect of internalizing the benefits and costs that an individual's actions confer or inflict on others. Despite the incompleteness of contracts, a modern economy's major markets—for labor, credit, and knowledge—can sometimes function tolerably well because social norms and other-regarding motives foster a positive work ethic, an obligation to tell the truth about the qualities of a project or a piece of information, and a commitment to keep promises. "The moral economy" is not an oxymoron.

The importance of norms and other social motives extends far beyond what we usually term market failures. It encompasses many of the arenas of social life in which the effects of one's actions on others is not governed by contract: the long-term climatic effects of one's lifestyle choices, the creation of drug-resistant superbugs through the opportunistic use of antibiotics, and the traffic congestion resulting from one's choice of a way to get around. The need for social norms to underwrite good governance is likely to increase as these and other problems pose ever-larger challenges to our well-being. The changing nature of work itself—from producing things to processing information and providing care, for example—further suggests that our economies will increasingly be characterized by contractual incompleteness.

The classical economists were right in thinking that ethical and other-regarding motives would be insufficient for the good governance of an economy in which many interactions are conducted between strangers. Nobody now doubts Smith's once-remarkable claim that a citizen's self-interest could be harnessed to "promote an end that was no part of his intention." But Joseph Schumpeter, who pioneered the economics of innovation and technical progress, was likewise right when he wrote that "no social system can work . . . in which everyone is . . . guided by nothing except his own . . . utilitarian ends."[48] In this passage he was not describing families or the polity, domains where the importance of ethical and other-regarding motives is widely recognized, but the workings of a capitalist firm.

Machiavelli anticipated Rousseau's injunction to take "men as they are" by more than two centuries (and mechanism design by more than four) in charging his republican lawmaker to devise a structure of governance in which people with "ordinary and natural humors" would nonetheless choose to act in ways that result in a well-governed republic. This was a major contribution to our understanding of how policies should be designed and laws ordered. But the same cannot be said of the radical extension of this good idea, first by Mandeville and subsequently by economists. Even today many in my discipline combine a professed indifference to the nature of individual preferences with excessive confidence in the ability of clever incentives to induce even an entirely amoral and self-interested citizenry to act in the public interest.

Ethical and other-regarding motives have always been essential to a well-governed society and are likely to be even more so in the future. Policies that ignore this fact and are indifferent to the preferences that motivate people's actions may compromise these essential predispositions. This is why policy makers should be concerned about the firemen's response to the commissioner's punitive incentives, and about the parents who arrived even later at the day care centers after the fines were imposed.

In the pages that follow, we will put ourselves in the shoes of Aristotle's Legislator, who shares these concerns and seeks to govern well, knowing that incentives and constraints, while essential to any social order, will never be sufficient and may have unintended adverse effects on ethical motivations. In the eyes of the Legislator, the policy tool kit based on the self-interest maxim, designed as it was for knaves and the wicked, may be part of the problem.

| | |

Moral Sentiments and Material Interests

An e-mail to me about the experiments that I report in this chapter recalled the "exciting and stimulating times" that my correspondent spent in the early 1950s as a young staffer in the Executive Office of the President. "People worked long hours," he told me, "and felt compensated by the sense of accomplishment, and . . . personal importance. Regularly a Friday afternoon meeting would go on until 8 or 9, when the chairman would suggest resuming Saturday morning. Nobody demurred. We all knew it was important, and we were important. . . . What happened when the President issued an order that anyone who worked on Saturday was to receive overtime pay . . . ? Saturday meetings virtually disappeared."

The e-mails were from Thomas Schelling, who, half a century after he left the White House, was awarded the Nobel Prize for convincing economists that their discipline should broaden its focus to include social interactions beyond markets. Was the young Schelling's experience in the Executive Office of the President atypical?

Incentives work. They often affect behavior almost exactly as conventional economic theory predicts, that is, by assuming that the target of the incentive cares only about his material gain. Textbook examples include the response to incentives by Tunisian sharecroppers and American windshield installers.[1] In these cases, the assumption of material self-interest provides a good basis for predicting the effect of varying incentives to increase the payoff of working harder. Their work effort was closely aligned with the extent to which their pay depended on it.

But whiteboard economics sometimes fails. Overtime pay did not induce Schelling and the other White House staffers to happily show up on Saturdays. Substantial rewards for high school matriculation in Israel had no impact on boys and little effect on girls, except among those already quite likely to matriculate.[2] Large cash payments in return for tested scholastic achievement in 250 urban schools in the United States were almost entirely ineffective, and incentives for student inputs (reading a book, for example) had modest effects.[3] In an unusual natural experiment, the imposition of fines as a way to shorten hospital stays in Norway had the opposite effect.[4] In contrast, hospital stays in England were greatly reduced by a policy designed to evoke shame and pride in hospital managers rather than to rely on the calculus of profit and loss.[5]

Jewish West Bank settlers, Palestinian refugees, and Palestinian students were asked how angry and disgusted they would feel, or how supportive of violence they might be, if their political leaders were to compromise on contested issues between the groups.[6] Those who saw their group's claims (regarding the status of Jerusalem, for example) as reflecting "sacred values" (about half in each of the three groups) expressed far greater anger, disgust, and support for violence if, in exchange for the compromise, their group received monetary compensation.

A similar reaction may explain Swiss citizens' response to a survey gauging their willingness to accept an environmental hazard: when offered compensation, they became more resistant to the local construction of a nuclear waste facility.[7] Many lawyers believe (and experimental evidence suggests) that inserting explicit provisions covering breach of contract increases the likelihood of breach.[8]

These examples cast doubt on the classical separability assumption that incentives and moral sentiments are simply additive in the implementation of desirable outcomes. I show in this chapter that laboratory experiments, played for significant sums of money, typically among anonymous subjects, suggest that moral and other noneconomic motives are sometimes crowded out by explicit incentives.

At the end of the previous chapter, I charged Aristotle's Legislator, who is aware of this problem, with the task of designing public policies in light of the crowding-out problem. The fact that appeals to material self-interest sometimes compromise moral sentiments would not worry the Legislator if there were little such sentiment to crowd out. But this is not the case. Natural observation and experimental data indicate that in most populations, few individuals are consistently self-interested, and moral and other-regarding motives are common. Moreover, we will see that these experiments predict what people do outside the lab. Among Brazilian fishermen, for example, those who cooperate in a public-goods experiment onshore adopt more environment-friendly traps and nets when they take to their boats.

Homo socialis

In the Prisoner's Dilemma game, defecting rather than cooperating with one's partner maximizes a player's payoff, irrespective of what the other player does. Defecting in this game is what game theorists call a dominant strategy, and the game is extremely simple; it does not take a game theorist to figure this out. So, assuming that people care only about their own payoffs, we would predict that defection would be universal.

But when the game is played with real people, something like half of players typically cooperate rather than defect.[9] Most subjects say that they prefer the mutual cooperation outcome over the higher material payoff they would get by defecting on a cooperator, and they are willing to take a chance that the other player feels the same way (and is willing to take the same chance.)

When players defect, it is often not because they are tempted by the higher payoff that they would get, but because they know that the other player might defect, and they hate the idea that their own cooperation would be exploited by the other. We know this from what happens when the Prisoner's Dilemma is not played simultaneously, as is standard, meaning that each person decides what to do not knowing what the other will do, but instead is played sequentially (one person chosen randomly moves first). In the sequential game, the second mover usually reciprocates the first player's move, cooperating if the first has done so, and defecting otherwise. Keep in mind the fact that avoiding being a chump appears to be the motive here, not the prospect of a higher payoff. We will return to it.

The experiments discussed in this and later chapters are listed in table 3.1 (the pages on which they are most fully described are given in the index). A more detailed, technical description of the games is in appendix 2.

The Prisoner's Dilemma is not the only game in which experimental subjects routinely violate the self-interest assumption.[10] Using data from a wide range of experiments, Ernst Fehr and Simon Gaechter estimate that 40 percent to 66 percent of subjects exhibit reciprocal choices, meaning that they returned favors even when not doing so would have given them higher payoffs. The same studies

Table 3.1. Values indirectly measured in experimental games

Game	Play of the game	Values measured
One-Shot Prisoner's Dilemma	Mutual cooperation results in highest average payoffs; but self-interested players will defect.	Players' reciprocity conditional on their beliefs about the actions to be taken by the other; effect of market framing on values
Gift Exchange	A transfer from one player to the other may be reciprocated or not.	Reciprocity and expectations of reciprocity
Trust (with and without fines)	The investor's transfer to the trustee is multiplied by the experimenter; the trustee may then make a back-transfer to the investor.	Investor: generosity or expectations of reciprocity. Trustee: reciprocity. Effect of prospective fines on investor generosity
Dictator	One player unilaterally transfers some amount to the second (passive) player. (This is not strictly a game.)	Unconditional generosity
Third-Party Punishment	A dictator game with a third party who observes the dictator's transfer and then may pay to reduce the payoffs of the dictator.	Third party: willingness to pay to punish violations of fairness in the treatment of others. First party: effect of expected punishment
Ultimatum	The proposer provisionally allocates a portion of the endowment to the responder, who may accept or reject. In the latter case, both players receive nothing.	Proposer: unconditional generosity or belief in the fair-mindedness of the responder. Responder: fairness, reciprocity

(*continued*)

Table 3.1. (*continued*)

Game	Play of the game	Values measured
Public Goods	A Prisoner's Dilemma with more than two players. Average payoffs are greatest when all contribute the maximum; but a self-interested player will contribute less (or in most cases, zero).	Altruism; reciprocity conditioned on the past actions of others
Public Goods with Punishment	After being informed of the contribution levels of each of the other players, each may pay to reduce the payoffs of any of the other players.	Contributor: unconditional generosity or belief in the willingness of others to punish unfairness, shame when violating a social norm. Punisher: fairness, reciprocity

Note: The indicated values provide plausible explanations of experimental behavior when this differs from behavior expected of an individual seeking to maximize game payoffs (and believing others to be doing the same). Appendix 2 gives more detail on the structure of these games.

suggest that 20 percent to 30 percent of the subjects exhibit conventional self-regarding preferences.[11] In Armin Falk and Michel Kosfeld's Trust game (described below) fewer than a fifth of experimental subjects made self-interested choices.

George Loewenstein and his coauthors distinguished three types of players in the experimental games they conducted: "*Saints* consistently prefer equality, and they do not like to receive higher payoffs than the other party even when they are in a negative relationship with the opponent . . . *Loyalists* do not like to receive higher payoffs in neutral or positive relationships, but seek advantageous inequality when . . . in negative relationships . . . *Ruthless competitors* consistently prefer to come out ahead of the other party regardless of the type of relationships" (emphasis in the original).[12] Of their subjects, 22 percent were saints, 39 percent were loyalists, and 29 percent were ruthless competitors. The remaining 10 percent did not fit into these categories.

As with Tolstoy's happy families, in this and other games there seems to be just one way to be self-interested—like Loewenstein's ruthless competitors—but many ways to depart from the standard economic model. Some are unconditionally altruistic, simply valuing the benefits received by others. Some express a conditional form of altruism: they reciprocate good deeds even when they cannot expect to benefit in any way. Others dislike inequality, apparently out of a commitment to justice. While *Homo economicus* is among the dramatis personae on the economic stage, experiments show that he is also often seriously outnumbered.

I use the term "social preferences" to refer to motives such as altruism, reciprocity, intrinsic pleasure in helping others, aversion to inequity, ethical commitments, and other motives that induce people to help others more than is consistent with maximizing their own wealth or material payoff. Social preferences are thus not limited to cases in which an actor assigns some value to the payoffs received by another person. I use a broader definition because moral, intrinsic, or other reasons unrelated to a concern for another's payoffs or well-being often motivate people to help others and adhere to social norms even when it costs them to do so. For example, one may adhere to a social norm not because of the harm that a transgression would do to another, but because of the kind of person one would like to be. Helping the homeless may be motivated by what James

Andreoni calls the "warm glow" of giving rather than a concern for the poor.[13] Being honest need not be motivated by the harm that the lie would do to others; it may be an end in itself.

Knowing that incentives may undermine one or more of these dimensions of social preferences provides a warning to the Legislator, but not much guidance. How do we design incentives and other policies in the presence of crowding out? To decide whether to use incentives, and if so, what kind, the Legislator has to know more about citizens' behavior in the absence of incentives and their response to the kinds of incentives that might be put in place. This requires an understanding of how incentives work and why they sometimes fail.

Crowding Out (and In)

To begin, the Legislator considers a paradigmatic problem facing policy makers: how to get citizens to contribute to some public good when it costs them to do so. This can be represented as a Public Goods game. An individual may choose to bear a cost in order to take an action—such as disposing of trash in an environment-friendly manner—that furthers some public good. The individual herself, like all citizens, will benefit from the public good, but let us assume that her cost in contributing is greater than the benefit she personally will receive. Thus, while the best outcome is for everyone to contribute (it maximizes the total payoff for the public), for each citizen, not contributing at all is the individually payoff-maximizing choice, no matter what the other citizens do. Not contributing is the dominant strategy for a payoff maximizer, just as it is in the Prisoner's Dilemma. Contributing is a form of altruism, that is, helping others at a cost to oneself.

The Public Goods game is thus a version of the Prisoner's Dilemma with more than two players. Other problems that often take the form of a public-goods problem are the voluntary payment of taxes, limiting one's carbon footprint, upholding social norms, producing new knowledge in the public domain, maintaining public safety, and acting to maintain the good reputation of one's group.

The citizen may be encouraged to contribute to the public good by a subsidy or other economic incentive. In what follows, I will use the term "incentive" (without the adjectives explicit, economic, monetary, and so on) to mean an intervention that affects the expected material costs and benefits associated with an action. In the standard economic model, the story ends here: the subsidy reduces the net cost of contributing to the public good, and as a result, more citizens will contribute or they will contribute more.

But some citizens have social preferences too, and these may motivate actions that benefit others even at a cost to oneself. How salient these preferences are relative to the citizen's self-regarding material motivations will depend on the situation in which the decision to contribute is made. Shopping and voting, for example, are different situations, and for most people the pursuit of self-interest is less likely to be considered an ethical shortcoming when shopping than when voting. In the case of the public good, the motives that are salient will depend on how the contribution is framed, including whether an incentive is provided to those who contribute. The incentive is part of the situation. I term these proximate motives to contribute the citizen's "experienced values."

The challenge facing the Legislator is that the framing provided by the incentive may affect the salience of the individual's social preferences, resulting in a level of experienced values different from would have been the case in the absence of the incentive. When this

ial preferences and incentives are not separable, and expe-
values may be influenced (positively or negatively) by the use
intives.

To see how, for any particular individual let the extent of the contribution be represented by a single number, and let the same be true of both explicit incentives and values. Nonseparability occurs when the presence or extent of the incentive affects the individual's experienced values.

This is illustrated in figure 3.1, panel A of which illustrates separability: the upper route from incentives to the contribution—the pathway via "cost of contribution net of incentive"—is the one stressed by the self-interest paradigm. The costs are a deterrent to contribution (shown by the minus sign on the arrow from cost to contribution). On this causal route, the incentive reduces the net costs of the public-spirited action and thus increases the actor's motivation to provide the public good.

The lower set of arrows in panel A—passing through "experienced values"—shows the effect of the citizen's social preferences on experienced values, and the effect of experienced values on the contribution to the public good, which is simply added to the effect of the subsidy. The effect of varying the incentive does not depend on the level of the social preferences, and correspondingly, the effect of varying the social preferences does not depend on the level of the incentive. This is what additivity (or separability) means.

Of course the self-interest paradigm may simply ignore the role of social preferences or even assume them to be absent. But as long as panel A is a good representation of the process of contribution, no harm is done in this, because the effect of the incentive is independent of the level of social preferences. The economists' policies will

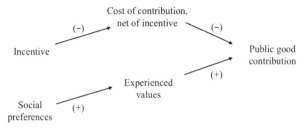

A. Separability: Incentives do not affect values

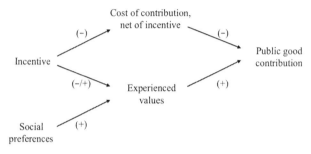

B. Non-separability: Incentives affect values

Figure 3.1. Incentives, experienced values, and contributions to the public good: The problem of nonseparability and crowding out Arrows are positive or negative causal effects. Crowding out occurs in panel B when there is a negative effect (–) from "Incentive" to "Experienced values."

work out as expected, even though *Homo economicus* is a misnomer for citizens who might better be termed *Homo socialis.*

Panel B illustrates the problem of nonseparability, which arises when this is not the case, because incentives have a negative effect on the individual's experienced values and hence indirectly have a negative effect on the citizen's contribution to the public good. Economists following John Stuart Mill in focusing on the citizen "solely as a being who desires to possess wealth" routinely ignore this indirect effect, either because they think it is not there or because it is not a part of economics. But it is definitely there, and because it affects how incentives work, it has to be part of economics.

Because of the effect of incentives on experienced values, the total—direct and indirect—effect of an incentive may fall short of what we would expect if we looked only at its effects on the costs and benefits of the targeted activity. In this case, we say that incentives crowd out social preferences. Then, incentives and social preferences are substitutes: the effect of each on the targeted activity declines as the level of the other increases. Where the effect on social preferences is positive, we have the synergy that the Legislator seeks: crowding in occurs, and social preferences and incentives are complements, each enhancing the effect of other.

The total effect of the introduction of an incentive on the public-goods contribution by an individual is the sum of the direct effect of the subsidy (which must be positive) plus the indirect effect of the subsidy operating via its effect on values (which may be of either sign) and the effect of values on the action (which we assume to be positive). We have separability when there is no indirect effect, either because social preferences are absent or because incentives do not affect their behavioral salience as expressed in "experienced values." This appears to be true of the effects of incentives on the work activity of American windshield installers, Tunisian farmers, and the other "textbook" cases mentioned at the beginning of the chapter.

Where the indirect effect is negative, meaning that the total effect falls short of the direct effect, then incentives and social preferences are substitutes (or are "sub-additive" or are said to exhibit "negative synergy" or "crowding out"). This may have been the true of the surprisingly modest or even absent effects of financial rewards for schoolwork mentioned at the outset.

Where the indirect effect is negative and large enough to offset the direct effect of the incentive, we have the attention-riveting cases in which incentives backfire, that is, they have the opposite of the intended effect, which I term "strong crowding out." The Boston firemen's and Haifa parents' responses to incentives are examples.

Where the indirect effect is positive, we have crowding in, that is, synergy between the two effects: then incentives and social preferences are complements rather than substitutes, and are sometimes termed "superadditive." (These four cases—separability, crowding out, crowding in, and strong crowding out—are characterized mathematically in appendix 1.)

How do we detect the crowding phenomenon in experiments? If an incentive were actually to reduce, rather than increase, contributions to the public good, we would surely have evidence of crowding out. But this kind of strong crowding out is just an extreme manifestation of the problem. So simply observing that an incentive has a positive effect is not evidence that crowding out is absent. Where crowding out is present but not "strong," the effect of the incentive will be in the intended direction, but not as large as it would have been if social preferences and incentives were simply additive. In this hypothetical case of separability, the effect of the incentive would be exactly what an entirely amoral and self-regarding person would do. So to test for the presence, nature, and extent of social preferences and their crowding out (or in), we use the predicted effectiveness of the incentive for such an exemplar of *Homo economicus* as our benchmark. Behavior deviating from the benchmark is evidence of social preferences and for their nonseparability from material incentives.

Here is an example of a subsidy that "worked" but induced almost entirely selfish behavior in people who, without the incentive, acted quite unselfishly. Juan Camilo Cardenas and his coauthors implemented an experimental "public bads" game called the Common Pool Resource game, which is very similar in structure to the real-world commons problem faced by his subjects—rural Colombian ecosystem users.[14]

In the experiment, Cardenas let the villagers choose how many "months" they would spend extracting resources from the hypothetical "forest" (the common pool resource). There was a level of exploitation (one month per year) that, if practiced by all, would maximize the total payoffs to the group. But in the experiment that Cardenas implemented, each individual would do better by extracting much more than this social optimum. The villagers immediately recognized the analogy between the experimental game, with its hypothetical forest, and their everyday challenges of making a livelihood from the real forest. There was nothing hypothetical about their payoffs in the experiment; they would earn substantial sums of money if they managed to cooperate.

This setup is similar to the Public Goods game, except that over-extracting resources is a "public bad": each subject in the experiment would earn higher material payoffs by overexploiting the "forest," irrespective of what the others did. But collectively, they would do best if each limited his or her extraction. The villagers could easily determine the payoffs that they would get for every combination of what they and the others did. Each villager was randomly assigned to one of fourteen groups in which they would play the experiment over a number of periods.

Cardenas and his coauthors followed two conventional practices in behavioral economics. First, the payoffs were real; some subjects went home with substantial sums of money. Second, participants played anonymously; even in treatments allowing for communication among the players, how much each extracted from the forest was known only to the experimenter and to the player herself.

In the first stage of the experiment, lasting eight periods, there were no incentives and no communication among the villagers. The villagers, on average, extracted 44 percent less of the experimental "resource" than the amount that would have maximized their individual payoffs. Cardenas and his coauthors then cleverly used this statistic—the difference between how much a villager extracted from the "forest" and the amount of extraction that would have gained her the greatest material payoff given what everyone else did—to measure each individual's social preferences. The rationale for their interpreting the statistic in this way was that her social preferences provide a plausible and parsimonious explanation of why she did not maximize her own material gain. The evidence from the first stage of the experiment, then, suggested that social preferences were quite common among the villagers.

But while striking, this was not the answer to the question Cardenas was asking. He wanted to know how either material incentives or communication among the subjects affected their extraction levels and, hence, what he could infer about the conditions affecting the social preferences of the villagers. Here is how he answered the question.

In the second stage of game, with nine periods of play, Cardenas introduced two new treatments. In nine of the groups, the villagers were allowed to communicate with each other briefly before playing anonymously. These groups extracted a bit less under the communication treatment than they had in the no-communication stage, thus deviating even a bit more from what a person who cared only about her own payoffs would do. Apparently, communication among the villagers somewhat enhanced the behavioral salience of their social preferences.

The experimenter explained to the members of the remaining five groups that they would have to pay a small fine (imposed by the experimenter) if it was found that they had extracted more of the resource than the amount that, had all members done the same, would have maximized the payoffs to the group. Call this amount the "social optimum" extraction level. To determine whether members had overextracted in this sense, they would be monitored (which would occur with a probability known to the villagers).

As expected, villagers in these groups initially extracted much less than those without the fine, showing that the penalty had the intended effect. But as the second stage of the experiment progressed, those in the groups subject to the fine raised their extraction levels. The prospect of the fine reduced how much an entirely selfish person would extract; but what Cardenas wanted to know was the effect of the incentive on the social preferences of the villagers, that is, on how much they deviated from what an entirely selfish person would do.

The result was a shocker: by the end of the second stage, their levels of extraction were barely (and not statistically significantly) less than what an entirely self-interested person would do. Remember: these are the very same villagers who in stage one, without incentives, extracted barely more than half of what would have maximized their personal gain.

Figure 3.2 shows the extent to which the villagers extracted less than would have maximized their personal gain for the two stages and two treatments (communication, fine) in the second stage of the experiment. The height of each dot thus indicates the extent of their social preferences. The incentive apparently worked, but it almost entirely sidelined whatever motives had led the villagers, in the absence

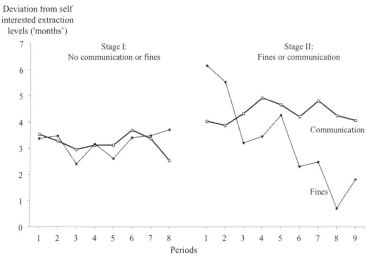

Figure 3.2. The effects of communication and economic incentives on the strength of social preferences In Stage I, both groups experienced the same treatment (no fines, no communication). In Stage II, one group of subjects ("Communication") was allowed to discuss the game and what they should do (play remained anonymous), while members in the other group ("Fines") were subjected to monitoring and a fine for overextraction (no communication). (Data from Cardenas, Stranlund, and Willis 2000.)

of the incentive, to forgo substantial individual gain by limiting their extraction levels for the benefit of the group. In other words, the fine worked as a substitute for the villagers' preexisting social preferences rather than an additional reason to protect the "forest."

For the moment, let's hold in abeyance questions about what would have happened if the fine had been large enough and the monitoring efficient enough to ensure that the villagers would have extracted exactly the social optimum amount from the forest, even though they had become entirely self-interested (having left their social preferences behind). The point here is that incentives work, but possibly with some collateral cultural damage. In chapter VI, I consider why we should worry about such damage.

Crowding Out: A Taxonomy for the Legislator

What was it that eclipsed the villagers' green-mindedness once the fines were announced? It seems that like the Haifa parents, the villagers took the fine to be the price of transgressing what had previously been a social norm; and they found the gains to be had by overextracting from the "forest" sufficient to justify the risk of being fined. But we do not really know, because the experiment measured what the villagers did, not what they were thinking and feeling about exploiting and maintaining their "forest."

But without understanding why the introduction of the fine sidelined social preferences among the villagers, it is difficult see how this problem could be avoided. Learning more about the crowding-out process, therefore, is the next challenge for the Legislator. He knows that he will eventually have to understand how the incentive affected what the villagers were thinking and feeling when they made their decisions, but for now he thinks that a taxonomy of crowding effects might allow him to extract a bit more information from experiments like those of Cardenas and his coauthors.

On the basis of how the Colombian villagers reacted, we may suspect that a person who is happy to give to a charity may be less inclined to contribute when a donation reduces her tax bill. But what is it that triggers this change? Is it the mere presence of the tax break (whatever its magnitude) that changes the meaning of the gift? Or is it the magnitude of the subsidy?

When the presence of the incentive (rather than its extent) is what affects the person's experienced values, we call this "categorical crowding out." When the extent of the incentive matters, we say that "marginal crowding out" has occurred. We will see that crowding *in* may also occur—that is, when an incentive enhances the experienced values of the individual—and this too may be either categorical or marginal.

The distinction between marginal and categorical crowding out might have helped the Boston fire commissioner avoid the Christmas call-in debacle. Thinking back, he probably realized later that a large-enough penalty for sick call-ins would have had the effect he wanted, even though his lesser penalties backfired. This would be the case if the crowding-out problem he faced were categorical (the mere presence of the penalties was the problem) rather than marginal.

To clarify these concepts, figure 3.3 shows the possible effects of a subsidy on a person's contribution to a public good when either categorical or marginal crowding out holds, and when crowding does not occur, that is, under separability. For each level of the subsidy (measured on the horizontal axis), the height of the line gives the level of the contribution—called the individual's best response to the given subsidy—that will maximize his utility (both from the incentives and from his values). For example, the line labeled "self-regarding contribution" gives the best response of some hypothetical self-regarding individual (with no social preferences to crowd out). He contributes a small amount simply out of self-interest and then contributes more in response to the subsidy. These lines are termed "best response functions"; their slopes are the effect of the subsidy on the level of contributions. (I have drawn these as straight lines, but that is a simplification.)

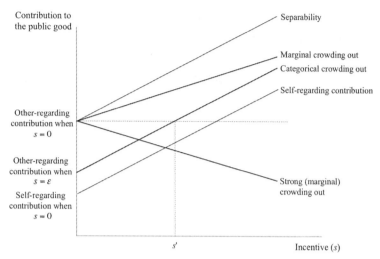

Figure 3.3. *Citizen's contribution to the public good under the nonseparability of incentives and values* Under separability (top line), experienced values and incentives are additive. Categorical crowding out shifts this line downward (s = ε means the subsidy is offered but that it is as small as can be imagined, ε representing an arbitrarily small number). Under strong crowding out, the use of the incentive is counterproductive; this holds for all levels of the subsidy under the strong (marginal) crowding-out downward-sloping line shown. Under categorical crowding out, incentives less than s' are also counterproductive, in the sense that contributions with the incentive are less than they would have been in the absence of incentives.

Look at the top line (labeled "separability") as a point of reference. This depicts another hypothetical individual, similar to the one modeled in panel A of figure 3.1. The social preferences and resulting experienced values of the individual induce her to contribute a substantial amount to the public good even when there is no subsidy (the vertical intercept of the top line). The slope of the top line is the effect of the subsidy when marginal crowding out is absent (because separability precludes this). The line labeled "marginal crowding out" is less steep, indicating that marginal crowding out has reduced the effectiveness of variations in the subsidy in altering the amount contributed. When strong marginal crowding out holds (the downward sloping line), the effect is negative (greater subsidy induces a lesser contribution to the public good). Marginal crowding in would be indicated by a line steeper than the separability line (not shown.)

The intercept at the vertical axis of the best-response function gives the citizen's contribution in the absence of any subsidy (the other-regarding citizen contributing more than the self-regarding when there is no subsidy.) The intercept labeled "other-regarding contribution when $s = \varepsilon$" gives the contribution when a subsidy is offered but it is very small (ε means a number as close to zero as you wish, but not zero). The difference in the vertical intercepts under separability and categorical crowding out shows the extent to which the mere presence of a subsidy per se diminishes social preferences.

Figure 3.3 would provide the Legislator with just the information he needs were he charged with selecting the subsidy. For each subsidy, it shows the contribution to the public good that could be expected depending on the nature and extent of crowding out. If estimates of the best-response function showed that citizens were other-regarding and that subsidies would create strong crowding out, the Legislator would stop using incentives. If the Legislator knew that an incentive would categorically crowd out social preferences, then he would either implement a subsidy larger than s' in the figure, or no subsidy at all. Any subsidy between 0 and s', he would see from the figure, would result in lower contributions to the public good.

The Legislator happily adds the best-response functions in figure 3.3 to his tool kit. Looking at the figure, he imagines the plight of the naïve legislator, who is unaware of the crowding-out problem and so believes that the top line ("separability") gives the relevant policy options. Unless crowding in should occur (not shown in the figure), the naïve Legislator will sometimes be disappointed when the results (the citizens' contributions) fall short of what he predicted by mistakenly using the best response based on separability.

Measuring Categorical and Marginal Crowding Out

This is not simply a thought experiment. A remarkable study shows that the effects of incentives can be estimated empirically and that both categorical and marginal crowding out do occur. Bernd Irlenbusch and Gabriele Ruchala implemented a public-goods experiment in which 192 German students faced three conditions: no incentives to contribute, and a bonus, given to the highest-contributing individual, that was either high or low.[15] Payoffs were such that even with no incentive, individuals would maximize their payoffs by contributing twenty-five units. The units given and received were later converted into equivalents in euros, so as with the experiment among Colombian villagers, the game was played for real money, which the students kept when the game was over.

In figure 3.4 we see that in the no-incentive case, contributions averaged thirty-seven units, or 48 percent above the twenty-five units that participants would have given if they were motivated only by material rewards. As with the Colombian villagers, the German students in the experiment evinced strong social preferences.

Contributions in the low-bonus case were a bit higher than in the absence of the incentive but not significantly different. The high-bonus case saw significantly higher contributions, but the amount contributed (fifty-three units) barely (and insignificantly) exceeded that predicted for self-interested subjects (fifty units). Again, the

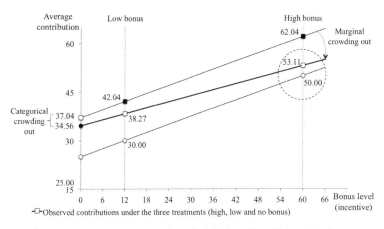

Figure 3.4. Categorical and marginal crowding out The experimental design is a Public Goods game comparing no incentive with two team-based compensation schemes with a low or high bonus for the highest contributor in the team. The maximum contribution level is 120. (Data from Irlenbusch and Ruchala 2008; also based on calculations described in the text.)

German students are strongly reminiscent of the Colombian villagers: incentives worked, yet there was collateral cultural damage: the bonus appears to have obliterated pre-existing social preferences.

Can we dissect the cultural damage and see why it occurs? Sandra Polanía-Reyes and I devised a way to do this.[16] We assumed that marginal crowding out affects the slope of the citizens' best-response function by a constant given amount (meaning that the function remains linear, like the lines in figure 3.3) We then were able to use the observed behavior in the high- and low-bonus cases to estimate the marginal effect of the bonus, that is, how much the incentive reduced the slope of the line. We found that a unit increase in the bonus was associated with a 0.31 increase in contributions. This contrasts with the marginal effect of 0.42 that would have occurred if subjects without social preferences had simply best responded to the incentive. Crowding out thus reduced the marginal effect of the incentive by 0.11, that is, by 26 percent of what it would have been under separability.

The estimated response to the incentive also gives us the level of categorical crowding out, namely, the difference between the observed contributions (37.04) in the absence of any incentive and the solid dot showing the predicted contributions (34.56) if an arbitrarily small incentive (the "ε incentive") had been in effect (the vertical intercept of the line in figure 3.4 through the observed points). The incentive thus categorically reduced contributions by 2.48. This categorical reduction in contributions is 21 percent of the extent of the social preferences of the subjects, measured by the excess in observed contributions over what an entirely self-interested person would have done in the absence of an incentive.

The total effect of the subsidy, including its direct and indirect effects, can be accounted for by using the causal logic seen in panel B of figure 3.1. (The details of these calculations and analogous calculations for the small bonus appear in appendix 3.) Here is the accounting for the high bonus compared to no bonus. The direct effect of the high bonus (the top arrows in fig. 3.1) was an increase in predicted contributions of 25 (from the 37.04 that the subjects contributed without the subsidy to the 62.04 that they would have contributed had separability been the case.) There were two indirect effects, one marginal and the other categorical. The categorical effect, as we have seen, was a reduction in contributions by 2.48 units. Marginal crowding out reduced contributions by 6.6 (that is, the reduction in the slope of the best-response function of 0.11 multiplied by the subsidy of 60). The total effect—the direct (25) minus the indirect

(9.08) was 15.92. Thus, the marginal crowding-out effect constituted the largest part of the negative indirect effect. With the small bonus, by contrast, categorical crowding out makes up most of the indirect effect and thus is the main source of crowding out.

Looking at figure 3.4, the Legislator can identify the policies and outcomes available to him. Were a naïve legislator to suppose, consistent with Hume's maxim, that his citizens were knaves, then the policy's effectiveness would be indicated by the lower line through the open dots. Were a less naïve legislator to recognize that citizens have social preferences (as Hume surely did) but that these and the incentives offered by the subsidy were separable (as Hume apparently also thought), then the policy-effectiveness curve would have been the top line (passing through the solid squares). The Aristotelian Legislator, who would know both that social preferences affect behavior and that the incentive may crowd them out, would know that the middle line represents his true options.

Categorical crowding out can be seen in other experiments. In one, reported willingness to help a stranger load a sofa into a van was much lower under a small money incentive than with no incentive at all; yet a moderate incentive increased the willingness to help.[17] This suggests that categorical crowding out was at work. Using these data as Polanía-Reyes and I did in the Irlenbusch and Ruchala study, we estimated that the mere presence of the incentive reduced the willingness to help by 27 percent compared with no incentive.

Another Cardenas experiment allows us to distinguish categorical and marginal crowding, but here we observe categorical crowding in.[18] This is our first evidence that incentives and social preferences can sometimes complement, rather than substitute for, each other. Because this is an aim of Aristotle's Legislator, it is worth going through the result in some detail.

As in his earlier study, Cardenas implemented an experimental Common Pool Resource (public "bad") game resembling the real-life conservation problem faced by his rural Colombian subjects. As in the other Cardenas experiment, in the absence of any explicit incentives, the villagers on average extracted less of the experimental "resource" than would have maximized their individual payoffs, providing evidence of a significant willingness to sacrifice individual gain in order to protect the resource and raise payoffs for the group. When they were made to pay a small fine if monitoring showed that they had overextracted the resource, they extracted even less than without the fine, showing that the fine had the intended effect.

But that is not the eye-catching result here: the fact that they deviated from what an entirely selfish person would have done by 25 percent *more* than in the absence of the incentive suggests that the fine *increased* the salience of the villagers' social preferences, resulting in their placing a greater experienced value on not overextracting the resource. The small fine crowded *in* social preferences; the incentive yielded a collateral cultural benefit.

Tellingly, increasing the initially small fine had virtually no effect. It seems that the fine thus did not work as an incentive (if it had, the larger fine should have had a greater effect than the smaller). In Cardenas's view, the very presence of the fine (whether high or low did not matter) was a signal that alerted subjects to the public nature of the interaction and the importance of conserving the resource. The main effect was due to how the fine framed the situation, not its alteration of the material costs and benefits of extracting from the forest. In Cardenas's view, the moral message rather than monetary motivation explains the effect.

The Legislator would like to know why, in the second Cardenas experiment, the small fine crowded in social preferences, while the opposite effect had occurred in the first experiment. The villagers were different of course, and the fine may have been framed differently. We will present other examples of fines as messages—some with positive effects, as here, and others with the more common crowding-out effect. These cases hold important lessons for why incentives are sometimes counterproductive and how, under well-designed policies, incentives can crowd in social preferences.

A Surprise for the Legislator

The Legislator knows that when the prices that structure private economic interactions fail to provide incentives for the efficient use of a society's resources, his task is to design optimal taxes, fines, or subsidies that will correct or attenuate the resulting market failure. Which policies are optimal will of course depend on the preferences of the citizens. But the evidence just presented suggests an added twist: the preferences that determine citizen's responses to the Legislator's incentives depend on the incentives themselves. As a result, optimal incentives depend on the nature of the citizens' preferences that result from this process (of imposing fines or providing subsidies), for these will determine the effects of the incentives.

The fact that preferences may depend on incentives complicates the Legislator's task, for he cannot simply take the citizens preferences as given, as economists normally do when designing optimal taxes, subsidies, and other incentives. But while this difficulty is a notch up in complexity, it is not some impenetrable chicken-and-egg problem.

For any policy being contemplated, taking account of crowding out just requires the structuring of incentives to take these indirect effects into consideration. The Legislator is thus not simply selecting, say, a tax rate, but rather a tax rate and a possibly altered distribution of preferences in the population that will result from the categorical and marginal effects of this incentive. It is the joint effect of the pair—tax rate, preferences resulting from the tax rate—that the sophisticated Legislator will consider when selecting his policy.

Armed with the idea that incentives and other policies may affect preferences, and using the conceptual apparatus illustrated in figures 3.3 and 3.4, the sophisticated Legislator can rethink the problem of optimal incentives. His intuition is that because crowding out reduces their effectiveness, he should use incentives less than would his naïve counterpart, who is unaware of these adverse incentive effects.

If crowding out is "strong," meaning that an incentive has an effect the opposite of its intent, the Legislator will of course abandon the use that incentive. So his intuition is correct in this case. But when crowding out blunts but does not reverse the effectiveness of incentives, it may be far from obvious to the Legislator whether the optimal use of incentives is greater or less than that which his naïve counterpart would use. Contrary to his intuition, the Legislator may find that in the presence of crowding out, he will make *greater* rather than lesser use of incentives.

To see why, consider a case in which the Legislator would like to meet a specific level of contribution or other public-spirited action—for example, that every citizen should take at least four hours of first aid training. The Legislator believes that training beyond four hours offers little additional benefit, and that those with less than four hours of training are not much more able to help others during emergencies than those with no training at all. This is an extreme version of decreasing returns: there is no benefit of additional time in training beyond four hours.

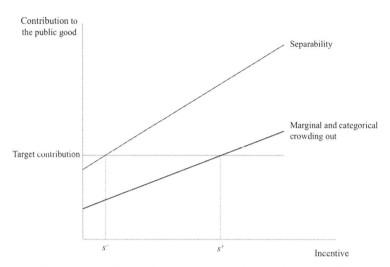

Figure 3.5. Underuse of the incentive by the naïve legislator The
*sophisticated Legislator, aware of the crowding-out problem, would
select the subsidy, s⁺, greater than that chosen by naïve legislator, who is
unaware that the incentive and social preferences are not separable, s⁻.*

Thus we have the situation depicted in figure 3.5. The target
(four hours in the above example) is the horizontal line, and because
the subsidy is costly to implement, the planner would like to find
the least subsidy that results in citizens hitting the target. The two
upward-sloping lines taken from the previous two figures give, respectively, the true policy options facing the sophisticated Legislator
(the lower line) and the options imagined by his naïve counterpart
(the upper line). It is clear from the figure that to meet this target,
the Legislator will need to adopt the subsidy s^+, which is greater than
s^-, the subsidy adopted by a naïve legislator who is unaware of the
crowding problem.

This surprising result may seem to be an artifact of our having
chosen a special "hit the target" kind of objective for the Legislator.

But it is not. The logic of the target case carries over to cases in which the benefits of the public good are continuously increasing as more of it is provided, but at a diminishing rate. Here is how the sophisticated Legislator will reason in this more general case.[19]

In the presence of crowding out, the Legislator knows that the true effectiveness of the subsidy is less than what his naïve counterpart believes; a simple comparison of the benefits (effectiveness) and the costs of implementing the policy would seem to recommend lesser use of the subsidy. This is correct; but there is a second, possibly offsetting effect.

Just as in the target case, because the incentive is less effective (either categorically or marginally) than it would be in the absence of crowding out, it follows that for any given level of the subsidy, the extent of underprovision of the public good will be greater. For any subsidy implemented in the presence of crowding out, the true best-response function of the citizen is always below the best-response function imagined by the naïve legislator (except possibly at $s = 0$, when the two lines coincide, if categorical crowding out is absent). As a result, the degree of public-goods underprovision anticipated by the sophisticated Legislator is greater than that anticipated by his naïve counterpart.

The sophisticated Legislator knows that a consequence of diminishing returns to the level of provision of the public good is that increases in its provision are especially beneficial when it is more underprovided. In this case, the benefit of further increasing the citizens' contribution is correspondingly greater in the eyes of the sophisticated Legislator than to the naïve legislator, who thinks that for any subsidy level, the provision of the public good will be greater. The Legislator thus has reason to adopt a greater subsidy than would be adopted by the naïve legislator. This is the second effect of taking nonseparability into account, and it may outweigh the first effect, which stems from the reduced effectiveness of the subsidy, and which, in the absence of the second effect, would lead the Legislator to adopt a lesser subsidy. The sophisticated Legislator will choose a larger subsidy if the greater benefit of changing the citizens' behavior (the second effect) more than offsets the diminished marginal effectiveness of the subsidy (the first effect).[20]

While it may seem odd that the sophisticated Legislator's recognition of the crowding-out problem would lead to greater rather than lesser use of the subsidy, it is not. Think about the doctor who discovers that a treatment is less effective than he thought. Will he prescribe a smaller dose? Not necessarily; even if he is attentive to the cost of the treatment for the patient, he may opt for a stronger dose, or else abandon the treatment in favor of an alternative. Like the doctor, the Legislator may use a greater level of subsidy precisely *because* it is less effective.

But if the treatment is less effective, the doctor or the Legislator might also seek other ways to accomplish the same end. Attendance at first aid courses might be promoted by direct appeals to people's social preferences, for example, by clarifying to citizens how important it is during natural disasters that most people know the elements of first aid. Where the Legislator has other options, knowledge of crowding out may lead him either to abandon the subsidy entirely or to combine it with direct appeals to citizen' social preferences.

The Lab and the Street

The experimental evidence for crowding out and the guidance it might give the Legislator would be of little interest if lab results did not predict behaviors outside the lab. Generalizing directly from experiments, even for phenomena much simpler than separability, is a concern in any empirical study, and it is often unwarranted.[21]

Consider, for example, the Dictator game, in which one experimental subject is provisionally given a sum of money and is asked to allocate any amount (including all, none, or some fraction of it) to the second player, whose only role is to be a passive recipient. The personal identities of the dictator and the recipient are not known to each other. Typically, more than 60 percent of dictators allocate a positive sum to the recipient, and the average given is about a fifth of the sum initially granted by the experimenter to the dictator.

But we would be sadly mistaken if we inferred from this that 60 percent of people would spontaneously transfer funds to an anonymous passerby, or even that the same subjects would offer a fifth of the money in their wallet to a homeless person asking for help. Another example: experimental subjects who reported that they had never given to a charity before allocated 65 percent of their endowment to a named charity in a lab experiment.[22] And one can bet that they did not empty their pockets for the next homeless person they encountered.

A possible explanation for the discrepancies between experimental and real-world behavior is that most people are strongly influenced by cues present in the situation in which they are acting, and there is no reason to think they respond any differently during experiments. An experiment about giving may prompt giving.

Human behavioral experiments raise four concerns about external validity that do not arise in most well-designed natural science experiments. First, experimental subjects typically know they are under a researcher's microscope, and they may behave differently from how they would under total anonymity or, perhaps more relevant for the study of social behavior, under the scrutiny of neighbors, family, or workmates. Second, experimental interactions with other subjects are typically anonymous and lack opportunities for ongoing face-to-face communication, unlike many social interactions of interest to economists and policy makers. Third, subject pools—to date, overwhelmingly students—may be quite different from other populations, due age effects and the processes of recruitment and self-selection.

Finally, the social interactions studied in most experiments are social dilemmas—variations on the Prisoner's Dilemma or Public Goods games—or tasks involving sharing with others, like the Ultimatum game and the Dictator game. In these settings, where social preferences are likely to be important, there is something to be crowded out. But while we would be right in concluding from experimental evidence that incentives may crowd out blood donations or participation in community-service projects, we might wonder whether this evidence has as much to say about the effect of incentives on our behavior when it comes to shopping or cleaning hotel rooms. We already know that it would be a mistake to think that crowding out would diminish the effect of incentives for hard work among Tunisian sharecroppers and American workers installing windshields.

It is impossible to know whether these four aspects of behavioral experiments bias the results in ways relevant to the question of separability. For example, in most cases subjects are paid a "show up" fee to participate in an experiment. Does this practice attract the more materially oriented, who may be less motivated by social preferences subject to crowding out? Conversely, experimenters do not generally communicate the subject of their research, but if potential subjects knew that an experiment was about cooperation, those who signed up might be atypically civic minded.

We can do more than speculate about these problems. Nicole Baran and her coauthors wanted to find out whether University of Chicago business students who had acted with greater reciprocity in an experimental game also reciprocated the great education the university had provided them, by contributing more to the university following graduation.

In the Trust game that Baran implemented, subjects in the role of "investor" were provisionally given a sum from which they were to transfer some amount to another subject, called the "trustee." This amount was then tripled by the experimenter. The trustee, knowing the investor's choice, could in turn "back-transfer" some (or all, or none) of this tripled amount, returning a benefit to the investor. Baran asked whether those who as trustees most generously reciprocated large transfers by the investor were also more likely to donate to a University of Chicago alumni fund. They were.[23]

Similarly, among the Japanese shrimp fishermen whom Jeffrey Carpenter and Erika Seki studied, those who contributed more in a public-goods experiment were more likely to be members of fishing cooperatives, which shared costs and catches among many boats, than to fish under the usual private boat arrangements.[24] A similar pattern was found among fishermen in northeastern Brazil, where some fish offshore in large crews, whose success depends on cooperation and coordination, but those exploiting inland waters fish alone. The ocean fishers were significantly more generous in Public Goods, Ultimatum, and Dictator games than the inland fishers.[25]

A better test of the external validity of experiments would go beyond simply noting whether subjects took part in a cooperation-sensitive production process like offshore or cooperative fishing, and would include a behavior-based measure of individuals' cooperativeness. The Brazilian fishers provide just such a test. Shrimp are caught in large plastic bucket-like contraptions; the fishermen cut holes in the bottoms of the traps to allow the immature shrimp to escape, thereby preserving the stock for future catches.

The fishermen thus face a real-world social dilemma: the expected income of each would be greatest if he were to cut smaller holes in his traps (increasing his own catch) while others cut larger holes in theirs (preserving future stocks). In Prisoner's Dilemma terms, small trap holes are a form of defection that maximizes the individual's material payoff irrespective of what others do (it is the dominant strategy). But a shrimper might resist the temptation to defect if he were both public spirited toward the other fishers and sufficiently patient to value the future opportunities that they all would lose were he to use traps with smaller holes.

Ernst Fehr and Andreas Leibbrandt implemented both a Public Goods game and an experimental measure of impatience with the shrimpers. They found that the shrimpers with both greater patience and greater cooperativeness in the experimental game punched significantly larger holes in their traps, thereby protecting future stocks for the entire community.[26] The effects, controlling for a large number of other possible influences on hole size, were substantial. A shrimper whose experimentally measured patience and cooperativeness were a standard deviation greater than the mean was predicted to cut holes in his traps that were half a standard deviation larger than the mean.

Additional evidence of external validity comes from a set of experiments and field studies with forty-nine groups of herders of the Bale Oromo people in Ethiopia, who were engaged in forest-commons management. Devesh Rustagi and his coauthors implemented public-goods experiments with a total of 679 herders, and also studied the success of the herders' cooperative forest projects.

The most common behavioral type in their experiments, constituting just over a third of the subjects, were "conditional cooperators," who responded to higher contributions by others by contributing more to the public good themselves. Controlling for a large number of other influences on the success of the forest projects, the authors found that groups with a larger number of conditional cooperators were more successful—they planted more new trees—than those with fewer conditional cooperators. This was in part because members of groups with more conditional cooperators spent significantly more time monitoring others' use of the forest. As with the Brazilian shrimpers, differences in the fraction of conditional cooperators in a group were associated with substantial increases in trees planted or time spent monitoring others.[27]

The evidence from a large number of experiments suggests that students volunteering for experiments are not more prosocial than other students; nor are they more prosocial than nonstudents. Indeed they seem to be less so. Students at Cardenas's university in Bogota were more self-interested, according to the results of his Common Pool Resource game, than were the villagers in the experiments just described. Kansas City warehouse workers were more generous in a giving experiment (the Dictator game) than were students at Kansas City Community College. Dutch students showed less aversion to inequality in their experimental behavior than did Dutch citizens who were not students.[28]

When Ernst Fehr and John List played a Trust game with students and with the chief executive officers of Costa Rican businesses, they found that the businessmen in the role of investor trusted more (transferred more to the trustee) and also reciprocated the investor's trust to a far greater degree than did the students, as can be seen in figure 3.6.[29]

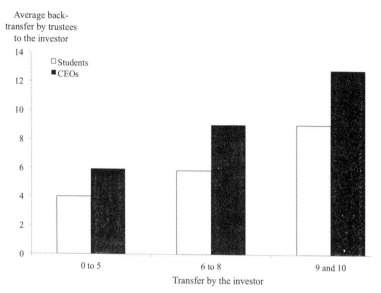

Figure 3.6. Reciprocation of trusting offers in the Trust game among Costa Rican students and CEOs For a given level of transfer by the investor, the CEO trustees back-transferred more than students. (Data from Fehr and List 2004.)

While these tests of the experimental validity of social preference experiments are encouraging, none directly test whether those who act as if they have separable preferences in the experiments do the same in outside the lab. Because testing for separability in natural settings is difficult, it is not clear how such a test would be conducted as a practical matter.

Moral and Material Synergies

It appears, then, that J. S. Mill took the field of political economy in the wrong direction when he narrowed its subject to the study of

MORAL SENTIMENTS AND MATERIAL INTERESTS

the individual "solely as a being who desires to possess wealth." Mill's surprising exclusion of ethical and other-regarding motives would have been a harmless simplification if these motives were really absent (not something that Mill would have ever supposed) or if the effects of incentives could simply be added to the effects of the excluded motives (which is what Mill must have thought). But as we have seen, neither of these justifications can be sustained.

Motives such as reciprocity, generosity, and trust are common, and these preferences may be crowded out by the use of explicit incentives. We have seen how information about the nature (categorical, marginal, strong) and extent of crowding out can guide the sophisticated Legislator in his choice of the level of incentives.

Happy though he is with these new additions to his toolbox— the citizens' best-response functions and what they say about the direct and indirect effects of incentives—the Legislator would surely want to go beyond simply designing appropriate policies and taking the crowding-out problem as a given. The Legislator could seek to frame incentives and other policies so that they crowd in, rather than crowd out, ethical and other-regarding motivations, as in Cardenas's second experiment in rural Colombia.

This thought gives him an addition to his toolbox: a crowding-in best-response function. Notice from figure 3.5 that were crowding in to obtain, the true best-response function of the citizens (not shown) would lie above the separability line imagined by the naïve legislator. It would have either a vertical-axis intercept above that of the separability line (categorical crowding in, as in the Cardenas experiment) or a steeper slope (marginal crowding in, indicating greater effectiveness of the subsidy) or both. But using this new tool requires turning the crowding problem on its head and creating a synergy between social preferences and incentives so as to make the subsidy *more* effective than the naïve legislator expected.

Is there some way that he could transform the nonseparability of incentives and social preferences from a curse to a blessing? To do this, the sophisticated Legislator will need more than the simple taxonomy (marginal versus categorical crowding out and crowding in) introduced here. He will have to penetrate the black box that has so far obscured the causal origins of crowding out. He must discover the cognitive processes that account for the nonseparability of material interests and moral sentiments.

I V

Incentives as Information

Machiavelli sought to design policies that would induce the self-interested to act as if they were "good." Hume wanted to harness the "insatiable avarice" of the citizen-knave in the interests of the public good. This remains an excellent idea.

But a constitution for knaves may *produce* knaves, and may cause the good to act as if they were "wicked." This is not news to successful businessmen such as David Packard:

> In the late 1930s, when I was working for General Electric . . . , the company was making a big thing of plant security . . . guarding its tool and parts bins to make sure employees didn't steal. . . . Many employees set out to prove this obvious display of distrust justified, walking off with tools and parts whenever they could.

When he founded Hewlett-Packard, he later wrote, he was:

> determined that our parts bins and storerooms should always be open . . . which was advantageous to HP in two important ways. . . . The easy access to parts and tools helped product

designers and others who wanted to work out new ideas at home or on weekends. . . . And open bins and storerooms were a symbol of trust, a trust that is central to the way HP does business.[1]

Like Packard, Aristotle's Legislator knows that goodwill is important for a well-ordered firm or nation. He also knows that goodwill may be eroded by policies that seem well conceived for a world in which feelings of trust and mutual concern do not exist or do not matter. Perhaps his greatest challenge is to develop policies under which social preferences will be synergistic with incentives that appeal to economic self-interest, each enhancing rather than diminishing the positive effects of the other. Even if the Legislator wants to adopt a more modest, "do no harm" creed and seeks to design incentives that are simply additive to social preferences, he will have to learn why crowding out occurs.

Learning about Preferences from Experiments

In 2011, Sandra Polanía-Reyes and I set out to collect all the evidence from experimental economics bearing on the assumption that social preferences and incentives are separable. We found fifty-one studies, which used over one hundred subject pools, more than twenty-six thousand subjects in all, and which were conducted in thirty-six countries.[2] The data set includes subjects playing Dictator, Trust, Ultimatum, Public Goods, Third-Party Punishment, Common Pool Resource, Gift Exchange, and other principal-agent games. These are all settings in which one's actions affect the payoffs to others, so social preferences may affect a subject's experimental behavior. In all but one of these games, the relation between the subjects is strategic, meaning that the payoff of each player depends on what the other player or players do, and each player knows this. The exception is the Dictator game, in which one player simply allocates a sum to a passive receiving player. (Recall that these games are described briefly in table 3.1 and in greater detail in appendix 2).

With few exceptions, however, the experiments were not designed to test the effects of incentives on preferences or to determine why these effects occurred, but instead to assess the nature and extent of nonselfish preferences. But as our analysis of categorical and marginal crowding out in the previous chapter shows, we found a method to test hypotheses about the effects of incentives on social preferences.

Because we will use the same method throughout, it is worth pausing to review its logic. The problem that Polanía-Reyes and I faced is that the experiments do not directly measure preferences; instead, what they measure is actions that subjects take under a varying set of constraints and expectations of material rewards. The task then is to use a subject's actions to reverse engineer what must have been her evaluations of the possible outcomes of the game—that is, the preferences that induced her to act in the particular way she acted in the experiment. This method is called "revealed preferences" in economics.

James Andreoni and John Miller used this method to reverse engineer an altruistic utility function from experimental data in a study titled "Giving according to GARP" (GARP is an acronym for "generalized axiom of revealed preference").[3] An important message from their paper is that altruistic preferences and their influence on social behavior can be studied by using the same analytical tools that have been developed for the study of, say, the shopping habits of an individual and her taste for ice cream. This is the reason why in explaining what people do (in the experiments or in natural settings), I interpret their actions as an attempt to bring about some desired end, given the options open to them. The method is conventional in economics, but the content is not: its application to social preferences takes the method in novel directions. Not the least of these, as we have already seen (in figure 3.1), is that a person's desired ends are not something fixed, but may be affected by the use of incentives.

A difficulty in inferring social preferences from experimental data arises because in a strategic interaction, it is generally the case that a subject's actions will depend not only on her preferences, but also on her beliefs about what others will do. Preferences, to be clear, are an individual's evaluations of the outcomes that her actions may bring about; beliefs are cause-and-effect understandings that translate her possible actions into their expected outcomes. Beliefs come in to play because the payoff that she receives in the above experiments (except the Dictator game) depends not only on what she does, but also on what others do.

To see how this complicates the problem of inferring preferences from the actions taken, recall the Trust game described in the previous chapter. When the investor transfers a significant portion of his endowment to the trustee (to be tripled by the experimenter, resulting in the trustee getting three times what the investor sent), we cannot jump to the conclusion the investor is generous. The reason is that his large transfer may have been motivated by self-interest combined with the belief that the trustee would back-transfer not less than half of what she receives. In this case, he would receive not less than $1.50 on every $1 sent, or a 50 percent rate of return on his "investment"; altruism need not necessarily be at work.

Perhaps we can, at a minimum, infer that the investor trusted the trustee. But even this is not the case, because his considerable transfer might have been based entirely on the belief that she was very poor and would keep every penny, which, combined with his generous preferences, would make this (for him) the best outcome of the game.

Despite difficulties in untangling beliefs and preferences as reasons for experimental behavior, well-designed experiments allow us to narrow the class of motives that may have been at work. In a one-shot (not repeated) Trust game, when the trustee returns a substantial amount to the investor, for example, that action clearly rules out self-interest. When, as in this case, a parsimonious explanation of the experimental behavior would be to attribute social preferences to the individual, I do so, in a phrase like "the subject apparently had motives other than self-interest," the "apparently" being a reminder that experiments do not directly test for preferences. But given the plausibility of the idea that one can sometimes recover preferences from observed behavior, I sometimes drop the "apparently" where the meaning is not likely to be misunderstood. In addition, we can often predict the actions that would be taken by an entirely selfish person, or one for whom social preferences and incentives were separable (that is, simply additive), as we did in figure 3.4.

To recover preferences from experimental results, we followed the same strategy used to study marginal and categorical crowding out in the Irlenbusch and Ruchala experiment. We observed the total effect of incentives on the actions taken by the subjects and then noted whether that result differed from the predicted direct effect (the top arrows in both panels of figure 3.1). If the total effect differed from the direct (material costs and benefits) effect, then we could infer that an incentive had somehow altered the subject's (unobserved) experienced values and had thereby affected her actions (via the bottom arrows in figure 3.1).[4]

INCENTIVES AS INFORMATION

This is what Polanía-Reyes and I found; and in most cases, the effect of incentives on experienced values was negative. The experiments show that policies premised on the belief that citizens or employees are entirely self-interested often induce people to act exactly that way. The challenge is to understand why.

The Meaning of Incentives

To help decipher the causes of crowding out, I will take a page from Friedrich Hayek, who taught economists to consider prices as messages.[5] When, say, the price of bread goes up because of a drought in the U.S. Midwest, the following sort of message is conveyed: "Bread is now scarcer and should be economized; you should put potatoes or rice on the table tonight." The genius of the market as a system of organizing an economy, Hayek pointed out, is that the message comes with its own motivation to pay attention; eating potatoes rather than bread will save money.

Incentives are a kind of price. We will see that had the authorities in Haifa consulted the Legislator, the message sent by a fine for lateness in picking up your child at the day care center would have been: "Your tardiness is inflicting costs on our staff, so you should try a little harder to come on time." But while the price of bread often conveys the right information at least approximately, the lateness price for the Haifa parents must have sent a quite different message from the one that would have prompted the parents to "economize" on lateness.

In addition to the distinction between categorical and marginal crowding introduced in the previous chapter, we can distinguish two causal mechanisms by which crowding (out or in) might take place.

First, incentives may affect preferences because they provide cues to the nature of the situation in which a person finds herself and hence may act as a guide to appropriate behavior, resulting in her applying a different set of preferences. ("If you are shopping, it is okay to be entirely self-interested; if you are with your family, it is not.") In this case, we say that preferences are situation-dependent and that the presence and nature of incentives are part of the situation.[6]

The second type of crowding out arises because incentives may alter the process by which people come to acquire preferences over their lifetime. In this case, we say that preferences are endogenous. Evidence from experiments may shed light on the effects of incentives on this process, but most experiments are far too brief (lasting a few hours at most) to capture the kind of social learning or socialization, typically occurring during childhood or adolescence, that makes preferences endogenous. I consider endogenous preferences in the next chapter. Here I use experimental evidence to consider cases in which preferences are situation-dependent.

Situation-dependence arises because actions are motivated by a heterogeneous repertoire of preferences—spiteful, payoff maximizing, generous—the salience of which depends on the nature of the decision situation. Our preferences are different when we interact with a domineering supervisor, shop, or relate to our neighbors. The boss may bring out spite, while the neighbors evoke generosity.

To see how this works, think about gifts.[7] Economists know that money is the perfect gift—it replaces the giver's less well-informed choice of a present with the recipient's own choice when she takes the money and buys the perfect gift for herself. But at holiday time, few economists give money to their friends, family, or colleagues. We know that money cannot convey thoughtfulness, romantic interest, concern, whimsy, or any of the other messages that gifts express. A gift is more than a transfer of resources; it is a signal about the giver's relationship to the recipient. Money changes the signal.

Can the same be said of incentives? It is commonplace in psychology to think that it can. Mark Lepper and his coauthors explain why: "The multiple social meanings of the use of tangible rewards are reflected in our everyday distinction among bribes and bonuses, incentives and salaries. . . . They carry different connotations concerning, for example, [i] the likely conditions under which the reward was offered, [ii] the presumed motives of the person administering the reward, and [iii] the relationship between the agent and the recipient of the reward."[8] All three pieces of information conveyed by incentives—"the likely conditions," "the presumed motives," and the "relationship"—may affect the social preferences of the incentives' target. Sometimes the news is not good.

Bad News

Incentives have a purpose, and because the purpose is often evident to the target of the incentives, she may infer information about the person who designed the incentive, about his beliefs concerning her (the target), and about the nature of the task to be done.[9] Incentives may affect preferences for reasons that are familiar to economists, as Mark Lepper and his coauthors say, because they indicate "the presumed motives of the person administering the reward." By implementing an incentive, one reveals information about one's intentions (payoff-maximizing versus fair-minded, for example) as well as beliefs about the target (hardworking or not, for example) and the targeted behavior (how onerous it is, for example.) This information may then affect the target's motivation to undertake the task.

The Boston fire commissioner's threat to dock the pay of firemen accumulating more than fifteen sick days conveyed the information that he did not trust that the firemen were doing their very best to come to work, especially on Mondays and Fridays. For the firemen, the new situation—working for a boss who did not trust them—seems to have altered their motivation. Of course, we cannot know just what caused the spike in sick call-ins. It could have been a very bad flu outbreak. That is why we use experimental information in addition to natural observation to try to understand why crowding out occurs.

This "bad news" effect commonly occurs in relationships between a principal, who designs incentives (a wage rate, a schedule of penalties for late delivery of a promised service, and so forth), and an agent, who is being induced to behave more in the principal's interest than the agent otherwise would. To do this, the principal must know (or guess) how the agent will respond to each of the possible incentives he could deploy. The agent knows this, of course, and hence can ordinarily figure out what the principal was thinking when he chose one particular incentive over other possible ways of affecting the agent's behavior.

Here is an example of how this sometimes does not work out well in practice. In this experiment, as in the trust game played with Costa Rican CEOs and students, German students in the role of "investor," the principal, were given the opportunity to transfer some amount to the agent, called the "trustee." As usual in the Trust game the experimenter then tripled this amount. Recall that the trustee, knowing the investor's choice, could in turn back-transfer some (or all or none) of this tripled amount, returning a benefit to the investor.[10]

But this version of the standard Trust game came with a twist. When the investor transferred money to the trustee, he or she was

Average back-
transfer of trustees

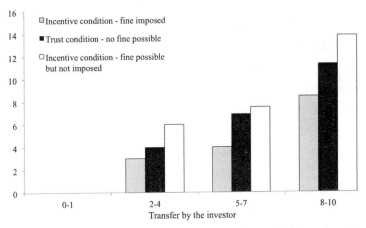

Figure 4.1. Forgoing the use of incentives apparently crowded in reciprocity in the Trust game (Data from Fehr and Rockenbach 2003.) Reciprocation was greatest when the fine was available to the investor but its use was renounced.

also asked to specify a desired level of back-transfer. In addition, the experimenters implemented an incentive condition: in some of the experimental sessions, the investor had the option of declaring that he would impose a fine if the trustee's back-transfer were less than the desired amount. In this "fine treatment," the investor had a further option, namely, to decline to impose the fine, and this choice (forgoing the opportunity to fine a nonperforming trustee) was known to the trustee and taken before the trustee's decision about the amount to back-transfer. There was also the standard "trust" condition, in which no such incentives were available to the investor. Figure 4.1 summarizes the results.

In the trust condition (black bars, no fines), trustees reciprocated generous initial transfers by investors with greater back-transfers. But stating the intent to fine a noncompliant trustee (grey bars) actually reduced return transfers for a given level of the investor's transfer.

The use of the fine appears to have diminished the trustee's feelings of reciprocity toward the investor. Even more interesting is that renouncing use of the fine when it was available (white bars) increased back-transfers (again, for a given amount transferred by the investor).

Only one-third of the investors renounced the fine when it was available; their payoffs were 50 percent greater than those of investors who used the fines. The bad-news interpretation suggested by Fehr and Rockenbach is that both in the trust condition and when the investor renounced the fine, a large initial transfer signaled that the investor trusted the trustee. The threat of the fine, however, conveyed a different message and diminished the trustee's reciprocity.[11] The fine option and the opportunity publicly to renounce its use provided the investor with an opportunity to send a trusting message to the trustee.

There are lessons here for the design of institutions and organizations. Crowding out as a result of the bad-news mechanism may be prevalent in principal-agent settings but can be averted where the principal has a means of signaling fairness or trust in the agent.

Polanía-Reyes and I wanted to know which subjects responded adversely to the threat of the fine. Our survey of the experimental evidence found that crowding out affects individuals who are intrinsically motivated or fair-minded. For payoff maximizers, it appears, there is nothing to crowd out. This unsurprising fact, like the positive effect of an investor renouncing use of the fines, has lessons for Aristotle's Legislator.

Moral Disengagement

Incentives may cause crowding out for another reason, one less familiar to economists. In most situations, people look for cues for appropriate behavior, and incentives provide these cues. A plausible explanation of some of the framing effects of incentives is that it occurs because market-like incentives trigger what psychologists term "moral disengagement," a process that occurs because "people can switch their ethicality on and off."[12]

In this case, the adverse indirect effect of the incentive does not work by conveying information about the principal, and it may be at work even in nonstrategic settings. Incentives provide information about (as Lepper and his coauthors put it) "the likely conditions under which the reward was offered" and hence about how the individual ought to behave. In the experimental evidence, moral disengagement can be distinguished from the bad-news cause of crowding out: in the former, incentives are implemented by a principal who is a player in the game, but in the latter, the targets of the incentive are not playing against the incentive designer. Instead, the incentives are introduced by the experimenter (as in Cardenas's experiments in rural Colombia) or possibly by peers in the game.

Situational cues may be very subtle, and our responses to them unwitting. When experimental subjects had the opportunity to cheat on a test and thus gain higher monetary rewards, less than quarter did so when the room was brightly lit, but more than half cheated when the room was slightly less well lit (the variations in lighting had no effect on whether one's cheating could be observed). In another experiment, subjects who wore dark glasses were much less generous to their partners in a Dictator game than were those outfitted with clear glasses.[13] Dark glasses and a darkened room, the researchers reasoned, gave the subjects a sense of anonymity. But it was entirely illusory: it is difficult to imagine that a subject could really think that wearing dark glasses would make him less observable, especially since the experiment was conducted at computer terminals in closed cubicles. Dogs, too, steal more when its dark, but the reason is probably not moral disengagement.[14]

The dark glasses were just a cue to anonymity and a sign that acting as if one were really anonymous would be okay. To see why this matters, imagine a survey question about personal pleasures asked in two different ways. First: "Please tell us about some experience that you enjoyed very much." Second: "Please tell us about some experience that you enjoyed very much. In answering this question, remember that there is absolutely no way that anyone will ever be able to associate your name with what you reply." The dark glasses, like the second version of the question could invite some kind of transgression.

Our degree of real anonymity changes dramatically as we move among family, the workplace, the marketplace, and other domains of social interaction. Alan Page Fiske provides a taxonomy of four psychological models corresponding to distinct kinds of social relationships: authoritarian, communal, egalitarian, and market, each with culturally prescribed patterns of appropriate behavior.[15] Depending on the information they convey, incentives may signal that the situation corresponds to one of these four types, and in part because the degree of anonymity differs, they may evoke distinctive responses. Because incentives are common in markets and markets are associated with anonymity, or at least with impersonal, arm's-length dealings with others, incentives may be a cue to imagined anonymity.

Here is an example, one that suggests that the moral-disengagement effects of market interactions are not simply a matter of anonymity taken literally. Armin Falk and Nora Szech entrusted University of Bonn students with the care of "their" healthy young mouse, showing each a picture of one of the very cute mice.[16] They then offered them a payment if they would allow the mouse to be gassed to death. Before making their decision, the subjects were shown a very disturbing video of a mouse being gassed.

In addition to this "individual treatment," they also implemented a "market treatment" in which the subject could sell her mouse to another student, who would then allow the mouse to be killed. They hypothesized that a student who was reluctant to surrender her mouse as simply an individual choice might be more willing to let the mouse die in the market treatment because the sale to another student distanced her from the deed.

Forty-six percent of the subjects in the individual (nonmarket) treatment were willing to surrender their mice for ten euros or less. When the mouse trustee could sell the mouse to a buyer, however, 72 percent were willing to let their mice die for that price or less.

Falk and Szech asked the subjects the minimum payment for which they would be willing to give up their mice. Using this information, they were able to calculate how much they would have had to offer the subjects in the individual treatment to get 72 percent of them to give up their mice—the same percentage of the subjects in the market treatment who had been willing to do so.

What they found was astounding: to get 72 percent of the subjects in the individual treatment to let their mice die, the subjects would have to have been offered 47.50 euros. Recall that in the market treatment, compensation of only 10 euros was sufficient for this number to let their mice go. This almost fivefold difference between the market and individual treatments in the experiment may be considered a measure of the moral disengagement created by the market setting.

Notice that it was not the incentives per se that reduced the price at which the market-treatment students would let the mice die. There were monetary incentives in both the individual and the market settings. What differed was that the subjects in the market setting could disengage morally.

It would be interesting to know how much saving the mouse would have been worth to subjects in a treatment in which an individual's mouse had been commandeered by another subject and destined for a certain death, but could be saved by purchasing it back. If the results were similar to those obtained with the other market treatment, then we could conclude that it was the arm's-length nature of the market setup, not the fact that it was a market per se, that accounted for the radical drop in willingness to pay to save the mouse in the market treatment.

A similar finding comes from Elizabeth Hoffman and her co-authors, who illustrated the framing power of names in an Ultimatum game.[17] In this game—another workhorse of behavioral economics—one player, called the proposer, is given a sum of money by the experimenter and asked to allocate it to the other player, called the responder. The responder, knowing how much the proposer was initially given, may either accept or reject the offer (which is the ultimatum giving the game its title). If the proposer accepts the ultimatum, the game ends and the two parties take home the sums of money determined by the proposer's split. But if the proposer rejects the ultimatum, the game still ends, but both go home empty-handed.

This game has been played throughout the world by hundreds of subject pools. In the next chapter, I describe some cross-cultural experiments that I conducted as part of a team of economists and anthropologists. Though results differ from culture to culture, responders commonly reject low offers. In postgame debriefings, some express anger at the unfairness of the proposer as a reason to prefer getting nothing rather than to allow the proposer to benefit from an unjust division of the pie.

INCENTIVES AS INFORMATION

The motivation of proposers who offer a large share of the pie to responders is more complicated. Offering a fifty-fifty split, for example, might be motivated by fair-mindedness or generosity, but it could also result when an entirely self-interested proposer believes that a respondent is fair-minded and will therefore reject a low offer.

Hoffman and her coauthors found that proposers' offers and responders' rejections of low offers were both diminished by simply relabeling the game the "Exchange" game and relabeling proposers and responders "sellers" and "buyers." The renaming did not in any way alter the incentives at work in the game. Instead, it affected the subjects' sense of appropriate behavior independently of the incentives. From the results, the new name appeared to diminish the respondents' standard of what constitutes a fair offer, or to reduce the salience of fairness in the respondents' minds. The proposers appeared to become either less generous or less concerned that responders might reject low offers.

The power of names has been confirmed in many (but not all) experiments since then. As may have been the case in the experiment by Hoffman and her coauthors, in some cases the framing effect appears to have altered subjects' beliefs about the actions of others rather than their preferences.[18]

Naming the game is not necessary for framing effects to occur. Incentives alone can create powerful frames. A year before the first U.S. reality-TV show, Andrew Schotter and his coauthors found, in a clever modification of the Ultimatum game, that market-like competition for "survival" among subjects reduced their concern for fairness. The subjects played the standard game no differently from how it is conducted in other experiments: proposers' substantial offers were accepted, and low offers were rejected. But when, in a subsequent treatment, the experimenters told the subjects that those with lower earnings would be excluded from a second round of the game, proposers offered less generous amounts, and responders accepted lower offers. The authors' interpretation was that "the competition inherent in markets . . . offers justifications for actions that, in isolation, would be unjustifiable."[19]

While this explanation is plausible, the experiment, like the others surveyed thus far, could not provide direct evidence for moral disengagement. Sometimes, however, we can directly measure how incentives cause ethical reasoning to recede in people's minds.

A large team of anthropologists and economists implemented both Dictator and Third-Party Punishment games in fifteen societies, including Amazonian, Arctic, and African hunter-gatherers; manufacturing workers in Accra, Ghana; and U.S. undergraduates.[20] Recall that in the Dictator game, an experimental subject is assigned a sum of money and asked to allocate some, all, or none of it to a passive recipient. The Third-Party Punishment game is a Dictator game with an active onlooker (the third party).

After observing the dictator's allocation to the second party, the third party can then pay to impose a fine on the dictator. Most third parties tend to punish stingy dictators. And dictators anticipate this. One would expect that in the presence of a third party, and therefore with the prospect of being fined, dictators would adjust their allocations upward compared to their allocations in the simple Dictator game, in which there is no possibility that stingy offers will be punished.

But this was not what happened.

Surprisingly, in only two of the fifteen populations studied were the dictators' offers significantly higher in the Third-Party Punishment game than in the Dictator game, and in four populations they were significantly *lower*. In Accra, where 41 percent of the dictator's allocations resulted in fines by the third party, the allocations in the Third-Party Punishment game were 30 percent lower than in the Dictator game. The incentives provided by the fine did not induce higher allocations; they had the opposite effect.

Were ethical motives crowded out? There is some evidence that this is what happened. In the standard game, dictators who adhered to one of the world's major religions (meaning, for this subject pool, Islam or Christianity, including Russian Orthodoxy) made allocations in the Dictator game that were 23 percent higher than those of dictators who did not follow one of these world religions. But in the Third-Party Punishment game, this "religion effect" virtually disappeared. Adherents of world religions behaved no differently from the unaffiliated. The presence of a monetary incentive appeared to define the setting as one in which the moral teachings of one's religion, including generosity as a value, were not relevant.

Another piece of evidence suggests that the incentive provided by the prospect of a fine from a third party increased the salience of economic concerns. In the standard Dictator game, the dictator's offer was uncorrelated with the dictator's economic need (in the real world). But in the Third-Party Punishment Game, the dictator's economic situation strongly (and significantly) predicted his or her offers. The incentives implicit in the Third-Party Punishment Game appeared to substitute economic motivations for religious or moral concerns. The results of these experiments were consistent with the expectation that crowding out operates through the effect of incentives on those with preexisting social preferences. It has no effect on those with little morality to crowd out.

The evidence on moral disengagement gives Aristotle's Legislator plenty to work with, for he knows that tangible rewards may be framed as "bribes and bonuses, incentives and salaries," as Lepper and his coauthors say, and one might add "and as prizes, fines, and punishments." He also knows that moral frames for social interactions are not difficult either to construct or to suppress.

Control: Incentives Compromise Autonomy

The third reason that incentives can crowd out social preferences is that people may respond adversely to the political nature of the incentives, which are often transparently an attempt to control the target.[21] Psychologists have explored how incentives (or constraints) can compromise a subject's sense of autonomy, explaining how this harm reduces an intrinsic motivation to undertake the targeted task.[22] The psychological mechanism at work appears to be a desire for the "feelings of competence and self-determination" that come from intrinsically motivated behavior.[23]

It is easy to see how incentives might convey the message that a principal (an employer, for example) wishes to control an agent (his employee). But most of the experimental evidence for this mechanism comes from nonstrategic settings (meaning that the experimenters, not a principal, implement the incentive). This self-determination mechanism thus differs from the previous two mechanisms—bad news about a principal and moral disengagement—because it arises from the target's desire for autonomy per se. It does not depend on the target's inferring the principal's desire to control the agent, on other negative information about the principal, or on clues about appropriate behavior.

Lepper and his coauthors in a different paper explained why "a person induced to undertake an inherently desirable activity as a means to some ulterior end should cease to see the activity as an end in itself." An incentive, they explained, may affect a person's perceptions of his own motivation: "To the extent that the external reinforcement contingencies controlling his behavior are salient, unambiguous, and sufficient to explain it, the person attributes his behavior to these controlling circumstances. But if external contingencies are not perceived . . . the person attributes his behavior to his own dispositions, interests, and desires."[24] In this perspective, the person is constantly constructing or affirming an identity and is acting so as to signal to herself that she is autonomous. The presence of the incentive makes the signal less convincing because it provides a competing explanation for her behavior.

In cases where people derive pleasure from an action per se in the absence of other rewards, psychologists say that the introduction of incentives may "overjustify" the activity and reduce the individual's sense of autonomy. An example is provided by the experiment mentioned in chapter I in which toddlers who were rewarded with a toy for helping an adult retrieve an out-of-reach object became less helpful than those who weren't given a toy. The authors of that study concluded: "Perhaps when rewards are offered children simply come to perceive a formerly self-sufficient activity as merely a means to some more valuable end."[25] The effect may be to reduce child's intrinsic motivation to help, and if the reward alone is insufficient, the child may simply stop helping.

In an iconic overjustification experiment, children were promised a reward for engaging in an activity that they had previously pursued enthusiastically for no reward. Children were selected for the experiment on the basis of their prior interest in painting and then asked whether they would like to draw with felt-tipped markers, under three conditions.[26] Under the "unexpected reward condition," after drawing for a period of time, the child was offered a "Good Player

Award" card with a red ribbon, a gold star, and the child's name on it. The second, "expected reward condition" differed in that the experimenter showed the child the award card and asked: "Would you like to win one of these Good Player Awards?" All assented and were given the award following the drawing session. In the third treatment there was no reward (expected or unexpected).

A week or two later, the experimenters observed the subjects' play choices in their ordinary school setting. Those who had anticipated a reward for choosing drawing took up painting only half as frequently as those who had not anticipated a reward. Moreover, those who had been promised a reward also painted less than they had done before the experiment. And during the experiment itself, the drawings produced by children who received rewards were judged to be of substantially lower quality than those done by the students in the control group. (The judges of artistic quality did not know which treatment groups the children were in.)

The researchers designed the experiment to isolate whether the negative impact occurred because an activity was rewarded or because the subject chose the activity knowing that it would be rewarded. The fact that it was the anticipation of the reward, not the reward itself, that affected the children's subsequent behavior suggests that the adverse effect was associated with compromised autonomy, not the receipt of rewards per se.

This interpretation is consistent with the observation that close supervision or arbitrary deadlines for completion of an otherwise enjoyable activity has almost the same negative effect as financial or other rewards. Lepper and his coauthors point out that the "detrimental effects of unnecessarily close adult supervision or the imposition of unneeded temporal deadlines suggest strongly that the effects . . . are the result of superfluous constraints on children's actions, not a specific function of the use of tangible rewards."[27] Thus it may not be the material reward per se that is the cause of crowding out. The Legislator knows that if true, this idea will have important implications for the design of public policy. We will return to it.

In contrast to psychologists' overjustification experiments, in which incentives are typically implemented by the experimenter, economists have studied strategic interactions in which the incentive is implemented by a player in the game. Here is an example.

Armin Falk and Michael Kosfeld implemented a principal-agent game with adult subjects to explore the idea that control aversion motivated by self-determination could explain why incentives sometimes degrade performance.[28] Experimental agents in a role similar to that of an employee chose a level of "production" that was costly for them to provide and beneficial to the principal (the employer). The agent's choice effectively determined the distribution of gains between the two, and the agent's maximum payoff came if he produced nothing at all.

Before the agent (the employee) made his decision, the principal could elect to leave the level of production completely to the agent's discretion or instead to impose a lower bound on the agent's production. (The levels of production required of the employee by these bounds were varied by the experimenter across treatments; the principal's choice was simply whether to impose it.) The principal could infer that a self-interested agent would perform at the lower bound or, in the absence of the bound, at zero. Thus imposition of the bound would maximize the principal's payoff.

But in the experiment, agents provided *less* production when the principal imposed the bound. Apparently anticipating this negative response, fewer than a third of the principals in the moderate- and low-bound treatments opted to impose the bound. This minority of "untrusting" principals earned, on average, half the profits of those who did not seek to control the agents' choice in the low-bound treatment, and a third less in the intermediate-bound condition. The use even of the upper bound reduced the profits of the principals, although not significantly.

These results are consistent with the adverse reaction to control by others seen in psychological experiments. But it may have resulted either from control aversion per se or from the "bad news" about the principal conveyed by his placing limits on the agent. Gabriel Burdin, Simon Halliday, and Fabio Landini used a clever experimental design to distinguish between these two reactions to control.[29] They first confirmed Falk and Kosfeld's crowding-out results by using an identical treatment. They then introduced a third party who could impose the lower bounds on the "employee" but who would not benefit in any way from the employee's "hard work," which, as before, would contribute to the principal's payoffs. If the adverse reaction to the lower bounds observed in the Falk and Kosfeld experiment was due to control aversion per se (rather than bad news about the principal), their third-party control treatment should have exhibited a similar negative reaction.

But it did not. Their interpretation is that the crowding out in the Falk and Kosfeld experiment was due primarily to the message that it sent about the principal and not to control aversion per se.

Consistent with the idea that incentives sometimes unintentionally are messages, the imposition of the lower bound in the Falk and Kosfeld experiment gave employees remarkably accurate information about employers' beliefs about them. In postplay interviews, most agents agreed with the statement that the imposition of the lower bound was a signal of distrust, and the principals who imposed the bound in fact had substantially lower expectations of the agents.

The untrusting principals' attempts to control the agents' choices induced over half the agents in all three treatments to produce at the minimum allowed, thereby affirming the principals' pessimism. This is an entirely new twist for Aristotle's Legislator. Looking up from the details of the control-aversion experiment to think about entire societies, the Legislator has a disturbing thought. In a real economy, he worries, if most employers have low expectations of their workers, they will adopt compensation and supervision policies that, like the imposition of the lower bound in the experiment, will evoke minimal performance from their workers. And the workers' slacking on the job will affirm the employers' dismal expectations.

Depending on the distribution of principals' prior beliefs about agents, he ruminates, a population with preferences similar to these experimental subjects' could support either a trusting and highly productive outcome or an untrusting one in which production barely exceeds the minimum that could be extracted by fiat. In either case, the prior beliefs are perpetuated, so either outcome could persist indefinitely.

This might not matter much, the Legislator tries to reassure himself, in an economy in which the imposition of limits would be sufficient to secure most of what employers cared about. The first example that comes to mind, unhappily, is cane harvesting and other work done by slaves, whose pace of work is easily observed and maintained by an overseer with recourse to severe punishments. He is relieved to come up with the assembly line next, whose pace is a kind of mechanical regulator of the work effort of employees. Those who fall behind are easily singled out. But he is at pains to think of any examples from a modern economy—that is, one based substantially on services, intensive in knowledge and interpersonal care—in which a high level of production could be enforced by the imposition of such lower bounds on otherwise unwilling producers.

Happily it occurs to him that a onetime intervention that induced employers not to impose lower bounds on work input might reveal to them that workers, under the right conditions, were willing to provide substantial input in return for more trusting treatment. With this new knowledge, employers would adopt new, more trusting treatments of their workers even after withdrawal of the intervention that induced them to give up the lower bound in the first place. Thus a onetime intervention could transform a vicious circle into a virtuous one. In this case, the policy would not work by changing workers' or employers' preferences; instead, it would force employers to act in a way that would alter workers' beliefs about them, in turn leading workers to act in ways that would induce the employers to adopt different beliefs about their work habits.

The same could be said of an intervention that would somehow induce workers to challenge employers' low expectations of them by providing more input than required, even when the lower bound was imposed. Economists use the term "equilibrium selection" to describe this kind of convention switching. The Legislator adds it to his tool kit.

Emotion, Deliberation, and Crowding Out

Can the Aristotelian Legislator go beyond the insights of the "incentives as messages" approach to explore the proximate neural basis for crowding out? Could he map how an incentive acts as a stimulus to our deliberative and affective neural activity, and use this information to design policies that would activate rather than deactivate the neural pathways associated with cooperative and generous behavior?

For example, we will see that on the basis of neuroimaging and other evidence, one might be tempted to conclude that incentives activate cognitive processes that are more deliberative and less affective, and that deliberation tends to result in self-interested action. Could we make incentives synergistic with social preferences by framing subsidies and fines in such a way to stimulate emotional and visceral responses rather than calculating ones?

I have my doubts, as you will see, but the idea is not as farfetched as it sounds. To start, there is some evidence that incentives and social rewards activate different regions of the brain. To identify the proximate causes of the crowding-out behavior in Fehr and Rockenbach's Trust game, described earlier, Jian Li and his coauthors studied the activation of distinct brain regions that occurs when trustees are faced with an investor who threatens to impose a fine for insufficient back-transfers. They compared these results with the neural activity in trustees who were not threatened with sanctions.[30] As in the Fehr and Rockenbach experiment, the threat tended to reduce rather than increase back-transfers made by the trustee for a given level of investor transfer.

The brain scan showed that the threat of sanctions deactivated the ventromedial prefrontal cortex (a brain area whose activation was correlated with higher back-transfers in this experiment) as well as other areas related to the processing of social rewards. The threat activated the parietal cortex, an area thought to be associated with cost-benefit analysis and other self-interested optimizing. Li and his coauthors concluded that the sanctions induced a "perception shift" favoring a more calculating, self-interested response.

If it were confirmed that incentives like the investor's threat of a fine in the Trust game activate brain regions associated with calculative self-interest, perhaps we could design incentives that do not have this effect. The "perception shift" in the subjects was between two quite different ways of responding to a stimulus: affective (meaning visceral or emotional) and deliberative (or cognitive). The philosopher-neuroscientist Joshua Greene describes these two processes as follows: "The human brain is like a dual-mode camera with both automatic settings and a manual mode."[31] The manual mode requires deliberate choice in picking the right settings; the automatic-setting option circumvents deliberation. In Greene's terms, deliberative or cognitive processes are the manual mode, and visceral and emotional ways of responding, which make up the affective processes, are the automatic mode. Psychologists call this idea "dual-process theory."[32]

In "Moral Tribes: Emotion, Reason, and the Gap between Us and Them," Greene provides a framework for thinking about incentives and morals. First, deliberative processes are outcome based (in philosophical terms, "consequentialist") and utilitarian, while affective processes support nonconsequentialist judgments (termed "deontological") such as duty or the conformity of an action to a set of rules. Second, these ways of behaving are associated with activation in different brain regions, respectively, the (deliberative) prefrontal cortex and the (affective) limbic system.

The neuroscientific evidence then implies that economic incentives induce consequentialist reasoning (activation of the prefrontal cortex) and implicitly reduce the salience of deontological judgments (deactivation of the limbic system). If this view is correct, then the crowding out seen in many behavioral experiments implies that consequentialist reasoning is often (but not always) less prosocial than deontological judgment.

There is some evidence that this dual-process approach can identify the proximate causes of behavior not only in the Trust game but also in the other experiments. Alan Sanfey and his coauthors, interpreted an earlier experiment by Sanfey's group in this way:

A neuro-imaging study examining the Ultimatum Game found two brain regions that were particularly active when the participant was confronted with an unfair offer, the anterior insula and the dorsolateral prefrontal cortex (dlPFC). Activation in these areas has been shown to correlate with emotional and deliberative processing, respectively, and it was found that if the insular activation was greater than the dlPFC activation, participants tended to reject the offer, whereas if the dlPFC activation was greater, they tended to accept the offer. This offers neural evidence for a two-system account of decision-making in this task.[33]

Struck by the activation of the insula, a region associated with negative emotions such as fear and disgust, and further associated with rejection of (presumably low) offers in the Ultimatum game, Colin Camerer and his coauthors comment: "It is irresistible to speculate that the insula is a neural locus of the distaste for inequality and unfair treatment."[34]

Dual-process theory may also explain why the effects of activation of both the affective and the deliberative processes may be less than additive. Deborah Small, George Loewenstein, and Paul Slovic found that a picture of a needy girl induced more charitable giving than did statistics on need, and that providing both statistics and the picture yielded less giving than the picture alone.[35] They concluded: "When thinking deliberatively, people discount sympathy towards identifiable victims but fail to generate sympathy toward statistical victims." Here the affective system appeared to promote generosity, but was overridden by the deliberative system when that process was stimulated by the presentation of statistics. In this case, the presentation of statistics may have activated the prefrontal cortex and the deliberative process, just as the threat of the fine did in Li's Trust game experiment, competing with and crowding out activation of more affective neural processing.

But it strikes me as unlikely that human goodness should emanate largely from the reptilian brain, namely, the limbic system and other brain regions in which humans are less distinctive than other animals, compared with our quite special prefrontal cortex. The idea that consequentialist reasoning is more likely to induce self-interest, and that deontological logic is more likely to favor ethical and other-regarding behavior, is far from obvious. If I take pleasure both in helping people in need and in eating ice cream, but cannot at the moment do both, it is not at all clear why activating my deliberative processes would lead me to go for the ice cream when my visceral response would be to help the person in need.

Why would incentives stimulate deliberation rather than emotion, and why would deliberation override positive social emotions such as sympathy? The first part of the question is easy: an incentive invites us to do cost-benefit calculations to determine whether the incentive is sufficient to motivate the targeted activity. These calculations are qualitatively different from our responses to emotions like sympathy, pain avoidance, or fear. If you have a painful burning sensation in your hand, you don't generally deliberate about whether getting away from the fire is to your benefit. But why might deliberation result in less prosocial behavior? This remains an open question.

Indeed it would be a mistake to think that deliberation is the enemy of generosity. A study by Linda Skitka and her coauthors showed that among American liberals (compared with conservatives), the deliberative process is more generous toward those affected with HIV-AIDS, and is less influenced than the affective process by considerations of "responsibility" for contracting the illness.[36]

To study the balance of affective and deliberative processes, Skitka and her coauthors overloaded the deliberative capacities of experimental subjects by inducing high levels of what psychologists call "cognitive load," as could be done, for example, by asking them to remember two seven-digit numbers (high load) as opposed to one two-digit number. In dual-process terms, high load is designed to degrade the deliberative process. Here is how Loewenstein and O'Donoghue interpreted the results: "The study found that subjects were less likely to advocate subsidized treatment under conditions of high [cognitive] load, which we would interpret as evidence that deliberative reactions are more concerned than affective reactions to AIDS victims. More interestingly, under conditions of high load, both liberals and conservatives were less likely to provide subsidized treatment to those deemed responsible (relative to those deemed not responsible), whereas under conditions of low load, liberals treated both groups equally whereas conservatives continued to favor groups who were seen as less responsible for contracting the HIV-AIDS."[37] They went on to suggest that the experiment might show that the "affective and deliberative reactions were consistent for conservatives—so cognitive load has no effect—but conflicting for liberals."

I suspect that the deliberation–self-interest coupling does not really work: deliberative processes can produce moral and other-regarding judgments and behavior. Taking seriously the golden rule is an example.

Correspondingly, the coupling of affective processes with generous and ethical motivations seems questionable. Self-interested behavior must have a solid foundation in our less deliberative processes.

As in all animals, visceral and other nondeliberative reactions in humans have evolved under the influence of natural selection. A good case can be made that among humans, natural selection may have resulted in a genetically transmitted visceral or emotional predisposition to help others even at a cost to oneself.[38] But it would be surprising if such "automatic" reactions did not also induce self-interested behavior such as pain avoidance, satisfaction of sexual desire, and flight from danger. One could expect, therefore, that self-interested behavior would be aligned with the neural pathways associated with emotion no less than with deliberation.

If this is the case, we would expect that the difference between self-regarding and other-regarding behavior does not map neatly onto either the deliberation-emotion distinction in cognitive processing or onto the prefrontal cortex–limbic system distinction in neuroscience. The neuroscientist Jonathan Cohen says that the deliberative prefrontal cortex "may be a critical substrate for *Homo economicus*."[39] Cohen is right about the calculative aspect of economic man. But the prefrontal cortex may be no more implicated than the affective limbic system in the self-interest attributed to *Homo economicus*.

The neuroscience of a dual-process theory of social preferences is a burgeoning field still in its infancy. But if a last word is to be had at this early date, it goes to Loewenstein and O'Donoghue: "[The] deliberative system has a stable concern for others driven by moral and ethical principles for how one ought to behave. The affective system, in contrast, is driven toward anything between pure self-interest and extreme altruism depending on the degree of sympathy that is triggered."[40]

It appears that incentives do make the deliberative processes more salient. But whether deliberation results in more generous behavior (as with liberals in the AIDS case) or less generous (as with the statistics about need and the picture of the needy girl) depends

Table 4.1. Dual-process theory and social preferences.

	Cognitive-processing style	
Preference type	*Affective*	*Deliberative*
Ethical, other-regarding	Sympathy for those harmed; anger at those who harm; "moral disgust" or fear of "sinful" acts	Account taking of the effect of one's actions on others; interpreting and acting on "moral teachings"
Self-regarding	Hunger, other appetites; fear of personal danger	Maximizing one's own expected gains, fitness, or well-being

Note: From the table it appears that there is no simple mapping between cognitive-processing styles and preference types.

on whether the imperative to generosity resulting from deliberation (such as a Benthamite utilitarian calculation) is stronger than the generosity-inducing emotions (such as sympathy) of the affective process. A taxonomy of these cases, showing the lack of a simple mapping between the deliberative-emotional distinction and social preferences, appears in table 4.1.

A Puzzle

The three reasons why incentives may crowd out social preferences—bad news, moral disengagement, and control aversion—provide some of the information that Aristotle's Legislator needs in order to design incentives that complement rather than substitute for a desire to uphold social norms and to act generously toward one's fellow citizens. In each case, policies can be devised to minimize the crowding-out problem and perhaps even induce crowding in. In considering the Legislator's policy options in the final two chapters, I provide examples of effective incentives that contain clearly conveyed mutually beneficial purposes (avoiding moral disengagement) deployed by peers who have nothing to gain personally (avoiding bad news) and that can complement rather than erode intrinsic motivation (avoiding control aversion).

But we cannot go there quite yet.

Evidence that social preferences are common, and that they underwrite mutually beneficial exchanges and other foundations of social life but are often crowded out by explicit economic incentives, presents us with a puzzle, one that if left unresolved might cast a shadow on my reasoning thus far. The adverse effect of incentives on generosity, reciprocity, the work ethic, and other motives essential to well-functioning institutions would seem to portend instability and dysfunction for any society in which explicit economic incentives are widely used.

Have societies somehow avoided the vicious cycle in which markets and other incentive-driven institutions erode the cultural foundations on which they depend, leading to the increasing use of incentives to compensate for the increasing deficiency of ethical and other-regarding preferences?[41]

Why did the Boston fire commissioner and the firemen not wind up in a kind of economic and cultural arms race to the bottom, in which the commissioner upped the ante by imposing ever more draconian pay deductions, and the firemen responded by acting in increasingly self-interested ways, until the firemen completely abandoned their sense of civic obligation in favor of precisely the opportunism the commissioner attributed to them at the outset?

And why would this dynamic not play out right across any market-based economy? Wouldn't we end up with exactly the constitution for knaves that Hume advocated, but in contrast to Hume's account, with a citizenry of knaves as well?

The experiments discussed so far, as well as casual observation, show that this is not our plight today. There are two possible explanations. The first is that I have misunderstood the crowding-out problem and perhaps overstated it. The second is that the corrosive effect of markets and incentives on social preferences indeed exists, but in many societies has been offset by other social processes allowing for the survival, and even flourishing, of a robust civic culture.

V

A Liberal Civic Culture

If incentives sometimes crowd out ethical reasoning, the desire to help others, and intrinsic motivations, and if leading thinkers celebrate markets as a morality-free zone, it seems just a short step to Karl Marx's broadside condemnation of capitalist culture: "Finally there came a time when everything that men had considered as inalienable became an object of exchange, of traffic and could be alienated. This is the time when the very things which till then had been communicated, but never exchanged, given but never sold, acquired but never bought: virtue, love, conviction, knowledge, conscience—when everything passed into commerce. It is the time of general corruption, of universal venality."[1]

But a century and a half later, "universal venality" fails to describe the cultures of northern Europe, where capitalism was born, or the North American and other offshoots of these populations. Or at least so it must seem to the parking enforcement division of the New York Police Department.

Diplomatic immunity from prosecution for traffic violations in New York City provides a natural experiment for testing Marx's prediction.[2] In deciding where to park and whether to pay any fines incurred, the diplomats of 146 nations differ markedly in how often they willingly break the law and inconvenience others by parking illegally and by not paying the resulting tickets.

In the five years before November 2002, the average number of violations per diplomat was 19, with the most flagrant violators being those from Egypt (140 violations per diplomat), Bulgaria (117), Albania (84), and Pakistan (69). Over the same period, the 31 diplomats from the United Kingdom, where capitalism was born, committed exactly zero violations, as did those from Sweden, Norway, Canada, and the Netherlands, the second birthplace of capitalism. Those from other early capitalist nations posted modest numbers of transgressions during this period: 1 per diplomat for Germany, 2.7 for Belgium. Some latecomer capitalist nations were likewise paragons of parking probity: Japan's 47 diplomats posted not a single violation, and Korean diplomats averaged just 0.4 violations.

Do not read too much into this. It is far from an ideal experiment. And as we will see, Adam Smith warned that unlike merchants, diplomats were not to be trusted. So perhaps the people with D license plates are not representative of their cultures.

But the puzzle is real in light of the experimental evidence suggesting that explicit economic rewards and penalties sometimes drive out social preferences. We will shortly turn to data more convincing than the parking transgressions of the world's diplomats, evidence based on cross-cultural comparisons of behavior. These experiments show that the oldest capitalist societies have sustained vibrant civic cultures characterized by widespread conformity to cooperative and generous social norms.

Were this a lecture, a person would at this point likely jump up and ask me something like "what planet are you on?" and follow that with a litany of counterevidence, everything from the unethical behavior of hedge fund managers to the fact that Americans bowl alone. I do not wish to exaggerate the cultural virtues of the oldest capitalist societies, but only to point to some apparent differences between them and many other societies in which the reach of market institutions has been more recent and more restricted.

The puzzle would be easily solved if the behavioral effects observed in experiments were either ephemeral or strictly limited in domain, if, for example, people's moral disengagement when offered incentives for a particular task at work did not spill over to other domains, such as family life or citizenship. But we will see that for better or worse, the economy is a great teacher, and its lessons are neither fleeting nor confined within its boundaries.

I will also offer reasons why living in a highly incentivized economy might have long-term adverse effects on the process of cultural evolution beyond those stemming from the negative situational cues sometimes associated with incentives as messages. The upshot is that the extensive use of incentives may adversely affect the evolution of civic preferences in the long run. In the terminology of the previous chapter, "endogenous preferences" are analogous to the sometimes-adverse effect of incentives on "situation-dependent" preferences.

These further thoughts about the puzzle thus only deepen the mystery. But perhaps the admirable civic cultures of many of the longest-standing capitalist economies owe more to the liberal social order in which these economies are embedded than to the extensive role of markets and incentives per se. This is the resolution of the puzzle that I propose.

By a "liberal society," I mean one characterized by extensive reliance on markets to allocate economic goods and services, formal equality of political rights, the rule of law, public tolerance, and few barriers to occupational and geographic mobility based on race, religion, or other accidents of birth. Some examples of liberal societies in the experimental studies I will introduce are Switzerland, Denmark, Australia, the United States, and the United Kingdom. Examples of societies that I do not term liberal (lacking at least one of the above attributes) are Saudi Arabia, Russia, Ukraine, and Oman as well as small-scale societies of hunter-gatherers, herders, and low-technology farmers.

The Economy Produces People

How people interact in markets and other economic institutions—who meets whom, to do what, with what rewards—durably shapes social norms and preferences, and these are then generalized to noneconomic domains of life. This has long been recognized. Marx was not alone in holding this view.

The royalist Edmund Burke lamented that the French Revolution had ushered in "the age of sophisters and economists": "Nothing is left which engages the affection on the part of the commonwealth . . . so as to create in us love, veneration, admiration or attachment. All the decent drapery of life is to be rudely torn off."[3]

Others have taken a more benign view of the cultural consequences of markets. The baron de Montesquieu wrote that "where there is commerce the ways of men are gentle."[4] But the idea that the economy produces people as well as goods and services is not in question.

The long-term effects on preferences to which Marx, Burke, Montesquieu, and others refer are quite different from the incentive effects we saw in the previous chapter, in which fines and subsidies affect preferences because they alter the situation in which a person finds herself, increasing the salience of some preferences and diminishing others. Making sense of Marx, Burke, or Montesquieu is easier if we recognize that incentives may also alter the process by which people come to acquire new tastes, habits, ethical commitments, and other motivations.

The way in which we come to have our particular preferences is much like the way in which we come to have our particular accents. The process takes place early in life, is for the most part unwitting, and depends critically on our social interactions with others. While midlife changes in preferences (like acquiring a new accent) may occur, the learning process is strongly attenuated after adolescence.

When it comes to the effects of incentives, the key difference between endogenous and situation-dependent (or framing-sensitive) preferences is that in the former case, incentives may affect a long-term learning process whose results persist over decades, even entire lifetimes. By contrast, when preferences are situation-dependent, a new situation—such as the withdrawal of an incentive—changes which preference in a person's repertoire will motivate behavior. Incentives affect preferences in both situation-dependent and endogenous preference cases, but the effects differ. In the former case, the incentive is a reversible signal about the principal or the situation; in the latter, the incentive alters the long-term, not easily reversed preference-learning process.

The developmental processes involved in learning new preferences typically include the effects of interactions over long periods with large numbers of others, such as the processes that occur in schooling, religious instruction, and other forms of socialization not readily captured in experiments. Conformism to widely practiced behaviors (and the adoption of the preferences that motivate them) is typically involved. We cannot, therefore, hope for the kind of experimental evidence on the evolution of preferences that is possible when we study the effects of incentives as messages about situations. But historical, social survey, and ethnographic data, while not directly related to the use of incentives, are quite consistent with the view that economies structured by differing incentives are likely to produce people with differing preferences.[5] Here is some of the evidence.

Over four decades, the social psychologist Melvin Kohn and his collaborators have studied the relationship between, on the one hand, a person's position in the authority structure of the workplace—giving as opposed to taking orders, designing incentives rather than being their target—and, on the other, one's valuation of self-direction and independence in one's children, as well as one's own intellectual flexibility and self-directedness.[6] They found that "the experience of occupational self-direction has a profound effect on people's values, orientation, and cognitive functioning."[7] The studies take account of the problem of reverse causation—the possibility that personality affects the occupational situation one ends up in rather than vice versa—and they provide convincing evidence that there is a causal arrow from job to preferences.

Kohn's collaborative study of Japan, the United States, and Poland yielded consistent findings across cultures: people who exercise self-direction on the job also value self-direction more in other realms of their life (including child rearing and leisure activities) and are less likely to exhibit fatalism, distrust, and self-depreciation.[8] Kohn and his coauthors reason that "social structure affects individual psychological functioning mainly by affecting the conditions of people's own lives." They note in conclusion: "The simple explanation that accounts for virtually all that is known about the effects of job on personality . . . is that the processes are direct: learning from the job and extending those lessons to off-the-job realities."[9]

Additional evidence comes from a study by the anthropologists Herbert Barry, Margaret Child and Irvin Bacon. They categorized seventy-nine mostly nonliterate societies according to the prevalent form of livelihood (animal husbandry, agriculture, hunting, or fishing). They also measured whether food could easily be stored—a common practice in agricultural and herding economies but not among foragers—and other forms of wealth accumulation, the latter being a major correlate of dimensions of social structure such as stratification.[10]

Barry and his coauthors also collected evidence on forms of child rearing, including obedience training, self-reliance, independence, and responsibility. They found large differences in child-rearing practices. These varied significantly with economic structure, controlling for other measures of social structure such as extent of polygyny, levels of women's participation in the predominant subsistence activity, and size of population units.

Where food storage was common, parents valued obedience rather than independence in children to a far greater extent than where storage was absent. The authors concluded, "Knowledge of the economy alone would enable one to predict with considerable accuracy whether a society's socialization pressures were primarily toward compliance or assertion."[11] The causal arrow is unlikely to run from child rearing to the type of economy, since the latter is dictated primarily by what combination of hunting and gathering, herding, or cultivation best provides a livelihood in the geographic area concerned.

These society-level studies cannot isolate the effects of incentives per se. The most that cross-cultural ethnographic studies can provide is evidence that preferences vary with economic structure. It is not difficult, however, to explain why differences in economic structure—and the extensive use of incentives in particular—might affect the evolution of preferences.[12]

Incentives and the Evolution of Preferences

Incentives and other aspects of economic organization affect the evolution of preferences because they influence both the types of people one encounters and the set of behaviors that are feasible and rewarding, given the kinds of tasks that people undertake.[13] The extensive use of incentives—say, a subsidy given to those who contribute to a public good—may impede the learning of prosocial preferences because of two uncontroversial aspects of the process of cultural evolution. First, people tend to adopt ways of behaving (including the preferences that motivate them) that they perceive to be common, independently of expected material payoffs of these behaviors. Second, the presence of incentives may lead people to interpret some generous and other-regarding acts as instead being expressions of self-interest induced by the subsidy.

The conformist element in cultural transmission (adoption of the behaviors that most others are doing) is in part the result of the powerful effect of mere exposure on social learning, which has been documented by the psychologist Robert Zajonc and subsequent authors.[14] For example, U.S. students were exposed, with low or high frequency, to a list of twelve nonsense English "words" ("kadirga," "zabulon"), as well as to an equal number of invented Chinese characters, and asked to rate them on a good-bad scale. With a single exception (one of the "Chinese" characters), the more that subjects were exposed to a word or character, the more likely they were to think that it referred to something good. The exposure effect is one of the many reasons that cultural transmission may have a conformist element, favoring the numerous over the rare, independently of the economic success associated with the behavior involved.

The second element in this explanation is that the presence and extent of incentives to contribute to a public project (or to engage in similar activities that benefit others) make the behavior (contribution) a less convincing signal of an individual's generosity, resulting in observers interpreting some generous acts as being merely self-interested. To see why this is so, we return to the psychologist Lepper and his coauthors: "When an individual observes another person engaging in some activity, he infers that the other is intrinsically motivated . . . to the extent that he does not perceive salient, unambiguous, and sufficient extrinsic contingencies to which to attribute the other's behavior."[15] The presence of incentives, however, may lead observers to think that a seemingly generous action was done not for the intrinsic pleasure of helping others but as an instrumental response to the incentive.

There are two reasons why the presence of an incentive may lead people to mistake a generous act—helping another at a cost to oneself—for a self-interested one. The first is that the incentive provides a competing explanation of the generous act: "he did it for the money." The second is that incentives often induce individuals to shift from an ethical to a payoff-maximizing frame (even, as we have seen, relocating neural activity to different regions of the brain). Knowing this, the presence of an incentive for an individual to help another may suggest to an observer that the action was self-interested.[16]

Taken together, these two facts—that incentives may reduce the perceived level of generosity in a population and that people tend to adopt common behaviors (and the preferences motivating them)—have an important implication. By reducing the perceived frequency of individuals who act out of generous preferences, the extensive use of incentives may lead, via the conformist effect on how we learn new behaviors, to the disadvantaging of generous traits relative to self-interested ones in the selection processes by which a culture persists and evolves.

The two causal mechanisms accounting for these possible adverse endogenous preference effects of incentives—conformism and "he did it for the money"—are empirically plausible. But I do not see any practical way of testing this explanation with historical data, since doing so would require finding something that almost certainly does not exist: a sample of otherwise similar societies with measurably different incentive structures, combined with data over a period of generations on social norms. But surprisingly, in light of their inability to capture long-term learning effects, experiments can isolate what appear to be short-term learning effects of incentives per se.

The Persistent Effects of Incentives

We already know that the adverse effects of incentives can sometimes persist even after the incentive is removed. Examples include the lasting tardiness of the Haifa day care parents and the reluctance of the child artists to take up painting long after having previously been promised a reward for their artwork. This is consistent with the idea that the effects of incentives on preferences go beyond situational cues and constitute part of a learning environment in which preferences are durably modified. This appears to be the case in other experiments, too.

Donning the hat of Aristotle's Legislator, Joseph Falkinger and his coauthors designed an incentive system to induce experimental subjects to contribute to a public good.[17] Recall that the Public Goods

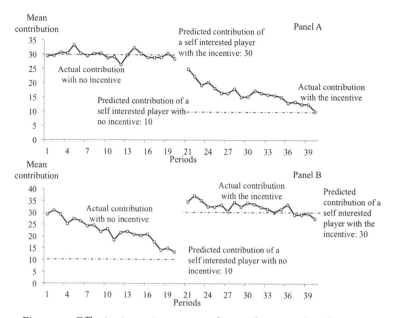

Figure 5.1. Effective incentives apparently crowd out social preferences in subsequent periods (Data from Falkinger et al. 2000.)

game is a multiperson version of a Prisoner's Dilemma; the dominant strategy for someone motivated solely by material self-interest is to contribute less than the amount that would yield the greatest payoffs for all were all to do the same.

The Falkinger incentive system worked: as can be seen in figure 5.1, it induced subjects to contribute almost exactly the amount that would be predicted for someone who cared only about maximizing her own material gains in the experiment. In panel A, the horizontal line at 30 is the predicted contribution level of an own-payoff-maximizing individual under the incentive system. The dots, indicating the actual mean contributions in each of the periods, show that the subjects acted almost exactly as the self-interest assumption predicts. This is not unexpected. We saw this in chapter III: when Irlenbusch and Ruchala offered a high incentive for a public-goods contribution, subjects contributed almost exactly what the economics textbooks predict for *Homo economicus* (figure 3.4). Cardenas et al. saw a similar result in the later periods of the treatment in which they imposed fines for overextraction from the "forest" (figure 3.2).

At this point (and without looking at the rest of the figure), it would be tempting to conclude that the subjects were indeed material-payoff maximizers. But this conclusion would be mistaken. Look at what happened in the Falkinger experiment during periods 21– 40 (in panel A): in the absence of the incentive, subjects initially contributed significantly more than 10, the amount that a self-interested payoff maximizer would contribute, even though by period 40 the subjects were contributing exactly what an own-payoff maximizer would give. This shows what by now should not come as a surprise, given the experiments discussed in chapter III: the motives that induced the subjects to contribute generously in the absence of incentives during the second 20 periods (at least initially) were entirely absent when, in the first 20 rounds, the incentives were offered.

Even more interesting, from the standpoint of the durable influence of incentives on preferences, is how the previous experience of an incentive system affects subjects' behavior after the incentives have been withdrawn. If the effect of an incentive were simply to provide a situational cue, then behavior in the absence of an incentive should not depend on one's prior experience with an incentive system. In Falkinger's experiment, however, this was not the case. In the absence of the incentive, the subjects who had previously experienced the incentive system (panel A, periods 21– 40) contributed 26 percent less than those who had never experienced the incentives (panel B, periods 1–20). It could be that the framing effect of the incentives persisted long enough to affect subsequent play, or it could be that the incentive actually altered the individual's preferences in some durable way. Because of the experiments' short duration, we cannot distinguish between these possibilities.

A durable negative effect of the experience of incentives occurred, too, in an experimental Gift Exchange game implemented by Simon Gaechter and his coauthors.[18] In the standard version of the game (before the introduction of fines and bonuses), the subject in the role of a principal like an "employer" chooses a "wage" to offer to his agent, the "employee." The employee then accepts the wage or not. "Workers" who accept the wage then select a level of "production" that is costly for the worker to provide (providing more reduces the worker's payoffs) and beneficial for the employer The game lasts just a single period, but it is implemented in a succession of periods, employers and employees being randomly rematched from the pool of subjects after each period.

In this setup, selfish workers would obviously accept any positive wage and then produce nothing, for there would be no way for the employer to retaliate or discipline a nonperforming worker. Knowing this, an employer who cared only about his own payoffs and who attributed the same preferences to the worker would offer a wage of zero; and the worker would reciprocate in kind. Both would then receive a payoff of zero, forgoing the positive profits and wages that would have occurred had a generous wage been offered and had the worker reciprocated with a substantial amount of effort. In light of the other experiments, you will not be surprised to find out that this is not at all what happened.

In addition to the standard (no-incentives) game, there were two "incentive" treatments. In both, the employer offered a contract specifying not just the wage but also a required level of output, with the stipulation that the wage would be paid only if the worker met the employer's output target. In the "fine" treatment under the incentive setup, failure to meet the target would be penalized by a wage reduction, while in the "bonus" treatment, meeting the target would be rewarded by a wage increase. The standard setup, without targets, bonuses, or fines, is called the "trust" treatment because a principal would offer a positive wage only if he trusted the agent to reciprocate by providing sufficient production.

The authors suspected—based on earlier experiments—that in the standard game (that is, without incentives of any kind) employers would indeed trust and workers would reciprocate. And initially they did, as the dashed line in the phase 1 panel of figure 5.2 shows. But the workers' production declined over time. By contrast, incentives

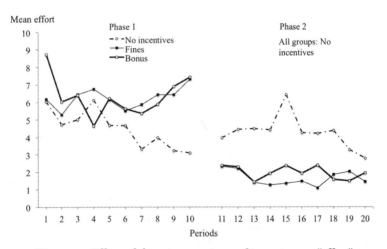

Figure 5.2. Effects of the prior experience of incentives on "effort"
During phase 2, no incentives were offered to any of the three
groups, and those who had experienced an incentive (either a
fine or a bonus) in phase 1 provided significantly lower effort.
(Data from Gaechter, Kessler, and Konigstein 2011.)

(either fines or bonuses, shown by the thin and thick lines) sustained substantial levels of production over the entire first phase.

But the authors wanted to know whether the experience of having first played the game under the fine or bonus treatments would affect how the subjects behaved in the absence of incentives. So in phase 2, all three groups played under the trust treatment, that is, with no incentives in place. The results are in the phase 2 panel of the figure.

In the absence of incentives, the subjects who had experienced either the bonus or fine treatment for the first ten periods produced far less than they had in the incentive treatments. Those who had not experienced incentives in the first phase (the dashed line, again) produced much more than those who had previously been exposed to incentives. For any wage offered by the principal, workers who had experienced incentives in the first period offered substantially (and statistically significant) lower levels of production when, in the second period, the incentives were removed. The experience with incentives appears to have diminished the subject's motivation to reciprocate the employer's trust or generosity in offering the wage. Remember: the employer who believed the employee to be entirely selfish would maximize his payoffs by offering a wage of zero.

I say "appears to have " because in this experiment as in most, we have no observations on the subjects' motivations. Remarkably, the best clues about motivational learning under the influence of incentives come from what may be the first experiment conducted on how incentives may crowd out ethical reasoning, designed by two political scientists.

Norman Frohlich and Joe Oppenheimer implemented a five-person Public Goods game under two conditions. In addition to the standard game (for example, the Falkinger experiment just described, but without incentives), they introduced an ingenious Rawlsian "veil of ignorance" treatment that aligned individual self-interest with the interests of all members of the group, thus abolishing the social dilemma normally constituted by a public goods game. In the Rawlsian treatment, each of the five players chose how much to contribute to the public good, but then received the payoffs of a randomly chosen player. Whatever he contributed, each player had an equal chance of receiving his own payoff or that of one of the other four players. In the usual game, as in the Prisoner's Dilemma, an individual maximizes her payoffs by contributing nothing. But in the Rawlsian treatment of the game, the best one can do is to contribute the amount that will maximize the average payoff of all five players, since doing so will maximize each player's own expected payoff. Players had no difficulty figuring out that this required contributing the maximum.

Ten groups played each of these treatments (conventional Public Goods Game and the Rawlsian "veil of ignorance" game), half of them with a brief period of discussion among the players before their (anonymous and simultaneous) play. In the other groups, no communication was allowed. All the groups then entered a second phase in which no communication was allowed and only the standard Public Goods game was played.

Not surprisingly, in phase 1 and in the absence of communication, subjects in the "veil of ignorance" game contributed much more than those in the standard game. Also unsurprisingly, when communication was allowed, contributions in both the "veil of ignorance" game and the standard game were significantly higher.

The authors, however, were more interested in phase 2 of the experiment, when everyone played the standard game. They wanted to know whether having played the "veil of ignorance" game would induce subjects to act more generously toward others. Those who had played behind the veil of ignorance, the researchers reasoned, would recognize the fair and socially optimal outcome (namely, full contribution) and would be more motivated than other players by fairness considerations when they came to play the normal game.

But this is not at all what happened.[19] In the groups that had not communicated in phase 1, there was no difference in contributions in phase 2 between those who had played the "veil of ignorance" game and those who had played the standard game. But among those who had communicated during phase 1, in phase 2 those who had played the standard game contributed twice as much as those who had played the "veil of ignorance" game.

The experience of having played a game in which self-interest was a good guide to what was best for all group members (the "veil of ignorance" treatment) apparently made people less able to articulate or respond to arguments of fairness when, in phase 2, they faced a real social dilemma and were allowed to communicate with one another. This may explain why the effect of communication in phase 1 was much greater in the standard game than among those playing behind the veil of ignorance. In fact, those who played the standard game with communication contributed slightly (but statistically significantly) more than those playing behind the veil of ignorance with communication. It may be that those whose play featured a real ethical dilemma (the standard game) had more to communicate than those who had been spared the dilemma by the veil of ignorance.

When surveyed, subjects who had played behind the veil recognized that they were playing fairly. But in phase 2, when they played the standard game, their self-reported concerns about fairness were uncorrelated with (and apparently had no effect on) how much they contributed. Notice that the effect of the veil of ignorance was not to eliminate fair-minded sentiments, but rather to sideline them, in the sense that those who were more fair-minded did not contribute more than those who were indifferent to fairness. By contrast, those who had played the standard game in phase 1 self-reported that they had played less fairly, but in phase 2, fairness concerns were a strong predictor of contributing larger amounts.

The Rawlsian treatment, like the Falkinger incentive system for the Public Goods game, is what economists call an incentive-compatible mechanism, meaning that under the set of incentives and constraints represented by the mechanism, self-interested individuals will implement a socially desirable outcome. In any such a mechanism, as in the Rawlsian veil of ignorance treatment, prices do the work of morals: the material incentives facing each player lead them to implement the social optimum. Here is how the authors explain the results: "The [Rawlsian] mechanism or any other incentive compatible device renders the need to invoke ethical concerns . . . moot . . . Both ethically motivated and selfishly motivated players can agree on the best strategy . . . As a result, when . . . players [who had experienced the Rawlsian treatment] subsequently have to make ethical decisions they are more likely to downplay the ethical components than are those regular players who have had practice confronting ethical issues."[20]

This "use it or lose it" interpretation of the eclipse of moral reasoning is entirely at odds with the view, common among economists, that incentive-compatible mechanisms such as ideal competitive markets or the veil of ignorance treatment in the experiment are to be admired precisely because they economize "the scarce resources of altruistic motivation," which might otherwise be used up.[21]

Taking account of the fact that ethical motivation is not just a resource to be economized but also one that can be diminished through nonuse, returns us to Marx's dismal prognostication about the cultural consequences of capitalism. Competition among self-regarding individuals for goods in competitive markets with complete contracts is widely advocated as an incentive-compatible mechanism with attributes similar to the Rawlsian veil of ignorance. This is the reasoning behind both Buchanan's indifference toward the condition of his fruit seller, and Gauthier's claim that morality has no role in evaluating competitive market outcomes. If Frohlich and Oppenheimer are right that citizens in such settings do not have to "flex their ethical muscles,"[22] then one wonders why Marx's prediction that the flowering of capitalism would be a "time of general corruption and universal venality" turned out to be mistaken.

The experimental evidence suggests that ethical crowding-out effects can be substantial and that the lessons of our economic experiences are sometimes long-lasting and tend to be generalized to other domains of life. This knowledge does not much help us resolve the puzzle with which we began.

My research took a surprising turn, one that only further deepened the puzzle, when, with a group of anthropologists and economists, I began to investigate whether societies where markets play a large role suffer a deficiency of social preferences, as would be expected from the above reasoning.

Markets and Fair-Mindedness

Three large cross-cultural behavioral experimental studies in populations with a broad range of economic and political systems have given us behavioral measures concerning individuals' cooperativeness, fair-mindedness, and other social preferences. In addition to the Third-Party Punishment game, Dictator game, Trust game, and Ultimatum game already described, the Public Goods with Punishment game (described below) provides behavioral measures of generosity, willingness to sacrifice personal benefits to uphold social norms, and readiness to contribute to a public good. These studies show that these behaviors flourish in market-based societies, though to varying degrees.

The most surprising evidence comes from an experimental Ultimatum game played by subject pools in fifteen isolated small-scale societies (not the same fifteen in the study described in chapter IV).[23] Recall that in this game one player proposes a division of a sum provided by the experimenter, and the responder can either accept her proposed share or reject it, neither player getting anything in the latter case. Entirely self-regarding proposers who believe that respondents are also self-regarding will anticipate that no positive offer will be rejected, so they will offer the smallest possible amount. This prediction from the assumption of self-interest has rarely been observed in hundreds of experiments in dozens of countries. Our study was no exception. Most proposers offered substantial amounts to the responder; low offers were frequently rejected.

In our study of hunter-gatherers, herders, and low-technology farmers (horticulturalists), the groups with greater average exposure to markets made more generous offers as proposers and were more willing to reject low offers as responders—meaning they were willing to receive nothing rather than accept a highly unequal division of the pie. The two least market-exposed groups—Tanzanian Hadza hunter-gatherers and Amazonian Quichua horticulturalists—offered a quarter and a third of the pie respectively, in contrast with the highly market-integrated Indonesian Lamalera whale hunters, who offered on average a bit more than half the pie to respondents. Considering all the groups, a standard deviation difference in our measure of market exposure was associated with about half a standard deviation increase in the mean Ultimatum game offer.

These were eyebrow-raising findings among anthropologists and other social scientists outside of economics, many of whom think that markets make people selfish. The *Wall Street Journal,* unsurprisingly, saw things differently. It headlined its January 24, 2002, front-page story about our results, "The Civilizing Effect of the Market." I spent the next couple of days answering agitated telephone calls from friends.

A second phase of this project (in which I was not involved) studied primarily rural peoples in Africa, Oceania, and South America.[24] (This was the project that produced the evidence about the crowding out of religion in the Third-Party Punishment game in Accra). Using improved data and techniques, the positive correlation between Ultimatum game offers and market exposure was replicated (at about the same magnitude), and the authors found a similar positive market correlation for offers in the Dictator and Third-Party Punishment games.

These results are not inconsistent with the experimental evidence presented in the previous chapter. The Accra workers for whom monetary incentives apparently reduced the salience of religion, resulting in less generous behavior, were among the most market-exposed in this study (they purchased all their food, for example, rather than obtaining it from hunting, gathering, or barter) and were also among the most generous, offering well above the average of the fifteen subject pools in the Dictator and Ultimatum games.

Unlike the first phase of the project, the second included one market-based liberal society, the United States, represented by a rural population in Missouri. We can gauge the Missourians' fair-mindedness in the Ultimatum game by the minimum offer (fraction of the pie) they would accept if the proposer offered it, as reported to the experimenter at the outset of the game. This "minimum acceptable offer," or MAO, can also be understood as the greatest amount the subject is willing to forgo in order not to accept an unfair offer. The MAO thus captures at once the subject's "willingness to pay" for fairness and the least advantageous division of the pie the subject considers fair enough not to trigger a rejection.

The MAO of the highly market-exposed Missourians was the third highest among the fifteen subject pools. Controlling for subjects' age, sex, schooling, and average income, the Missourians' minimum acceptable offer was 2.6 times the average of the other groups. In the Dictator game, virtually all the Missourians offered half the pie, making them, at least by this measure, the most egalitarian of all the populations. Rural Missourians tend to vote Republican; but from this experimental evidence, they appear to be more concerned about economic inequality than the Hadza hunter-gatherers, whose practices of food sharing and lack of political hierarchy were the inspiration for James Woodburn's classic paper "Egalitarian Societies."[25] Recall that the Hadza subjects offered a quarter of the pie on average in the Dictator game, and their MAO in the Ultimatum game was less than half of the Missourians'.

Cultural Differences in Cooperation and Punishment

It would help address our puzzle if we had an explanation why rural Republican and highly market-exposed Missourians are more oriented toward fairness in the Ultimatum game than the group that perhaps more than any other has exemplified the egalitarian foraging way of life. Evidence that may help comes from experiments with an unusually diverse set of (also, coincidentally, fifteen) subject pools, including some from liberal societies (the United States, the United Kingdom, Switzerland, Germany, Denmark, Australia). Other pools came from Turkey, Russia, Saudi Arabia, China, Oman, and South Korea. In addition, this study provides an idea that may help resolve the puzzle with which we began. The cultural differences among the subject pools may be somewhat attenuated, however, because unlike the herders, hunter-gatherers, and farmers in the other cross-cultural studies, the subjects here were university students, who may be more culturally similar around the world than those not exposed to the same set of life experiences.[26] The experiment implemented (by the same experimenter) in these sites is a Public Goods with Punishment game.

This is a modification of the Public Goods game, the n-player Prisoners' Dilemma introduced in the previous chapter. The players are each awarded an endowment by the experimenter and given the opportunity anonymously to contribute some, all, or none of it to a common pot (the public good). After all the contributions are made, the amount in the pot is doubled (or in some experiments, tripled) and then distributed equally to the players, irrespective of their contributions. In most versions of this game, the group size and the multiplication factor (that is, doubling or tripling the amount in the pot) are set so that each individual will maximize his or her payoff by contributing nothing, irrespective of what the others do. Yet the total payoff for the entire group is greatest if everyone contributes his or her entire endowment.

For example, if there are five members of the group and the multiplication factor is two (the amount in the pot is doubled by the experimenter before being redistributed to the subjects), then by contributing 1 to the public pot, the pot to be distributed increases by 2, of which I will get my 1/5 share. So by giving up 1, I would increase my payoff from the eventual distribution out of the pot by 2/5, which clearly does not justify forgoing the 1 if one is an own-payoff maximizer. Yet if everyone contributes 1, each will receive 2.

The punishment modification of this game is that after all players have made their allocations, each is provided with information about the other players' contributions (the identities are not given, just an ID number known only to the experimenter). Each player is then given the opportunity to sacrifice some of his or her own payoff in order to reduce the payoff to any other member in the group. This is the "punishment option," but it is of course not described in those terms, in order to avoid framing the action as morally motivated.

This procedure is followed in each of the periods of the game (often ten). The presence of an option to punish a player who violates a norm of generosity toward others makes the Public Goods with Punishment game similar to the Third-Party Punishment game played in Accra, which we saw in the last chapter. In that game, however, the punisher was a third party, not one whose payoffs were directly affected by the behavior of the possible target of punishment.

This game provides information on three behaviors motivated by social preferences: willingness to contribute to a public good (public generosity) and to penalize those who do not (upholding social norms), both at a cost to oneself, and the degree of positive response to punishment by others (shame at one's violation of a social norm). Where all three of these dispositions are present, contributions to the public good are substantial.

The results of this experiment when played around the world are summarized in figure 5.3. The grouping of the subject pools by the authors of the study (though somewhat arbitrary) dramatizes the considerable cultural differences evident in the experimental play. In each of the six panels, the leftmost set of (mostly downward trending)

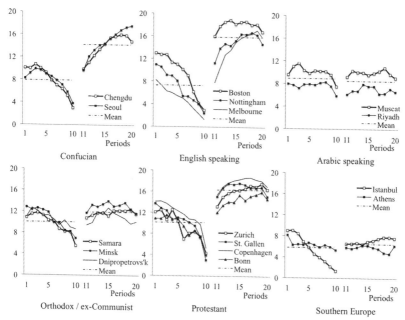

*Figure 5.3. Cultural differences in mean contributions with
and without a punishment option in a Public Goods game*
In each of the panels, the left observations are the treatment without
punishment, and those on the right are from the same game with the
punishment option. (Data from Gaechter, Herrmann, and Thoni.
2010; the cultural categories are from the original source.)

lines of dots shows the average contributions in the first ten periods
of the game, when there was no punishment option. The line of dots
on the right of each panel records average contributions when the
punishment option was introduced.

As expected, cultural differences in game play among the subject
pools were significant. But in all of them (as is common in other
experiments with the Public Goods game), subjects contributed substantial amounts in the first period.[27] In the absence of the punishment option, however, cooperation soon unraveled. When available,

the punishment option was widely used, especially in the early periods, and the contributions stayed consistently high in all fifteen subject pools as a result. In the treatment with punishment, the subject pools with the highest average contributions were (in order) Boston, Copenhagen, St. Gallen (Switzerland), Zurich, and Nottingham; the lowest average contributions were in Athens, Riyadh, Muscat (Oman), Dnipropetrovs'k (Ukraine), and Samara (Russia).

Average contribution levels in the subject pools correlated positively with measures (for the populations in which the experiment as conducted) of rule of law (the correlation coefficient between these two measures was $r = 0.53$), democracy ($r = 0.54$), individualism ($r = 0.58$), and social equality ($r = 0.65$). Positive correlations were also found, as expected, with survey measures of trust ($r = 0.38$).[28]

Voluntary contribution to a public good is surely a plausible measure of the civic virtues that Marx thought would die out in a market economy. The same is true of rejections of stingy offers in an Ultimatum game, because they show that people will sacrifice their own material gain to punish those who violate social norms of fairness. That these behaviors are stronger in nations with a greater extent of market interactions is puzzling. Understanding why these cross-country correlations occur will cast further doubt on the idea that market-based economies necessarily promote "universal venality."

Sustaining Social Order in Liberal and Other Societies

The difference between the cooperating and free-riding subject pools in this cross-cultural study—between, on the one hand, Boston and Zurich, and, on the other, Athens and Muscat—lies in the use of punishment and the response to being punished. In the experiment without the punishment option, subjects in Samara,

Dnipropetrovs'k, and Muscat contributed more than those in Boston, Nottingham, and Zurich. The reason these subject pools did less well in the punishment version of the game is that a significant amount of punishment was directed not only at shirkers but also at high contributors. This may have been done in retaliation for punishment received in earlier rounds by subjects who believed (correctly) that the high contributors were doing most of the punishing (figure 5.4). The authors termed this practice—punishment of those contributing the same or more than the subject—"antisocial punishment." Other experiments have found the same patterns.

The extent of antisocial punishment was significantly and inversely correlated with the societal measures mentioned above: rule of law ($r = -0.53$), democracy ($r = -0.59$) individualism

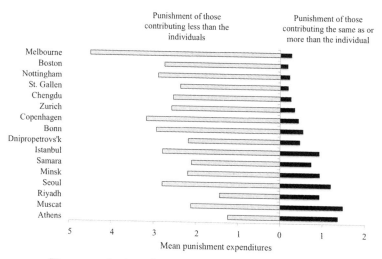

Figure 5.4. Antisocial punishment in a Public Goods game
To the right of 0 are punishments imposed on those who contributed the same or more than the punisher (antisocial punishment).
(Data from Herrmann, Thoni, and Gaechter 2008b.)

($r = -0.63$), and social equality ($r = -0.72$). In the five highest-contributing subject pools (Boston, Copenhagen, St. Gallen, Zurich, and Nottingham), shirkers who were punished responded by significantly increasing their contributions in subsequent periods. In only one of the five lowest-contributing pools (Athens, Riyadh, Muscat, Dnipropetrovs'k, and Samara) did shirkers respond positively to punishment. In the other four, their response was not significantly different from zero.

A plausible explanation for these differing uses of punishment and the responses of its targets is that punishment works only if it is regarded as legitimate and conveys the signal that the target has violated widely held norms. It appears that the punishment of free riders, even by complete strangers, is legitimate and evokes shame, not anger, in Boston and Copenhagen, but is seen differently in Muscat and Samara.

The results of an experimental exploration of the effect of legitimacy on the efficacy of punishment by Archan Ertan, Talbott Page, and Louis Putterman are consistent with this interpretation. Before playing the Public Goods game, each group of experimental subjects in Providence, Rhode Island, was invited to deliberate and then vote on whether peer punishment should be allowed, and whether it should be restricted in any way. This is very unlike the highly individualistic setup of the more common Public Goods with Punishment game, in which the punishment decision is made individually and simultaneously. But the novel communication aspect of the experimental protocol adopted by Ertan and his coauthors matches real-world practices of cooperation and norm enforcement. As is clear from ethnographic and other studies, persuasion, gossip, and ridicule play an important part in sustaining social norms; the punishment of transgressors is rarely carried out by an individual acting alone.[29]

Here is what the experimenters found: "No group ever allowed punishment of high contributors, most groups eventually voted to allow punishment of low contributors, and the result was both high contributions and high efficiency levels."[30] Apparently, majority determination of the punishment system made the punishment of shirkers not just an incentive but also a signal of group norms.

This result suggests an explanation for the contrasting levels of cooperation sustained by peer punishment in experiments with subject pools from liberal and other societies. Consider the structure of what anthropologists call a "lineage-segmented" society. Lineages are the fundamental social unit, composed of families sharing a (perhaps quite distant) common ancestor. In these societies, families mitigate risks by providing and seeking help during times of need. In addition to risk pooling and redistribution, lineages are responsible for the moral instruction and behavior of their members and for the rectification of any transgressions toward either members or nonmembers, including punishment and compensation where appropriate.[31] Punishment by a nonmember for a member's misbehavior may itself be considered a transgression requiring rectification or inviting retaliation. Ernst Gellner's description of pastoralists as "a system of mutually trusting kinsmen" is an example. These lineages are "strong, self-policing, self-defending, politically participating groups . . . They defend themselves by means of indiscriminate retaliation against the group of any aggressor. Hence they also police themselves and their own members, for they do not wish to provoke retaliation."[32]

In liberal societies, by contrast, the tasks of moral instruction and maintenance of order are routinely entrusted to individuals who are unrelated and, at least initially, unknown to those whom they teach, police, or judge. In an inversion of the moral code of lineage-segmented societies, the legitimacy of these teachers, police, and court officers is based on their anonymity and lack of relationship to those they interact with. This legitimacy is enhanced by uniforms, academic degrees, and official titles acquired (at least ideally) through a process of fair competition, not family favor.

Perhaps this explains why, when Boston subjects who contributed less than the average in the Public Goods game were punished, they substantially increased their contributions, while under the same conditions, subjects in Dnipropetrovs'k actually reduced theirs (though not by a significant amount). While the incentive to contribute more was no doubt salient in both cases, the message that the incentive sent may have differed. Boston subjects may have read the fine as disapproval by fellow citizens, while those in Dnipropetrovs'k may have seen it as an insult.

My hypothesis is that the different ways that order is maintained in liberal and lineage-based societies are part of the explanation of the cross-cultural differences observed in the experiments. It has yet to be tested empirically, but if it were borne out, it would direct attention not to the cultural consequences of markets but rather to liberal political, judicial, and other nonmarket institutions as the key to liberal civic culture. This differs from the usual explanation of the civic culture of liberal societies, namely, the *doux commerce* hypothesis, which credits the exchange process itself.

Doux Commerce?

While living in England (1726–29), Voltaire was astounded that at the London Stock Exchange, "the Jew, the Mohammedan, the

Christian deal with one another as if they were of the same religion, and give the name infidel only to those who go bankrupt . . . The Presbyterian trusts the Anabaptist and the Anglican takes the Quaker at his word"; and "upon leaving this peaceful and free assembly, some withdraw to the synagogue, . . . others retire to their churches . . . others to have a drink . . . and everyone is happy."[33] Perhaps he was observing "the civilizing effect of markets," which the *Wall Street Journal* celebrated with the help of our experiments.

Understanding why people in the more market-exposed societies in our study made more generous offers in the game, and were more likely to reject low offers, requires two pieces of information. First, in many of the populations we studied, interactions with strangers are often fraught with danger. But this is less true where regular market exchanges occur, for the simple reason that some of the strangers one meets in a market provide opportunities for mutual gain. Second, our experimental subjects played anonymously, which may have cued them to play in a way that would have been appropriate toward strangers. A plausible explanation of the more generous and fair-minded experimental behavior seen in the more market-oriented societies, then, is that people learn from their market experiences that fair dealing with strangers is often profitable. Maybe the members of the London Stock Exchange who so impressed Voltaire had learned something similar.

This possible explanation for the civic values exhibited by market societies suggests that there may be something to the key hypothesis of *doux commerce* thinkers such as Voltaire and Montesquieu. Adam Smith comes closest to providing a causal mechanism that would explain why markets might foster a robust civic culture. He contrasts the probity of merchants with the untrustworthiness of ambassadors: "When a person makes perhaps twenty contracts in a day, he cannot gain so much by endeavoring to impose on his neighbors, as the very appearance of a cheat would make him lose. When people seldom deal with one another, we find that they are somewhat disposed to cheat, because they can gain more by a smart trick than they can lose by the injury which it does their character."[34]

Smith is describing a reputation-based variant of a large class of game-theoretic models: in cases where contracts are incomplete or promises unenforceable, frequent, repeated exchanges with known individuals allow for retaliation against opportunistic behavior. The availability of punishment provides incentives that induce otherwise self-regarding individuals to adopt norms such as honesty and diligence toward their partners, thereby underwriting exchanges whose the mutual benefits would otherwise be compromised by malfeasance.[35]

If Smith is right, markets with a restricted number of people, in which exchanges take place repeatedly over a long period, might promote honest dealing. And just as Kohn showed that lessons learned at work about authority and independence are generalized to child-rearing values and other realms, social norms associated with markets might become more generally diffused. Perhaps this explains why, when the anthropologist showed up with an odd game to play and real money on the table, the subjects from more market-exposed populations were more concerned about fairness and were more generous to their partners compared with other groups.

Smith's argument that repeated interactions with many individuals all known to one another may promote honest dealing makes sense. But it does not explain why markets should provide a more favorable setting for this dynamic than institutions such as families, states, or teams of people who regularly work together. In these non-market settings, the number of people with whom one interacts is smaller than in most markets, and the repetition of interactions much greater. So Smith's reasoning should apply with greater force outside the market. I return to Smith's honest merchant in the next chapter. For now, let me say that I do not think Smith's version of the *doux commerce* hypothesis (or any of its variants) adequately accounts for the civic-minded citizenry of many of the highly market-oriented societies. Instead, I think that the explanation has everything to do with nonmarket aspects of liberal social orders.

A Liberal Civic Culture

Here is my proposed resolution of the puzzle of the robust civic cultures in societies in which markets play a major role. I will first explain the reasoning (extending my joint work with Ugo Pagano and his joint work with Massimo D'Antoni), and then present some evidence.[36]

Liberal states have neither the information nor the coercive reach to eliminate opportunism and malfeasance. But they can and do protect citizens from worst-case outcomes such as personal injury, loss of property, and other calamities. The result, writes Norbert Elias, is a "civilizing process" based on the fact that "the threat which one person represents for another is subject to stricter control"; as a result, "everyday life is freer of sudden reversals of fortune [and] physical violence is confined to the barracks."[37] This attenuation of calamity is accomplished through the rule of law, occupational and other forms of mobility allowing people an exit option when faced with cataclysmic loss, and, more recently, social insurance.

By reducing risk, these aspects of liberal society become substitutes for the kinds of familial and parochial ties on which lineage segments and other traditional identities rest. Because these ties become less valuable, they are less likely to be sought and maintained. The result is a cultural environment favorable to the evolution of universal norms, which apply to strangers as well as to the clan. In addition, de facto insurance against worst-case outcomes may free people to act on their social preferences by ensuring that those who conform to moral norms of generosity or cooperation will not be exploited by their self-interested fellow citizens.

While this risk-reduction aspect of liberal society affects the entire panoply of social interactions, I will illustrate it by showing how it would promote trust in a market exchange. (A game-theoretic model of this argument appears in appendix 4.) Consider a population composed of a large number of people who interact in pairs in an exchange in which they may either behave opportunistically (for example, by attempting to steal the other's goods) or trade goods for their mutual benefit. Call these strategies "defect" and "cooperate." Suppose a defector takes the goods of a cooperator but runs the risk of getting a beating for his behavior; in this case, cooperating is a best response to being paired with a known cooperator. Defecting is always the best response to a defector, because the defector can fully exploit the undefended cooperator. Though mutual cooperation maximizes total payoffs (and also the individual payoffs for both individuals), a trader paired with an unknown stranger would defect in the absence of a reasonable assurance that the stranger is a cooperator.

Put yourself in the shoes of a trader facing an unknown potential trading partner. How confident would you need to be that your exchange partner is trustworthy (that is, will not defect) in order for you to cooperate? This "minimum degree of confidence required to trust the other" will depend on the consequences of inadvertently cooperating with a defector. If being exploited by a defector inflicted serious costs on you as a hapless cooperator, you would cooperate only if you were virtually certain that he was trustworthy. If, on the other hand, the worst that could happen to you as a naïve cooperator was not that bad, you would be much more willing to take a chance on trusting an unknown person.

The rule of law and other aspects of the liberal state make the consequences of mistakenly trusting a defector much less dire. As a result, the rule of law lowers the bar for how much you would have to know about your partner before trusting him. Thus, the rule of law could promote the spread of trusting expectations and hence of trusting behavior in a population. John Rawls provides a complementary argument: "when it is dangerous to stick to the rules when others are not," "public institutions" may penalize defectors, thereby reducing their numbers. This lowers the probability that a cooperator will be exploited by a defector, and so minimizes the would-be cooperator's motivation to preemptively defect as a strategy to reduce risk.[38]

Markets, of course, are part of this story. In the example above, the occasion for a trusting relationship between buyer and seller would not have arisen without the possibility of mutual gain through exchange. The synergistic effects of markets and the rule of law in favoring the evolution of trust among strangers may account both for Voltaire's observations of cooperation among men of different religions on the London Stock Exchange, and for the surprising results of our cross-cultural experiments. A summary of the causal model I have just described is in figure 5.5.

The other way that the rule of law may support social preferences is by protecting those who conform to social norms from exploitation by defectors. This protective effect may occur not only because defectors are fewer under the rule of law (Rawls's argument) but also

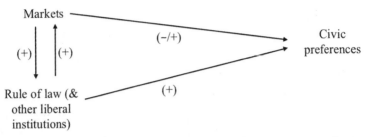

Figure 5.5. Markets, liberalism, and civic preferences Arrows indicate causal effects, with (+) and (−) indicating, respectively, "enhances" and "undermines." The (+) on the arrow from markets to civic preferences recognizes the force of the doux commerce arguments that markets may facilitate cooperative relationships with strangers (as suggested by the cross-cultural experiments).

because the knowledge that defectors will be punished for their transgressions may reduce the appeal of preemptive defection by someone who would otherwise prefer to cooperate.

This second crowding-in effect is evident in an experiment conducted by the social psychologists Mizuhu Shinada and Toshio Yamagishi among students at Hokkaido University. They cooperated more in a Public Goods game when they were assured that others (but not they, themselves) would be punished if they did not contribute sufficiently, even though the punishment had no effect on the subject's own material incentives to defect or contribute.[39]

The subjects apparently wanted to be cooperative, but wished even more to avoid being exploited by defectors. Iris Bohnet and her coauthors call this motive "betrayal aversion."[40] The assurance that defectors would be punished by a third party reduced a subject's fear that a defector would gain at her expense. Similar synergies occur in natural settings: social norms support the observance of traffic regulations, but these may unravel in the absence of state-imposed sanc-

148

tions for flagrant violations. These or similar synergies may account for the few experiments in which material incentives and moral motives appeared to be complements rather than substitutes, the former enhancing the salience of the latter.

In addition, the emergence of the rule of law appears to have been associated with a parallel shift from trust in kin and other particular individuals to generalized trust, consistent with Yamagishi's "emancipation theory of trust."[41] Guido Tabellini, for example, showed that generalized (rather than familial) trust appears to thrive in countries with a long history of liberal political institutions.[42] In a large sample of immigrants to Europe, the strong inverse association between measures of political participation, such as signing petitions or participating in demonstrations or boycotts, and the extent of one's obligation to respect and care for one's children and parents was also consistent with this view.[43]

The substitution of generalized trust for familial or parochial norms appears to have been at work during the expansion of the eleventh-century Mediterranean trading system, in which familial, communal, and other parochial systems of so-called collectivist contract enforcement were eclipsed by more universalistic, state-based, individualist systems.[44] These are some of the reasons why market-based societies may exhibit high levels universalism in the definition and application of social norms.

Markets may have assisted the "civilizing process" in other ways. The spread of markets often contributed to the emergence of national states bound by the rule of law, and if my argument is correct, this dynamic favored the evolution of generalized trust. In addition, expansion of markets favored the proliferation of more universal social norms by promoting the national systems of schooling-by-strangers that Gellner termed exo-socialization.[45] Gellner writes that markets can regulate the division of labor at the national level only if parochial traditional cultures are replaced by more universal values consistent with the extensive interaction with strangers in market environments. The resulting national standardization of language and culture facilitated occupational and geographic mobility, rendering individuals' income-earning assets less specific to place and craft. The result was to complement the other literal and de facto forms of insurance provided by liberal institutions.

I have suggested that the puzzle of vibrant civic cultures in many market-based societies may be resolved by paying attention to how geographic and occupational mobility, the rule of law, and other aspects of liberal societies preserve social order by sustaining civic virtues. If I am right, then the kinds of incentives and constraints that people face in a liberal democratic and market-based society sometimes lead to a kind of crowding in of social preferences rather than the crowding out more commonly seen in experiments.

This result was just what Aristotle's Legislator is hoping to accomplish. He does not seek to design some incentive-compatible mechanism that would allow him to set aside concerns about public morality. Instead, he wants to develop public policies that would allow incentives and constraints to work synergistically rather than at cross-purposes with peoples' ethical and other-regarding dispositions.

It is time, thinks the Legislator, to visit a few economics faculties to see what help they can offer on this score. Recalling some unpleasant rebuffs from economists in the past, he will be surprised by the warm welcome he now receives.

V I
The Legislator's Dilemma

"The superiority of liberalism has been mathematically demonstrated" was *Le Figaro's* headline, slightly embellishing what Gerard Debreu had actually said in an interview with the newspaper in 1984.[1] The basis for Debreu's remarks was the first fundamental theorem of welfare economics, to which he (along with Kenneth Arrow and others) had contributed a third of a century earlier. But as we will see, research in economic theory since their "invisible hand theorem" suggests a quite different conclusion about what the math demonstrated.

Many years after Debreu's *Figaro* interview, renewed discussions between Aristotle's Legislator and his colleagues in economics are friendly enough. Since Richard Titmuss's *The Gift Relationship* (1971) was published, economists have been intrigued—but mostly not persuaded—by his claim that policies based on explicit economic incentives may be counterproductive because they induce people to adopt a "market mentality," and that such policies thus compromise preexisting values that lead people to act in socially beneficial ways.[2]

At the time of the book's publication there were two reasons to doubt Titmuss. First, little hard evidence showed that social preferences such as altruism, fairness, and civic duty were important

151

influences on individual behavior or were in any way essential to the functioning of a market-based economy. Second, even had these social preferences been thought to be important influences on behavior, Titmuss's book offered scant evidence that explicit economic incentives would undermine them.[3]

Another reason that most economists did not share Titmuss's concern was the then-burgeoning field of mechanism design. This body of research, an extension of the earlier Marshall-Pigou tradition in what is called welfare economics, addressed market failures by means of green taxes, training subsidies, and other incentives. Recall that market failures are situations in which people's uncoordinated actions result in Pareto-inefficient outcomes. This outcome, in turn, is defined as one for which there exists a technically feasible alternative outcome, given existing resources and technologies, in which at least one person is better off and nobody is worse off. Mechanism design held out the promise that even among entirely self-regarding citizens, well-designed incentives could, along with market prices, implement Pareto-efficient outcomes. As a result, at the time Titmuss's book appeared, virtue was something economists thought they could safely ignore, just as J. S. Mill had advised them to do over a century earlier.

Economics Discovers Aristotle

Research in the intervening years has upset this complacency. As we have seen, experimental and other evidence has made it clear that ethical and other-regarding motivations are common, and moreover, as Titmuss claimed, that they can be crowded out by incentives. At the same time, economists were discovering that simple textbook metaphors like James Buchanan's fruit stand, at which "both parties agree on the property rights," were a poor guide to understanding a modern capitalist economy. Economic theory turned to the study of the exchange process when contracts are incomplete, that is, when it was not the case that everything that matters can be stipulated in an enforceable agreement. New models of the labor market, for example, recognized that work itself was not something that could be contracted for, so getting a job done well depends at least in part on the employee's intrinsic desire to do the job well. Similarly, in the credit market even the best contract cannot guarantee the repayment of a loan if the borrower is bankrupt; lenders need to trust the borrower's account of the project that the loan will finance.

The new microeconomics of labor, credit, and other markets enumerated the ways that, as Arrow said, social norms and moral codes could induce economic actors to internalize their actions' costs and benefits to others when contracts failed to do this. The employee's work ethic would induce her to internalize the cost that she would impose on her employer by keeping in touch with her Faccbook friends while on the job. The borrower's sense of honesty would deter his misrepresenting the riskiness of the project for which he was seeking a loan that would, in all likelihood, never be repaid if the project failed. Economists were coming to see why prices alone could not always do the work of morals.

Another advance in economic theory—in the seemingly unrelated field of macroeconomics—raised doubts about the "constitution for knaves" policy paradigm. A generation ago, Robert Lucas rocked economics with a simple observation: taxes and other governmental interventions in the private economy affect not only (as intended) the costs and benefits of citizens' actions, but also their beliefs about the future actions of others (including the government). Thus, just as in the case of citizens' experienced values, as illustrated in figure 3.1, incentives may have an indirect effect (in this case, via citizens' beliefs) as well as direct ones. For example, announcing stiffer penalties for the nonpayment of taxes provides an incentive to pay up, but it also may convey the information that noncompliance is common, leading formerly honest citizens to cheat.

Lucas reasoned that the effect of a policy intervention can be predicted only if one takes into account these indirect effects on beliefs, and then studies the joint outcome in which citizens' beliefs and the targeted economic actions are both mutually dependent. His point was that a new economic policy is not an intervention in a frozen model of how the economy works, but rather a change in the workings of the model itself: "Given that the structure of an econometric model consists of optimal decision rules of economic agents, and that optimal decision rules vary systematically with changes in the structure . . . relevant to the decision maker, it follows that any change in policy will systematically alter the structure of econometric models."[4] He concluded: "Policy makers, if they wish to forecast the response of citizens, must take the latter into their confidence." This idea was taken to be so important that economists now capitalize it, bestowing an honor on the Lucas Critique withheld even from the invisible hand. Here I apply Lucas's logic to cases in which incentives affect not only beliefs (as Lucas stressed) but also preferences.

Not surprisingly in light of these and other developments, economics began to change. Albert Hirschman chided his fellow economists who, he said, propose "to deal with unethical or antisocial behavior by raising the cost of that behavior rather than proclaiming standards and imposing prohibitions and sanctions," probably because "they think of citizens as consumers with unchanging or arbitrarily changing tastes in matters civic as well as commodity-related behavior." Economists, according to Hirschman, disregard the fact that "a principal purpose of publically proclaimed laws and regulations is to stigmatize antisocial behavior and thereby to influence citizens' values and behavioral codes."[5] Michael Taylor, a political scientist, took up Hirschman's idea that legal structures shape preferences and social norms. And he went further, turning Thomas Hobbes's justification of state authority on its head and suggesting that Hobbesian man might be the result of, and not a reason for, the Hobbesian state.[6] Reading Hirschman and then Taylor in the 1980s set me to work on the project that resulted in this book.[7]

I was far from alone. At a meeting of the American Economics Association in 1994, Henry Aaron pointed out "the failure of economists to take the formation of preferences seriously," and went on to suggest that the Lucas Critique be extended accordingly.[8] The economist Bruno Frey titled a paper "A Constitution for Knaves Crowds Out Civic Virtue."[9] The political scientist Elinor Ostrom, soon to be honored with a Nobel in economics, like Taylor worried about "crowding out citizenship."[10] The discipline of economics, which had spurned Titmuss a generation earlier, eventually rediscovered him. The subtitle of a paper in a top economics journal in 2008 asked "Was Titmuss Right?" (The authors concluded he was right about women but not men.)[11]

Economists, at least some of them, not only reread Titmuss but also rediscovered (or, more likely, discovered) Aristotle. What should his Legislator do, given this new knowledge about the possible antisynergy between incentives and the social motives they now recognized as essential to a well-functioning economy and society? The new turn of research in economics, while recognizing the crowding-out problem, did not provide much of an answer. It had not yet systematically exploited the burgeoning experimental evidence for its policy implications, nor had it pursued the logic of recent developments in economic theory that would help clarify the Legislator's dilemma and perhaps suggest a way out. These are the Legislator's remaining tasks.

Mechanism Design: Can Prices Do the Work of Morals?

Not all economists were convinced that the importance of social preferences and the crowding-out problem warranted a new approach to policy. One could, they might insist, take on board the new experimental evidence and advances in theory without abandoning the self-interest-based policy paradigm.

Suppose that a policy maker, they reasoned, recognizes the need to address market failures and also understands that explicit incentives may crowd out the ethical and other-regarding motives. A holdout for the self-interest paradigm could go on to concede that these social preferences might otherwise induce actors to internalize the costs and benefits that their actions confer on others, thus mitigating the market failure that arises when contracts are incomplete. But the policy maker might nonetheless be confident that he could devise systems of subsidies, penalties, and constraints to implement socially desired outcomes, even if social preferences had been crowded out to the point that citizens were entirely amoral and self-regarding.

To think this possible, one would have to bar strong crowding out (so as to preclude cases in which incentives were counterproductive) and concede that the policy maker herself must not be entirely self-interested. But given these two caveats, a constitution for knaves just might do the job, as Hume recommended, even (as Hume never intended) in a world of not-at-all-hypothetical but instead very real, flesh-and-blood knaves.

This remains the canonical model of policy making in economics, and it is worth exploring whether it could possibly work. We will see that it could not.

To do this we need the theory of mechanism design.[12] Founding works in this branch of economics appeared at about the same time as Titmuss's book.[13] Since then, the growing concern with environmental, public health, and other kinds of market failures has given new urgency to the mechanism designer's attempt to give "the invisible hand a helping hand," as the *Economist* put it in 2007, struggling to explain the challenging mathematics of the field when three of its leading scholars—Leo Hurwicz, Eric Maskin, and Roger Myerson—were awarded the Nobel Prize.

Helping the invisible hand inevitably requires that government play a role in the economy, but there is nothing Big Brother–ish about mechanism design. And surprisingly, this is where it runs into trouble.

The theory begins with recognition of the necessarily limited reach of the policy maker. The task of the mechanism designer is to provide a set of contracts, property rights, and other social rules— called a mechanism—that will attenuate or eliminate market failures. But both realism and a commitment to individual privacy require that the policies proposed can be implemented even when important bits of information about individuals are known only privately and hence cannot be used by the mechanism designer to implement the incentives, constraints, or other aspects of the proposed policy.

This privacy-of-information restriction excludes utopian solutions in which the designer could simply wish away the underlying reason for the market failure. If the proposed mechanism could use information about how hard a person worked, for example, or about a buyer's or seller's true valuation of some good or service, then the same information could have been used to write a complete private contract between the parties. And that contract would have eliminated the market failure that the mechanism designer had been called in to address.

To correct the problem of free riding in a work team, for example, a mechanism designer cannot simply propose an enforceable contract that all must work hard and well, or even that each member must truthfully report how hard she worked. If the mechanism designer could do this, then the team members could have done the same and simply paid team members according to how hard they worked. There would have been no need for the mechanism designer in the first place.

To its practitioners three conditions for an acceptable solution then define the challenge of mechanism design. The first is that the resulting allocation be Pareto-efficient.

Second, policies must rely on individuals' voluntary participation in their economic activities. They must be free to choose their own courses of action, guided by their own preferences, including opting out of any possible exchange or other interaction. In economic language, the outcome must satisfy the individual's "participation constraint"; each must regard participating in the mechanism as better than not doing so, meaning that participation is voluntary. The outcome must also be "incentive compatible," meaning that whatever the individual does while participating must be motivated by the individual's own preferences.

Third, there can be no restrictions on the kinds of preferences people may have. So the mechanism must work even if individuals are entirely self-interested and amoral.

Call these three conditions *efficiency, voluntary participation,* and *preference neutrality.* The first imposes a minimal collective-rationality condition (minimal because it ignores, for example, considerations of justice). The second rules out the confiscation of property or mandatory participation in an exchange. Along with the second, the third expresses the standard liberal commitments to individual liberty and the state's neutrality on matters concerning individuals' conceptions of the good.

The last has recently come to be termed liberal neutrality, expressed by Ronald Dworkin's dictum that "political decisions must be . . . independent of any particular conception of the good life, or of what gives value to life."[14] Peter Jones likewise writes: "It is not the function of the state to impose the pursuit of any particular set of ends upon its citizens."[15] Neutrality in this sense is not universally advocated by liberals. My broad interpretation of liberal neutrality—the permissibility of an unrestricted set of preferences—would be objected to by some, for example, who would point out that a preference for domination of others might be judged impermissible without violating liberal neutrality. But I use the requirement of an unrestricted set of preferences here simply to allow individuals the systematic pursuit of material self-interest, which could hardly be objected to under the liberal neutrality doctrine.

If mechanism design had succeeded in its quest for privacy-respecting rules that eliminated market failures while respecting the two quintessentially liberal requirements of voluntary participation and preference neutrality, *Le Figaro* could hardly have been faulted for its headline about what the math had demonstrated. Moreover, the holdout for the self-interest paradigm would have been vindicated. So if mechanism design had found its holy grail, we would have to conclude that a constitution for knaves would work, at least in this limited sense, however unpleasant it might otherwise be. But more than four decades of research in mechanism design has showed quite the opposite.

A (Liberal) Constitution for Knaves

A mechanism is a set of rules that the designer might impose on a population to influence the behaviors that determine how an economy's resources are used. The fines and subsidies in the previous chapters' experiments are found in the mechanism designer's toolbox. So too are such familiar ways of determining resource use as majority rule, buying and selling in competitive markets, and, as we will see, more exotic rules as well. The setup defining the mechanism designer's task is strikingly like the problem faced by Machiavelli's benign ruler, "who would found a republic and order its laws," and was charged with governing well through the imposition of enlightened laws upon a citizenry of "natural and ordinary humors."[16]

This context of an enlightened ruler and self-interested subjects is exactly the setting for the "rotten kid" theorem devised by Gary Becker, another Nobel in economics. He identified conditions under which an altruistic household head (the mechanism designer) could impose a rule governing his transfers of income within the family that would induce all family members to act as if they cared no more for their own well-being than for each of the other family members: "Sufficient 'love' by one member guarantees that all members act as if they loved other members as much as themselves. As it were, the amount of 'love' required in a family is economized: sufficient 'love' by one member leads all other members by 'an invisible hand' to act as if they too loved everyone."[17]

The theorem works, Becker explains, because the altruistic family head can arrange things so that every family member will "internalize fully all within-family 'externalities' regardless of how selfish . . . these members are." Thus, under the right rules governing how income is distributed within the family, entirely self-interested family members will act as if they were entirely altruistic. This is a particularly dramatic case of prices doing the work of morals.

And it is exactly what the *Economist* had in mind: Becker provided an analogue for the invisible hand in family relationships, where Adam Smith's variant does not work. Becker concludes, "Armed with this theorem, I do not need to dwell on the preferences of the nonheads"—even, apparently, the rotten one after whom the theorem is named. I studied Becker's theorem at about the time I haplessly issued a price list for household chores that my not-at-all-rotten kids had previously done voluntarily. I did not see the connection at the time. You already know how that turned out.

Exported to the world of public policy, Becker's rotten-kid theorem suggests that well-designed public incentives could dispense with virtue entirely as a foundation of good government (at least among "nonheads"). Just as importantly, it spares the policy maker or constitution writer the liberal embarrassment of having to foster in citizens some particular values—a concern for the environment, for future generations, or even for one's own family, for example—over others.

But just as proof of the invisible hand theorem demonstrated how implausible were the axioms required to advocate a laissez-faire policy on efficiency grounds, modern mechanism design has clarified the limits of even the cleverest ways of giving the invisible hand a helping hand via public policy. Soon after the publication of Becker's celebrated paper, for example, it was shown that the rotten-kid theorem relied on highly unrealistic mathematical assumptions, which limited its application to a set of rather special cases, quite remote from the general problem faced by family heads and mechanism designers.[18] There would be no simple shortcuts for those who would "found a republic and order its laws."

To see why a constitution for knaves could not work, let me set aside the objection that the constitution writer or mechanism designer had better not be a knave, and that a life surrounded by knaves would be unpleasant even for knaves. The basic idea in mechanism design is to align individual incentives with the objective of efficiency, defined over a large group of people. This may be done, as we saw in chapter II and as Becker explained, if we can find a way to induce each person to act as if he or she internalized all of the benefits and costs to others resulting from his or her actions. This is the condition of Robison Crusoe on his island; he alone "owns" the results of the work he has done, the risks he has taken, and the knowledge he has gained. Getting people to act as if they were like Robinson Crusoe alone on his island is the name of the game.

Just how difficult it is to do this for a large group of individuals with unrestricted preferences will be clear from the problem that arises in any process where people contribute to a joint output. Think about a group of software engineers working together to write code for new applications. To pose this as a problem of mechanism design, consistent with the preference neutrality condition, we suppose that each team member is interested only in his or her own material pay-off, however determined. The mechanism designer (standing outside the team a bit like the legendary philosopher-king) can observe the team's total output but cannot see how hard each member has worked (respecting the privacy-of-information restriction).

The problem for the designer is that if each team member receives as compensation simply an equal share of the output of the team, then a worker's payoff for providing one unit of additional output will not be one unit of compensation, as it would be for Robinson Crusoe, but instead, because the additional unit will be shared among all of the team, $1/n$ units, where n is the number of team members. Under this shared-output compensation rule, working is analogous to contributing to a public good.

Each worker owns only a small fraction of the full benefit that his efforts have created, so if he can choose on his own (the voluntary-participation condition), he will provide less effort for the team than would be efficient, because he will not take into account the benefits that his effort confers on other team members. In this situation, every worker could be better off if each worked a little harder. Of course the designer knows that they would voluntarily work harder if they altruistically valued the contributions that their efforts made to the material payoffs of the other team members, but the preference-neutrality and voluntary-participation conditions prohibit him from imposing other-regarding preferences on the team or from compelling members to act counter to their preferences.

A mechanism that works for these individuals should result in each team member's acting as if she were Robinson Crusoe, owning the results of her work. Each would then work up to the point where the discomfort of working a little harder was exactly compensated by the additional benefit of her work to the members of the entire team (more technically, the marginal disutility of work is equal to the marginal benefit that she gains from work). But if the designer cannot require the team members to provide any particular lcvel of work (that is private information), meeting this objective seems to be impossible.

But it is not. The designer need only announce that he will pay each member the *entire value* of the output of the team, minus a constant sum to be determined by the designer. This bizarre mechanism ensures that any contribution by a member to the output of the team will be exactly compensated, giving each member the Robinson Crusoe incentives of an isolated individual who owns the entire fruits of his labor. The subtraction of a constant sum is necessary to allow the designer to balance the team's budget; otherwise, he would be paying out n times the team's total output.

Problem solved?

Not yet. To see why, we can introduce some real-world risk. Suppose the team's realized production depends not only on the sum of the team members' efforts but also on chance events affecting production but not controlled by team members. Call these positive or negative chance events "shocks," and suppose, realistically, that like each member's effort, they are not observable by the designer, so he cannot determine whether the team's unexpectedly low output in some year comes from bad luck or from shirking workers. The contract offered by the designer would have to ensure that team members received an *expected* income (averaging over "good" shocks and "bad") at least as great as their next-best alternative (the wage in some other job, unemployment insurance, or something similar).

But given the fluctuating level of total output as a result of a positive shock, for teams of any significant size each member's *realized* income (total output minus some large constant sufficient to balance the budget) in any period could be many times larger than the workers' next-best alternative. That is not the problem, however. The hitch is that shocks can also be negative, so realized income could also be much less than what the team member would have received in some alternative employment. It could, in fact, be a large negative number, meaning that the member would have to pay the mechanism designer rather than the other way around.

The problem arises because in order for this clever and odd mechanism to work, the pay of each member has to be keyed to the entire team's *realized* output, and both negative and positive shocks to total output would realistically dwarf any individual's average compensation in the long run. A contract under which, in some periods, a team member would not be paid and instead would be required to pay the team a substantial multiple of her expected salary is not likely to be attractive to many workers. No contract of this type would be voluntarily accepted by the team members, thus violating the condition of voluntary participation.

If the team members could borrow an unlimited amount of money in the bad years, they might be okay with such a contract. But this could never be the case, because a similar problem arises in the credit market: the contracted repayment of the funds is not enforceable if the team member is without funds. Thus, implementing the optimal contract for the team members just displaces the mechanism designer's challenge to the analogous problem in the credit market: the incompleteness of contracts, where he would confront similar obstacles to a solution.

The Liberal Trilemma

This is not the end of the story, of course. Far more complicated mechanisms might address the problems that confront the designer's simple "pay each the whole output" plan. But the verdict of the now-vast literature of mechanism design is that the designer's problems are endemic, not specific to the team-production example. In 2007, when the Prize Committee of the Royal Swedish Academy of Sciences honored Maskin, Hurwicz and Myerson for their contributions to mechanism design, it explained what the field had discovered.

A paper by Hurwicz, the committee explained, had proved the following "negative result" concerning voluntary participation: in the presence of private information, "no incentive compatible mechanism which satisfies the participation constraint can produce Pareto-optimal outcomes." Referring to Maskin's joint work with Jean Jacques Laffont, and Myerson's joint work with Mark Satterthwaite, the committee members wrote: "In a large class of models Pareto efficiency is incompatible with voluntary participation, even if there are no public goods."[19] Mechanism design, it appeared, had failed in its quest for mechanisms to address market failures that would have Pareto-efficient outcomes while respecting preference neutrality and voluntary participation.

A good example of the problems that account for these "negative results" is illustrated by one-shot buyer-seller interactions called "double auctions" because both buyers and sellers are looking for the counterpart who will give them the best price. In a double auction, prospective buyers and sellers are paired, each knows how much they value the good held by the prospective seller, and they simultaneously announce prices: for the seller, the least price at which she will part with the good, and for the buyer, the highest price he is willing to pay. If the seller's announced price is less than the buyers, then a trade will occur, the actual price being either of the two announced prices or some price in between. If the seller's announced price exceeds the buyer's, then no transaction takes place.

The double-auction setting is important because it is generally thought that Pareto efficiency is not difficult to sustain in this type of interaction, even without the help of a mechanism designer, because it features none of the familiar impediments to efficient bargaining and market exchange, such as ill-defined property rights, incomplete contracts, or, as in the case of public goods, the nonexcludability of some aspect of the goods involved. Barring these impediments, a large number of buyers or sellers knowing only their own preferences and the prices offered or asked by their trading counterparts should be able to bargain their way to an efficient allocation, eventually exhausting all potential gains from trade and hence, by definition, implementing a Pareto-efficient outcome.

But surprisingly, this is not the case. The problem is that when traders meet, they have no incentive to reveal their true valuations of the goods that may be exchanged, since, as is plausible to assume, these stated valuations will influence the eventual price at which they transact if they make a deal.

Knowing this, the prospective seller of a good will overstate the lowest price at which he will sell, and the would-be buyer will understate the highest price at which she is willing to buy. As a result, the buyer's announced price will sometimes fall short of the seller's announced price, so no trade will take place, even when the buyer's true valuation of the good is greater than the seller's. This means that some mutually beneficial exchanges will not be consummated. Buyers and sellers will walk away with money left on the table; Pareto efficiency will elude the bargainers.

The key result of investigations of the double auction is that if traders care only about maximizing their expected gains, it is never in either party's interest to truthfully reveal his or her evaluation. This is the case even if the other party is reporting truthfully. The fact that individuals may benefit by misrepresenting their preferences also prevents a benign social planner from eliciting the information he needs in order to provide incentives for the efficient provision of a public good.[20]

Kalyan Chatterjee invented an ingenious mechanism for which a trader's best response (the action that maximizes her payoffs) is to truthfully report her valuations, with the result that all mutually beneficial trades occur.[21] The mechanism implementing this Pareto-efficient outcome requires upfront payments between the traders that depend only on the announced values, irrespective of whether a trade ensues. The size of the payments depends on the losses that each trader's misrepresentation of the true valuation would have imposed on the other, had the other responded truthfully. Chatterjee describes this mechanism as "the payment to each player of the expected externality generated by his action."

The payment is effectively a tax on false representation of individual's valuation of the good, a tax just sufficient to make truthfulness the best response. The clever part is that Chatterjee figured out how this could be done without violating the privacy of the traders' true valuations of the good.

But as you have come to expect by now, there was a hitch. Given their true valuations, some traders would do better by refusing to make the upfront payment and instead withdrawing from the mechanism. But if they withdraw, the mechanism does not work. The mechanism therefore works only if either the parties (improbably) do not know in advance how much they value their own goods or, barring this odd situation, if participation is involuntary (violating the voluntary-participation constraint).[22] This Big Brother aspect of the Chatterjee solution ruled it out.

Figure 6.1 summarizes what I call the liberal trilemma. What mechanism design has discovered is that the three conditions of liberal constitutional design and public policy—neutrality with respect to preferences, voluntary participation, and Pareto efficiency—are not generally compatible. Let's consider each dyad—each pair of vertices of the triangle in the figure—and see why the excluded vertex is not feasible. Between each pair of liberal desiderata, the phrase in parentheses is the consequence of realizing the two desiderata connected by this side but excluding the third.

If voluntary participation is combined with preference neutrality—the base of the triangle—as we have just seen from the example of the double auction, some would-be mutually beneficial exchanges

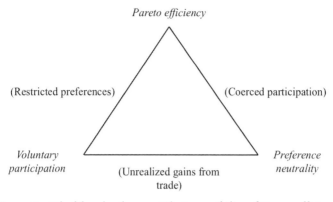

Figure 6.1. The liberal trilemma: The impossibility of Pareto efficiency, preference neutrality, and voluntary participation

will not occur, so there will be unrealized gains from trade, violating Pareto efficiency. Pareto efficiency and preference neutrality are jointly feasible—the right-hand side of the triangle—if people can be compelled to participate in a mechanism (like that designed by Chatterjee) even if they would prefer not to, violating the voluntary-participation condition. Finally, voluntary participation and Pareto efficiency are jointly feasible if the traders were predisposed to report honestly their true valuations. Individuals would then never walk away from a potential mutually beneficial trade, but demanding that traders place a sufficiently high value on honesty requires a violation of preference neutrality.

One way out of the trilemma is to abandon liberal neutrality. If the traders were altruistic, they would value the losses—not only their own but also those suffered by their trading partners because of forgone mutually beneficial trades. Because this would lead them to take account of the costs that their actions inflict on others, it would attenuate the resulting market failures. What degree of altruism would be needed to ensure that all mutually beneficial trades were implemented?

One's intuition is that if both traders were perfectly altruistic, then they would not care at all about the price (they would treat others' gains as equivalent to their own) and so would not misreport their true valuations. This is true. But Sung-Ha Hwang and I have shown, surprisingly, that it is sufficient for only one of the traders to be entirely altruistic; explaining why this is the case, however, would take us away from the lessons of the liberal trilemma.[23]

Recent research has not overturned the conclusion that preference neutrality, voluntary participation, and Pareto efficiency are not jointly possible, even in a very simple exchange of goods. Thus, even if we assume that those who design public policy are paragons of civic virtue, an assumption that the self-interest-based policy paradigm would like to dispense with for the rest of the population, mechanism design fails to produce a constitution for knaves fit for a liberal society. Among the reasons is the liberal aversion to requiring people to participate in economic transactions against their will, and to allowing states to favor some kinds of preferences over others.

Another source of the trilemma is the limited extent to which intrinsically private information may be placed in a mechanism designer's hands. This is not only true as a practical matter but also, at least in a liberal society, a highly valued limit on the authority of states. Machiavelli stated the core message of the trilemma in his *Discourses* when he concluded that inducing the truly bad to act as if they were good "would be either a very cruel endeavor or altogether impossible," and would require "extraordinary means, including violence and a resort to arms."[24]

The literature on mechanism design reads like one piece of bad news after another. The negative results were important contributions, and as they accumulated, some in the field beat a strategic retreat, weakening the standard of efficiency in order to resolve the trilemma by the stroke of a pen. Again the Nobel committee: "Thus in settings where participants have private information, Pareto optimality in the classical sense is in general not attainable, and we need a new standard of efficiency."[25] Thus, mechanism design has (for the most part) abandoned the standard Pareto criterion in favor of "incentive efficiency," which simply means "the best that can be done given the way people respond to incentives," or in other words, given existing preferences. By this new standard, an outcome like the unrealized gains from trade in the double auction would be deemed efficient. But it is clear that the operation succeeded only because the patient disappeared.

This seemingly technical watering down of the field's time-honored objective is a concession to the inconvenient fact that preferences indeed matter. We saw how they mattered in the case of the hypothetical team of software developers, in which a bit of altruism among the members would have attenuated their failure to reach an efficient outcome. Many of his fellow economists may now agree, perhaps ruefully, with Tim Besley: "Perhaps then the solution can only lie in creating better people."[26]

The time has come, the Legislator muses, to take a second look at liberal neutrality.

A Second-Best World

The Legislator thus has some difficult tradeoffs to consider. The trilemma has affirmed that he was right to worry about the nature of people's preferences. From earlier chapters, he knows that policies that would more effectively harness self-interest to public ends may compromise the ethical and other-regarding preferences on which the success of the Legislator's constitution must also depend. And as we will see, the reverse is also true: policies that support the proliferation and expression of ethical and other-regarding motivations will sometimes reduce the effectiveness of explicit incentives in implementing efficient outcomes.

The resulting conundrum facing the Legislator is just a novel application of a venerable yet paradoxical idea in economics: policies that address market failures by moving the economy in the "right" direction may be misguided unless they go all the way and implement the ideal market and property rights on which the invisible hand theorem is based. This "all or nothing" advice to the policy maker is called the general theorem of the second best.[27]

Here is the idea in its original economic application. In a competitive economy of the type represented by the invisible hand theorem, recall that prices are signals to buyers that ideally measure the true scarcity of the good, as measured by its social marginal cost— that is, the cost of making an additional unit of the good available, taking account of not only the costs borne by the producer and seller of the good (the private marginal cost), but also any costs borne by all others.

The key assumption under which the theorem is true—that everything that matters in an exchange is subject to a contract enforceable at no cost to the parties of the exchange—ensures that competition among buyers and sellers will result in prices equal to the social marginal cost of each good. In other words, everything that matters will have a price, and the price will be right. Where the social marginal cost of a good exceeds its private marginal cost—for example, because of the costs of environmental damages for which the producer is not liable—the mechanism designer can tax the good by an amount equal to these excluded costs so that the price (now including the tax) will equal the social marginal cost.

But suppose there are two violations of the "price equals social marginal cost" rule. Imagine, for example, that a certain firm has a monopoly on some good; it restricts sales and profits by setting prices above the marginal cost of production. This is the first market failure.

The firm's production of the good contributes to environmental degradation, so the private marginal cost of production to the firm's owners is less than the social marginal cost. This is the second market failure.

Now consider what happens if we address one of these market failures—for example, by breaking up the monopoly into smaller competitive firms so that the excess of price over marginal cost will be reduced. The second-best theorem shows that this may take the economy further away from an efficient outcome. The reason is that the competitive firms that would then make up the industry would produce more than the erstwhile monopoly because, not being monopolies, they would not benefit by restricting sales. They would expand production until their marginal cost equaled market price. This would correct the standard problem of monopolies: firms sell too little in order to profit from high prices. But the increased production would worsen the environmental problems. Letting the company remain a monopoly might have been a better policy. If adopting optimal antitrust and environmental policies simultaneously ("going all the way") is for some reason precluded, one cannot be sure that either policy alone would improve things and could well make things worse.

The intuition behind this result is that distortions caused by violation of one of the efficiency conditions may be attenuated by offsetting distortions induced by other violations. The remarkable result is that bringing the economy closer to fulfillment of the standard efficiency conditions may result in a net loss of efficiency.

A similar result arises from the nonseparability of incentives and social preferences. It follows from a now-familiar logic. Where market failures arise because contracts are incomplete, socially valuable norms like trust and reciprocity may be important in attenuating these market failures. In these cases, public policies and legal practices that more closely approximate the idealized incentives associated with complete contracting—fines imposed for insufficient back-transfers in the Trust game, for example, or for lateness at the Haifa day care centers—may exacerbate the underlying market failure by undermining these norms. The result is a less efficient allocation.

The theory of mechanism design has led us to doubt whether efficient outcomes can be implemented in an entirely self-interested population. So norms such as trust and reciprocity will remain socially valuable under any conceivable set of mechanisms, because there is no constitution for knaves that works. "Going all the way" is not an option. Aristotle's Legislator thus lives in a second-best world in which interventions that would be appropriate in an ideal world may not only underperform. They may make things worse.

One of these trade-offs stems from the cultural downside of policies designed to perfect the workings of markets and to extend their role in determining how a society uses its human and material resources. To understand these concerns, we return to the idea in the previous chapter that markets and other social institutions are teachers—that is, they are environments that induce people to learn new motivations and to discard old ones. The concern now troubling the Legislator is that markets that approximate the ideal assumptions of the invisible hand theorem might provide an inauspicious environment for learning social norms, which, we have seen, are essential to market functioning.

Look at markets through this lens. To see how markets—at least those in economics textbooks—differ from other institutions, I will define two of the dimensions that characterize institutions as learning environments: first, interactions may be either durable or ephemeral, and second, they may be either personal or anonymous. A key characteristic of markets, first advanced by Max Weber and since stressed by Buchanan and other advocates of an expanded role for markets, is that they require neither personal affection nor long-term relationships among people engaged in exchange.[28] Markets, in this view, work well when they are both ephemeral and anonymous.

Contrast this with what the mid-twentieth-century sociologist Talcott Parsons called the "two principal competitors" of the market: "requisitioning through the direct application of political power" and "non-political solidarities and communities."[29] Parsons was not good at naming things: we can call these two allocational systems, respectively, states and communities.

The former ("requisitioning through political power") is in some respects as impersonal as a market—at least ideally. But there are differences too. Membership in a state is not typically something one chooses, but is instead an accident of birth. Entry and exit costs are high (often requiring a change in citizenship or at least residence). Moreover, the interpersonal contacts through which state allocations work are far from ephemeral.

Unlike states or markets, directly interacting communities with stable membership—often described by the terms "organic solidarity," "clan," "generalized reciprocity," or "gemeinschaft"—are neither ephemeral nor impersonal.[30] Parsons's "non-political solidarities and communities" are based on long-term face-to-face interactions among known partners.

Table 6.1. Idealized markets as learning environments

Quantitative	Qualitative dimension	
dimension	Anonymous	Personal
Ephemeral	Markets	Racially segmented markets
Durable	Bureaucracies	Communities, clans, families

Note: The rows refer to the extent to which parties to an interaction may expect future interactions, while the columns refer to the irrelevance or importance, respectively, of the individual's identity as an influence on the transaction.

Table 6.1 presents these three ideal types, along with a fourth: ephemeral and personal social interaction, in which one's race or some other marker of identity is important. Racially segmented day-labor markets are an example, since they are personal (the participants' ethnic identities matter), but the contact among participants is not ongoing.

Seen in this light, markets do not look like a school for generosity or concern for others. In their study of generosity toward the needy, George Loewenstein and Deborah Small found that emotional concern is greater for "victims who share our own affective state, who are geographically or socially proximate, who are similar to us or are presented in a vivid fashion."[31] It is rightly called a feature of markets, not a bug, that they allow for mutually beneficial interactions among individuals who share none of this closeness or vividness. But this aspect of market interactions may also attenuate concern for the good or harm to others arising from one's actions.

Although many markets are impersonal or ephemeral—spot markets for day laborers, for example—labor markets also include the lifetime employment famously practiced by some Japanese firms, and the intimate relationships within a small family-owned firm.

To see why these differences matter, return to Adam Smith's observation that merchants are trustworthier than ambassadors. His reasoning was that merchants are likely to interact repeatedly with many people, each of whom knows how the merchant treated others. Cheating one of them, Smith observed, would result in a costly loss in reputation for the merchant. Ambassadors, on the other hand, whose interactions are more ephemeral, "can gain more by a smart trick than they can lose by the injury which it does their character."

Smith versus Smith

Smith's reasoning about the probity of merchants and the untrustworthiness of ambassadors seems to be correct. I am not sure whether he is right about the results, but he could be: don't forget that Costa Rican CEOs were more reciprocal than students in the Trust game, and many in the diplomatic corps at the United Nations are no paragons of parking probity. Also, we will see from a series of experiments and natural observations that the more that markets deviate from the spot market, with its idealized "flexibility" and arm's-length impersonality, the greater is the tendency to form loyalties with exchange partners and to reciprocate their fair treatment and trust.

The sociologist Peter Kollock wanted to know how the extent of trust among people might depend on the kind of market in which they interacted. He investigated "the structural origins of trust in a system of exchange, rather than treating trust as an individual personality variable."[32] He wanted, that is, to see how trust might endogenously emerge in a market. He designed an experiment in which goods of variable quality were exchanged. In one treatment, the quality of the good was subject to contract (enforced by the experimenter), and in another treatment it was not, so quality became a matter of trust. He found that trust in and commitment to trading partners, as well as a concern for one's own reputation and others', emerged when product quality was not subject to contract, but did not emerge when quality was contractible.

Like Kollock, Martin Brown and his coauthors used a market experiment to explore the effects of contractual incompleteness on trust and loyalty among traders.[33] The goods exchanged varied in quality, and higher-quality goods were more costly to provide. In the complete contracting condition, as in Kollock's study, the experimenter enforced the level of quality promised by the supplier, while in the incomplete contracting condition, the supplier could provide any level of quality, irrespective of any promise or agreement with the buyer. Since buyers and sellers knew the identification numbers of those they interacted with, they could use information acquired in previous rounds to decide with whom they wished to interact, the prices and quality to offer, whether to switch partners, and the like. Buyers could make a private offer to the same seller in the next period (rather than broadcasting a public offer) if they wanted to initiate an ongoing relationship.

The complete and incomplete contracting conditions yielded very different patterns of trading. With complete contracting, 90 percent of the trading relationships lasted less than three periods, and most were one-shot. But only 40 percent of relationships under the incomplete contracting condition lasted less than three periods, and most traders formed trusting relationships with their partners. Buyers in the incomplete contracting condition offered prices considerably in excess of the supplier's cost of providing a particular level of quality, thus deliberately sharing the gains from exchange.

The differences between complete and incomplete conditions were particularly pronounced in the game's later rounds, suggesting that traders learned from their experiences and updated their behavior accordingly. As in the Kollock experiment, people learned to trust trading partners when contracts were incomplete and remained loyal to them (not switching when better deals were available elsewhere). This did not occur when contracts were complete.

The experiments document a synergistic relationship between incomplete contracts and social preferences. As we have seen, social preferences contribute to well-functioning markets when contracts are incomplete. In addition, the experiments show that exchanges conducted via incomplete contracts produce conditions—such as the durable and personal interactions that Smith found in the daily lives of merchants but not ambassadors—under which people tend to adopt social preferences.

Incomplete contracts cause market failures, as economists know, but they also encourage trust, which, as Arrow says, may be essential to attenuating market failures. This is part of the Legislator's dilemma. But it could be the basis of a kind of virtuous circle: the trust that is essential to mutually beneficial exchange when contracts are incomplete appears to be learned in precisely the kinds of trading relationships that evolve when contracts are incomplete. The virtuous circle's vicious cousin also exists, of course: lack of trust among trading partners will induce traders to make contracts as complete as possible, thereby making the evolution of trust unlikely.

We saw this in the control-aversion experiment of Falk and Kosfeld (in chapter IV): "employers" who did not trust their "employees" designed contracts that were as complete as the experiment allowed, thereby inducing "employees" to perform minimally, and fulfilling the employer's expectations. If contracts could be made complete, then the disappearance of trust would not be an impediment. But from our exploration of the liberal trilemma, we know that this is not generally possible.

The complementarity of trust and contractual incompleteness illustrates the main message of this new application of the theory of the second best. Exchanges are durable and personal because market participants do not abandon their current exchange partner the moment a better deal appears. Economists call this "market inflexibility" and rightly (if one can set aside the problem of sustaining trust and other social norms) consider it an impediment to efficiency. But what are the consequences of making markets more "flexible," as would occur in Brown's experiment if traders were not allowed to know the identity of their partners, meaning that long-term loyalties could not develop? The population could well tip from the virtuous cycle to the vicious one.

To see how policies to implement a more impersonal and ephemeral ideal market may degrade the economy as an environment in which ethical or other-regarding preferences are learned, return to Smith's claim that merchants are trustworthier than ambassadors. His reasoning can be understood as a repeated Prisoner's Dilemma.[34] We know that if social interactions are sufficiently long-lasting and people sufficiently patient, individuals with conditionally cooperative preferences (strictly: initially predisposed to cooperate and then to retaliate against those who did not cooperate in the previous round) will do better than noncooperators as long as most people are conditional cooperators. If, as seems plausible on empirical grounds, those who do well materially in a society are more likely to be copied, then long-lasting economic interactions with such individuals will support a society of conditional cooperators. The emergence and persistence of the probity of Smith's merchants could well be explained by a similar process of cultural evolution.

But Smith's reasoning leads in an unsuspected direction. Consider a group of villagers whose livelihood depends on a common-pool resource like a forest or a fishery that is subject to tragedy-of-the-commons-type overexploitation. These people could be the Colombian forest users whom we encountered in chapter III in the experiments of Juan Camilo Cardenas and his coauthors. Recall that these villagers cooperated especially well in sustaining their experimental "resource" when they could communicate with one another.

Suppose that in real life the resource has been sustained over centuries because most villagers are conditional cooperators, resisting the temptation to free ride on the restraint of their fellow villagers because a defection by one would provoke a defection by all. This is probably among the reasons why so many small communities of fishers, farmers, and forest users have averted the "tragedy of the commons."[35]

It works because everyone in the village knows that they will interact with one another in the future, as will their grandchildren. Their common ownership of the natural asset increases the expected duration of these interactions, because those who leave the village surrender their claim on the asset. This provides the ideal conditions for effective disciplining of defectors in the management of the common-pool resource. Protected from exploitation by defectors, conditional cooperation in this population would be a sustainable social norm.

Privatizing the asset—giving each member a marketable share in the forest, for example—provides each with an incentive to sustain the resource and monitor those who would overexploit it. But by allowing the sale of one's share, privatization also makes it easier to leave. This undermines the conditions that sustained cooperation. It reduces the expected duration of interactions, so the value of avoiding retaliation is reduced, possibly by enough to make overexploitation the more rewarding strategy. Those who remained conditional cooperators in this setting would experience frequent exploitation by their defecting fellow villagers. Privatization would thus favor the evolution of self-regarding preferences. One might not have anticipated this being the endpoint of Smith's parable about the merchant.

Privatization versus Cooperation

The example is hypothetical, but similar processes are not difficult to come by in the field studies of historians, economists, and anthropologists. A curious twist in the history of land rights in highland Peru provided Ragnhild Haugli Braaten with a natural quasi experiment illustrating these effects.[36]

In an area long dominated and managed by the owners of large haciendas, a leftist military coup in 1968 initiated a series of land reforms, making farmers the de facto owners of the land they tilled. Because the government wanted to promote cooperative ownership of the land, it also initiated a time-consuming titling process in which communities were given formal joint ownership of the land. Eventually, all rural landholders' rights were to be recognized in this manner. Though pushed in varying degrees by local land-reform officials, the recognition of joint land titles in the *communidades campesinas reconocidas* (as they were termed) drew little interest from the campesinos; the formal legal status of the land had no practical import for the farmers at the time. There was no market in land in any case, and land rights appear to have been understood as jointly held in all communities.

When civilian rule was reestablished ten years after the coup, the joint titling process was halted in midstream. In both the "recognized" villages and those that the military government had failed to reach before being thrown out, farmers continued their independent cultivation as de facto owners. In both sets of villages, too, a traditional community assembly of almost entirely male household heads deliberated questions of governance.

Among the assembly's tasks was the organization of *faenas,* communal work parties that maintained the farmers' complex irrigation systems, roads, public buildings, and other common resources. The assembly also specified the number of workdays each household was required to contribute and disciplined those who reneged on their community labor responsibilities. Their admonishments were backed up by the real threat that the land tilled by the free rider could be confiscated. In addition, men volunteered to help neighbors in a traditional custom of reciprocal sharing of farmwork called *ayni.* The joint titling appeared to change little about the farmers' lives; most farmers did not know whether their community was "recognized."

Things started changing dramatically in the late 1990s, however, with the introduction of formal legal titles to private individual landholdings, including the right to sell titles. For the first time, there was a market in land ownership, and farmers could use land as collateral for loans. By 2011, the Special Land Titling and Cadaster Project had issued a million and a half individual titles. But the new laws did not apply to the recognized communities, because they already held formal joint ownership. By the time Braaten arrived in the highlands to implement her Public Goods game experiments, the ownership status of each community was well known, and differences between the individually titled areas, called "private communities," and the jointly titled areas had become apparent.

Braaten wanted to know whether the form of land ownership was associated with differences in the degree of cooperation among the campesinos. She interviewed 570 people and performed a Public Goods experiment with them; half were from seven jointly owned communities and half from eight "private" communities. Other than their different land-rights histories, the two sets of communities hardly differed in literacy, land area per household, degree of poverty, mean income, elevation above sea level, and even degree of trust (as measured by agreement with the standard survey statement "One can trust the majority of people"). But compared with those holding jointly titled land, people in the private communities volunteered less than half the number of *faena* days to the communal projects, and substantially and significantly fewer days to *ayni,* the system of reciprocal farming help, as well.

The campesinos immediately recognized the resemblance between Braaten's experimental Public Goods game and the *faenas.* Among men, those from the joint-ownership villages contributed over a third more to the experimental public good than those from the private communities, controlling for individual and community characteristics. (Women from the joint-ownership communities were indistinguishable from those from the private communities, a finding that Braaten attributed to the fact that the communal governance institutions, as well as both *faena* and *ayni* work, were almost entirely male activities.) She concluded that the "recent formalization of individual land rights has . . . weakened the traditional forms of cooperation."

As with individual land titling, the development of modern labor markets in the Peruvian highlands appears to have turned the traditional contributions of communal labor into an activity for chumps. Those exploiting the exit option afforded by a regional labor market increased their payoffs by simply ignoring what had once been a community norm.[37] Other ethnographic and historical studies—from India, medieval traders in the Mediterranean (already mentioned), Mexican and Brazilian shoemakers—suggest that Braaten's conclusion may have broad relevance.[38]

It would be a mistake to infer from Braaten's study and the other evidence that the privatization and clarification of land and other property rights designed to allow for more complete contracts will fail to contribute to the economic development of the communities involved. But it is safe to conclude that efforts to perfect the workings of markets may have collateral cultural effects that make people less likely to learn or retain the exchange-supporting norms and other values essential to good governance.

The Legislator's Dilemma

The Legislator's visits to economics faculties have left him with five uncomfortable facts about incentives: incentives are essential to a well-governed society; incentives cannot singlehandedly implement a fully efficient use of economic resources if people are entirely self-interested and amoral; ethical and other social preferences are therefore essential; unless designed to at least "do no harm," incentives may stand in the way of "creating better people"; and as a result, public policy must be concerned about the nature of individual preferences and the possibility that incentives may affect them adversely. The last point is not something to be celebrated by anyone committed to the idea that in a liberal society the government ought to stay out of the business of cultivating some values and discouraging others. But the Legislator does not see how it can be avoided.

He also knows that in the second-best world that he faces, devising good policies in light of these facts will be a challenge. Just like the incentives in our experiments, the kinds of policies advocated by economists to make markets work more efficiently in an economy of knaves—roughly, by putting a price on everything—may compromise exactly those ethical and other-regarding motives that are essential to a well-governed society. The functioning of markets

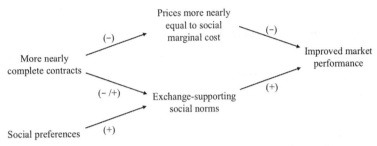

Figure 6.2. The Legislator's dilemma in improving market performance

themselves may, as a result, be degraded by these market-improving policies when, as is typically the case, there is no way to guarantee every aspect of an exchange by means of an enforceable contract. Some of the economist's standard remedies to make markets work better may make them work worse.

This is the Legislator's dilemma. He sketches figure 6.2. Implementing the conditions—such as clearly defined private property rights, competition, flexibility, and mobility—under which markets would work well if contracts were complete may compromise those social norms permitting mutually beneficial exchange when contracts are not. But the economic and social institutions that promote these social norms may impede market functioning because they widen the distance between the economy and the ideal world of the invisible hand.

To figure out how to address the challenge of this second-best world, Aristotle's Legislator returns to his roots.

VII

A Mandate for Aristotle's Legislator

When the Athenian citizens' assembly decided in 325 BCE to set up a colony and naval station in the Adriatic, far to the west of Greece, they took on an enormous project requiring thousands of people and 289 ships.[1] And they had little time to spare: the window for safe navigation around the Peloponnesus would close in a matter of weeks. Neither the personnel nor the ships were at the moment under public orders; the settlers, oarsmen, navigators, and soldiers would have to be recruited from their private lives, and the ships outfitted for the mission (some would carry horses, since cavalry were involved). We know how they accomplished this because the assembly's decree was preserved.

Trierarchs (ship commanders and equippers), appointed from among Athens's wealthy, were required to bring a fully outfitted ship to the docks at Piraeus by a given date. Those who felt unjustly burdened could appeal their assignment (called a liturgy). They would do this by challenging some other (also presumably wealthy) individual to either take on their liturgy, or else to exchange with the challenger all their real and personal property holdings. If the target of the challenge refused to do either, then a popular jury would determine which man's estate was the larger and should therefore bear the costs of the liturgy. By allowing citizens to use private information about their own and their neighbors' wealth to mitigate injustices in the assignment of the liturgy, this ingenious provision limited opposition to the provisioning of the mission.

The decree continues that the assembly would honor the " first [trierarch] to bring his ship [to Piraeus] with a crown of 500 drachmas and the second with a crown of 300 dr[achma]s and the third with a crown of 200 dr[achma]s," adding that "the herald of the Council [of 500] is to announce the crowns at the contest of the Thargelia [a festival] . . . in order that the competitive zeal . . . of the trierarchs towards the demos may be evident." The daily wage for a skilled worker at the time was about one drachma, so these were substantial rewards, even though they represented a tiny fraction of the total cost of executing a liturgy. Others responsible for the timely dispatch of the mission would also be honored.

Lest there be any doubt about the elevated purpose served by these incentives, the decree spelled out the expected benefits of the Adriatic naval base: "the demos may for all future time have its own commerce and transport in grain" as well as a "guard against the Tyrrhenians" (Etruscan pirates).

And for those unmoved by honors and rewards, there was a warning: "But if anyone to whom each of these things has been commanded does not do them in accordance with this decree, whether he be a magistrate or a private individual, the man that does not do so is to be fined 10,000 dr[achma]s," with the proceeds going to honor Athena. (The winners of prizes for the timely arrival of the ships at Piraeus most likely would have given them as offerings to Athena, too.)

Collectively, the Athenian polis was an accomplished mechanism designer; and its members would have laughed at the idea that material incentives and moral sentiments were simply additive. They would have found the idea that the incentives they offered might crowd out the Athenians' civic virtues more risible still.

The "crown" they promised to the first trierarch who outfitted a ship was a prize, not a fee for service; their exhortations and incentives were complements, not substitutes. They were the first Aristotelian Legislators, though there is no evidence that Aristotle himself was involved. (He died three years after the Adriatic mission began.)

Recall the experiment in which imposing fines on parents arriving late to pick up their children at day care centers in Haifa resulted in a doubling of the number of tardy pickups. Now imagine that the Athenians had traveled to Haifa in a time machine and had been asked to help design the day care centers' policy for dealing with late parents.

The sign that the day care centers posted on their doors read: "Since some parents have been coming late we (with the approval of the Authority for Private Day Care Centers in Israel) have decided to impose a fine on parents who come late to pick up their children. As of next Sunday a fine of NIS 10 [about $3 at the time, in Israeli new shekels] will be charged every time a child is collected after 16.10."

Had the Athenians been consulted, they certainly would have not approved. Instead, their sign would have announced: "The Council of Parents wishes to thank you for arriving on time to pick up your children, since this reduces the anxiety that the children sometimes feel and allows our staff to leave in a timely manner to be with their own families. We will recognize all parents who have a perfect record unblemished by lateness for the next three months with an award of NIS 500, to be given at our annual parents and staff holiday party, with an option to contribute your award to the school's Teacher of the Year celebration."

But that would not have been all: "Those who arrive more than ten minutes late, however, will pay a fine of NIS 1,000, with the payment of the fine publicly transmitted also at the holiday party. In the unlikely event that the occasion for such a fine arises, the payment will also support the Teacher of the Year celebration." And the message would have ended with: "Of course, sometimes it is impossible, for reasons beyond your control, to arrive on time; and should this occur, you may explain the circumstances before a committee of parents and staff, and if the lateness was unavoidable or if the fine would cause extreme hardship, the lateness will be publicly reported but no fine will be imposed."

In fairness to the Haifa children's centers, the cryptic sign informing the parents of the fines was not their idea of good public policy. It was part of an experimental design intended to avoid framing lateness as a moral issue, which would have confounded the effect of the fine. But if the intent was to discover the effect of fines per se on lateness, then the design must have been based on the assumption that the parents' response to the fines would not depend on how the new policy was explained.

I wonder what would have happened if the doors of the day care centers had carried messages like the one the time-traveling Athenians proposed, explaining the ethical problem of lateness but without announcing a fine. Would parents have been moved to pick up their kids on time? And then, if the message had also warned that a fine would be imposed for lateness, would this have enhanced the salience of the moral message, crowding in social preferences and causing a greater reduction in tardiness than the moral message alone? Would this Athenian version of the experiment have reversed the crowding out that occurred in the absence of moral framing?

It might have.

That is the upshot of what we saw in chapters IV–VI. The problem of crowding out may arise when the information that an incentive conveys is off-putting about the person imposing the incentive, or when it frames the problem as one in which self-interested motives are acceptable or even called for, or when the incentive compromises the autonomy of its target. The problem, we will see, may be the information, not the incentive itself, and there may be ways that the information conveyed by the incentive could be more positive.

We also saw that in the presence of an incentive, generous actions such as helping others may be misunderstood as self-interested, even when they are not, and that this may result in people adopting self-interested preferences to a greater extent than they would in the absence of the incentive. But like the adverse information sometimes conveyed by incentives, this problem might be attenuated by providing ample opportunity for the display of civic-minded motives, as the Athenian assembly did.

The Legislator is beginning to wonder whether incentives per se are really the problem, and whether instead the crowding-out problem may arise from the relationship between the person imposing the incentive and its target, or from the meaning of the incentive. If he is to draw up his mandate as a policy maker and one who "orders the laws," the Legislator will need to study cases in which incentives and social preferences worked in tandem rather than at cross-purposes. Then he will be ready to update Hume's maxim about the constitution for knaves.

Getting and Becoming

I asked you to put away for later use the fact (from chapter III) that in a sequential Prisoner's Dilemma, the second mover most often mimics the first mover, reciprocating cooperation or defection depending on what the first mover did. The fact that second movers reciprocate cooperation means that they place a positive subjective value either on jointly cooperating per se or on the payoffs received by the other player, whose trust and cooperativeness were evident in his first move. This value is sufficient to offset the higher payoff the second mover could receive by defecting on the cooperator, which is why they cooperate.

When second movers defect on defecting first movers, they are taking the action that maximizes payoffs under the circumstances, but evidently are *not* doing so from exclusively acquisitive motives. The same individuals would have forgone payoffs in order to co-operate with a cooperator, as we have seen. But cooperating with a defector has a different meaning, identifying the second mover as a "loser," someone easily taken advantage of. Thus, part of the motivation behind the "mimic the first mover" pattern is something that reciprocating says about the second actor herself: "I am the kind of person who rewards those who cooperate and stands up to defectors who would exploit the cooperation of others."

When people engage in trade, produce goods and services, save and invest, vote and advocate policies, they are attempting not only to *get* things, but also to *be* someone, both in their own eyes and in the eyes of others.[2] Our motives in other words are constitutive as well as acquisitive.

This idea, commonplace among psychologists and sociologists, was missed by most economists until George Akerlof and Rachel Kranton alerted the discipline to the possibility in their *Identity Economics* (2010).[3] Sometimes constitutive and acquisitive motives are closely aligned, as with Adam Smith's merchant, who (one imagines) would like to act in ways that let him see himself as an honest man, a reputation that would also underwrite profitable exchanges with others. Similarly, the second mover in the sequential Prisoner's Dilemma game who defects on a defecting first mover is both making a statement about who she is and also maximizing her payoffs.

Distinguishing between acquisitive and constitutive motives and determining which is at work in cases like this can have important implications for the advocacy and design of public policy. Here is an example. Proponents of tax-financed redistribution to the poor often represent their programs as a kind of insurance for voters in the middle of the income distribution, who would not currently be beneficiaries. It is likely that proponents adopt this kind of rhetoric because they think opposition to redistribution programs stems from voters' self-interest. This supposition is equivalent to viewing a second mover's defection solely as a payoff-maximizing strategy, and overlooking its constitutive aspect.

But in the United States and elsewhere, much of the opposition to income redistribution is ethical, not self-interested, and is based on beliefs that the poor are undeserving. In a U.S. Gallup survey analyzed by the economist Christina Fong, among poor people who do not expect their economic situation to improve, those who believe that lack of effort causes poverty tend to oppose redistribution.[4] Analogously, among the securely well off, who expect their incomes to rise in the future, those who believe that poverty is the result of back luck voice strong support for redistribution. Support for redistribution to the poor is also high among white respondents who believe that race is important to one's chances of getting ahead in America, and to men who feel likewise about gender.

There are two lessons here for the Legislator about political rhetoric and policy advocacy, extending beyond redistribution to matters of climate change, foreign policy, and other highly charged topics.

The first is that appeals based entirely on self-interest will fail to tap the social preferences that might lead people to support the policy in question. Canvassers for a signature drive in Albuquerque, New Mexico, to increase the minimum wage were well prepared with arguments that the change would support the local economy. But they found that the quickest way to get the job done was simply to let the resident know the dollar amount of the current minimum wage, a fact commonly met with disbelief, outrage, and a heartfelt signature.[5]

The second lesson is less obvious: an appeal to self-interest is inviting the voter to ask: "What's in it for me?" The effect may be to reduce the salience of the voter's ethical and other social concerns. This kind of moral disengagement appears to have occurred in a number of the experiments reviewed in chapter IV. Thus, appeals to self-interest not only may fail to tap citizen's social preferences, but may even sideline them. This is just another example of the problem of nonseparability of moral sentiments and material interests, with which we began.

There are lessons here too about the use of incentives. Acquisitive and constitutive reasons for actions may sometimes clash. And we know from experiments and from observing ourselves and others that being good sometimes trumps doing well. Responding to an incentive in the manner intended (that is, as a payoff maximizer) may make the responder a victim. But not always. A self-interested response to an incentive may constitute the actor as a good citizen or an intelligent shopper, indicating that constitutive and acquisitive motives were closely aligned. The same reasoning, we will see, suggests how we can make incentives and social preferences synergistic.

How acquisitive ends interact with the constitutive motives that J. S. Mill advised economists to ignore may explain why incentives sometimes work exactly as economists predict on the basis of unmitigated self-interest—and sometimes don't. Recall that in the Trust game implemented by Fehr and Rockenbach, in which the investor could announce that he would fine the trustee if the trustee's back-transfer was not sufficient, the announcement reduced the trustee's level of reciprocity.[6] Back-transfers from the trustee were lower under the threat of the fine (figure 4.1).

On closer scrutiny, however, the incentive represented by the threat of the fine seems not to have been the problem. When we look at the data from the experiment to see who among the trustees responded negatively to the incentive, it appears that strong crowding out was almost exclusively a reaction not to the incentive per se, but to the apparent greed of the investor. Crowding out occurred when the back-transfer demanded of trustee would have given most of the joint surplus (total payoffs for the two) to the investor. There was no backlash against the fines threatened by investors who asked for back-transfers that allocated both the investor and the trustee substantial shares of the surplus. In these cases, the use of fines by evidently fair-minded investors reduced back-transfers by an insignificant amount compared with back-transfers in the experiment in which fines were not an option.

The key difference was the message sent by the fine. Where the stipulated back-transfer would have captured most of the surplus for the investor, the fine conveyed greed. Where it would have split the surplus more equally, the fine conveyed a commitment to fairness, and perhaps the investor's desire not to be exploited by the trustee. The use of the fine to enforce a seemingly unfair demand provided an acquisitive motive to comply, but to the trustee, it also may have transformed the meaning of conceding. Complying with the investor's stipulated back-transfer no longer made the trustee a cooperative and ethical person, as it would have had the investor's demands been modest. It labelled the trustee as a person easily manipulated, or a victim.[7]

Thus, I suspect that it was the relationship between the investor and the trustee, not the threatened fine per se, that was the source of strong crowding out. That suspicion is reinforced by a diametrically opposite reaction to fines in a Public Goods with Punishment experiment. The imposition of fines by peers who have to pay to levy them, when they had nothing to gain personally from doing so, appear to have crowded in social preferences. We have already seen (in chapter V) evidence that peer punishment works. But this result could have occurred simply because of the direct effect of the incentive on the willingness to contribute, without having any effect on the subjects' experienced values. We would like to know whether the incentive heightened the salience of the subjects' social preferences, crowding them in, or whether instead the positive response to the punishment by peers was simply based on self-interest

Recall that in this game once each member's contributions to a public good are revealed, fellow group members have the opportunity to pay (reduce their own payoff) to inflict a punishment on (reduce the payoffs of) one or more members in their group. In some variants of this experiment, the game is repeated a number of times and group membership is shuffled after each period; in subsequent periods, a punisher it is extremely unlikely to be in the same group with a past target of her punishment. In this so-called stranger treatment, the punisher cannot benefit if the target of his punishment responds by subsequently contributing more. Both the punisher and target know this, and importantly, the target knows that the punisher knows this. The target knows, therefore, that punishment in this case is an altruistic act that benefits others (the members of the target's group in future periods) at the punisher's expense; hence, it

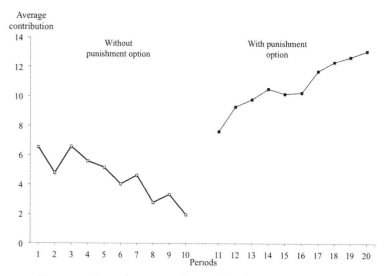

Figure 7.1 Contributions without and with peer punishment in the Public Goods game (stranger treatment) The contribution that maximizes average payoff is 20. In the treatment with no punishment, the contribution that maximizes an individual's payoff is 0, and this is true irrespective of what others contribute (not contributing is the dominant strategy). (Data from Fehr and Gaechter 2000a.)

cannot be seen as a sign of the punisher's intent to get a larger slice of the pie.

Figure 7.1 shows the period-by-period contributions in a stranger treatment of the Public Goods game implemented by Fehr and Gaechter. The first ten periods were the standard game with no punishment option; peer punishment was allowed in the subsequent periods. When punishment was not an option, contributions were initially quite generous but then declined to virtually nothing at the end of ten periods, as is standard in this game. When the punishment option was introduced, contributions started at around the level of the first period of the no-punishment treatment, but then steadily rose. (The results are the same if the ten rounds with the punishment option are played first, followed by ten rounds of the standard Public Goods game.) Recall that this is exactly what happened in the "English-speaking," "Protestant," and "Confucian" populations in the cross-cultural study described in chapter V, but not in the "Southern Europe," "Arabic-speaking," and "Orthodox/ Ex-Communist" populations (figure 5.3).

Why is the fine counterproductive when imposed by an over-reaching investor in the Trust game, but so effective in many subject pools when imposed by peers in the Public Goods game? A plausible explanation is that when punished by a peer who had nothing to gain by doing so, players saw the fine as a signal of public-spirited social disapproval by fellow group members. If this were the case, targeted free riders would feel shame, which they would redress by contributing more. If so, the incentive (the prospect of peer-imposed fines) has crowded in social preferences. (The positive effect might be even greater for free riders who escaped punishment, because they get the moral message without being angered by fellow group members' social disapproval.)

But is this crowding-in explanation true?

The higher contributions in the presence of fines could have occurred because when would-be free riders took into account the likelihood of punishment for low contributions, their self-interest may have dictated their contributing more. If so, this would not be evidence of a fine crowding in a social preference. The increase in contributions instead would suggest that fines sometimes substitute for social preferences.

Curious, my coauthors and I explored this possibility. In our Public Goods with Punishment experiment, we found that the responses of targeted free riders could not be explained by self-interest alone.[8] The punishments meted out by their peers were not sufficient to offset the gains of free riding and would not have induced an expected payoff maximizer to contribute more. Nonetheless, the experience of being punished strongly affected free riders' subsequent behavior: those who contributed below the mean and were punished for it contributed much more subsequently. For this to have happened, the erstwhile free rider must have had some moral qualms about his self-interested behavior, and having it publicly recognized brought genuine shame, which he attenuated by contributing more.

Additional direct evidence comes from experiments in which purely verbal messages of disapproval had a substantial positive effect on free riders' subsequent contributions.[9] Abigail Barr found this among the rural Tanzanians who played her variant of the Public Goods game. After each round the subjects were given the opportunity to comment on what had transpired in the game. Free riders often received verbal rebukes from other subjects ("Now I know why I never get offered food when I drop by your house!"). The targets contributed more in subsequent rounds. Free riders who escaped rebuke responded even more positively.

Like the fines imposed by seemingly civic-minded peers in the more standard Public Goods with Punishment game, rebukes from neighbors may have raised the salience of the subjects' constitutive motives. It became more important to affirm one's generosity, in the eyes of one's neighbors and oneself alike, than to take home a few more Tanzanian shillings.

Results from a variant of Falk and Kosfeld's "control aversion" experiment (described in chapter IV) are also consistent with the interpretation that crowding out does not follow from the use of incentives per se but rather from the relationship between the incentive's target and the designer, and particularly from the presumed intent of the designer. Recall that control per se may not have been what the "employees" found objectionable: when a lower bound on their efforts was imposed by a third party who did not stand to benefit, the negative response of the employees did not materialize.

More relevant to the design of public policy: when agents themselves (rather than a principal) implemented controls on their fellow members, the negative control-averse response also did not occur.[10] Apparently, the imposition of controls by peers, especially if it is the result of a deliberative process legitimated by voting, poses no threat to people's desire to constitute themselves as autonomous individuals. Indeed, the deliberation and adoption of policies protecting each group member from exploitation by free riders may be an essential part of a constitutive program for a person who values self-direction.

Can this framework provide the Legislator with a guide to policy?

Moral Lessons: Are Incentives to Blame?

At the outset, I cited an early example of the self-interest-based policy paradigm, Jeremy Bentham's advice to "make it each man's *interest* to observe . . . that conduct which it is his *duty* to observe." It is a guide to how proper incentives should harness self-interested individuals' objectives for public ends. But Bentham also understood the constitutive side of action and the need to design incentives that, unlike the Haifa day care center fines, complement moral sentiments rather than substitute for them: "A punishment may be said to be . . . a moral lesson, when by reason of the ignominy it stamps upon the offence, it is calculated to inspire the public with sentiments of aversion towards those pernicious habits and dispositions with which the offence appears to be connected; and thereby to inculcate the opposite beneficial habits and dispositions."[11]

Before pursuing the idea of punishment as a "moral lesson," let's briefly recall its long and checkered history. Public executions and whippings, pillories, ducking stools, branding, and even burning all have been advocated on these grounds. In some U.S. jurisdictions, punishments designed to shame the convicted have been instituted for commercial and sex offenses (embezzlement and prostitution) and minor crimes such as shoplifting. Some people are required to publicly display signs advertising their transgression: "I am a convicted thief" or "I got caught possessing cocaine" or "Convicted: DWI."[12] A community-access TV channel in Kansas City ran a popular show called *John TV,* which displayed the names and photographs of men convicted of soliciting prostitutes. In the UK, the National Health Service announced that it would list the names, labeled with a red flag, of general practitioners who repeatedly missed early signs of cancer in their patients; green ratings would be given to doctors with a record of timely recommendations that their patients see a specialist.[13]

In addition to compromising people's dignity, these punishments seem poorly designed to accomplish the educative role that Bentham advocated. Bentham quite explicitly sought to inspire public aversion not of the transgressors but of the "habits and dispositions" accounting for the transgressions.

Other unconventional forms of punishment are more attuned to this end. At a compulsory "School for Johns" in San Francisco, former prostitutes explain the hardships of that life; a burglar was required by a Memphis judge to permit his victim to enter the burglar's home unannounced (accompanied by a police officer), choose an item of a value equivalent to the stolen object, and take it. Both punishments made the offense more personal and vivid to the convicted, which, following the reasoning of Loewenstein and Small, should have corrected the moral disengagement that apparently allowed the transgression.[14]

Setting aside these eye-catching punishments, the Aristotelian Legislator returns to the seemingly intractable dilemma posed by the fact that incentives are at once a necessary part of good governance yet may undermine its normative foundations. But recall that I told you (in chapter IV) that we would return to the idea put forward by Lepper and his coauthors that these negative effects may not be "a specific function of the use of tangible rewards." They were referring to the compromised autonomy of the once-avid young artists whose intrinsic pleasure in painting had been diminished by the promise of an award. But the idea has far wider reach.

From an economic point of view, the small tax on plastic grocery bags enacted in Ireland in 2002 resembles the fine for lateness at the Haifa day care centers: it slightly raised the cost of an action that the incentive sought to deter. But its effect could not have been more different: in just two weeks following its introduction, the use of the plastic bags dropped by 94 percent.[15] The tax may have crowded in social preferences: for many Irish men and women, carrying a plastic grocery bag home appeared to have joined wearing a fur coat in the closet of antisocial practices.

The difference between the lateness fine and the plastic bag tax is instructive. In Haifa, the announcement of the fine included no justification for the punishment. There was no "moral lesson." The absence of an explicit normative justification of the fine invited a default frame: lateness was for sale. Maybe the modest level of the fine conveyed to the parents that their lateness was not really very costly to the school. Moreover, in the eyes of other parents, one might be late for reasons beyond one's control, not out of deliberate disregard for the inconvenience it caused teachers. The announcement of the fine said that "some parents" were arriving late, which perhaps told parents that they would not be unique were they to arrive late, and therefore that lateness was not a particularly serious transgression of the generally observed social norm of punctuality. Finally, at least among parents, the only observers of one's tardy arrival at the day care were themselves also late.

The Irish plastic bag tax, by contrast, was preceded by extended public deliberation and a substantial publicity campaign dramatizing the bags' role in blighting the environment. Unlike an occasional lateness at the day care center, which might be beyond a parent's control, the use of a plastic bag required a deliberate and highly public act of commission by the shopper. In the Irish case, the monetary incentive was combined with a message of explicit social obligation, and it apparently reminded people of the larger social costs of using and disposing of the bags. In Haifa, the fine seems to have said, "Lateness is okay as long as you pay for it," while in Ireland the message was something like "Don't trash the Emerald Isle!"

To sharpen the difference between the two cases, let's imagine what would have happened if time-traveling members of the Athenian assembly, instead of modern behavioral economists, had designed the day care policy toward tardy parents. Table 7.1 contrasts the actual experiment with my guess about what would have happened had the Athenians made it there in time to help out.

Look at the "Athenian's moral message" row in the table. While the message alone would have had some positive effect ("better" rather than "status quo"), its impact, I would be willing to bet, would

Table 7.1. Lateness at the Haifa day care centers: The actual and (imagined) Athenian experiments compared

	No fine	Fine (actual)	**Effect tested**
No moral message (actual)	Status quo	Worst	Fine without message
Athenian's moral message	Better	Best	Fine with message
Effect tested	Message without fine	Message with fine	

Note: The "status quo" cell is the situation without fines or messages, that is, before the day care centers sought to address parental lateness. Introducing the fine (as the centers did) delivered the "worst" outcome, namely, more lateness. If the incentives and the moral message were additive in their effects (that is, if the two were separable), then the effects of the fine would be independent of whether it was accompanied by a moral message, and correspondingly, the effect of the message would be independent of whether it was accompanied by a fine.

have been enhanced by the fine. And in the "Fine (actual)" column, the message would have changed the fine's effect from negative to positive. In other words, in the absence of the moral message, the fine crowded out social preferences, and with the moral message, the parents' ethical concerns were crowded in. In this case, the fine and the moral message were complements rather than substitutes.

The entries in the "Athenian's moral message" row of the table are not entirely fanciful. A similar crowding-in process was apparently at work in a public goods experiment by Roberto Galbiati and Pietro Vertova.[16] Consistent with the crowding in resulting from the presence of a small fine in the Cardenas experiment described in chapter III, Galbiati and Vertova found that the effect of a stated (nonbinding) obligation to contribute a certain amount to a public good was greater when it was combined with a weak monetary incentive than when no incentives were offered. But a stronger monetary incentive did not increase contributions, and also had no effect on behavior in the absence of the stated obligation. The authors' interpretation is that the explicit incentives enhanced the salience of the stated obligation. This is exactly how Cardenas explained a similar result in his experiment with Colombian villagers (in chapter III.).

A Mandate for Aristotle's Legislator

These experiments, along with Bentham's reasoning, suggest that policy makers can sometimes find ways to turn the separability problem on its head, making incentives and morals complements rather than substitutes. Does this provide any practical advice to the policy maker?

I think it does.

Table 7.2 shows the main policy implications of the fact that the material inducements and constraints stressed by the conventional policy paradigm are messages as well as incentives; that incentives may impede the evolution of social preferences in the long run; that these moral sentiments are an essential foundation of good government; and that both crowding out and crowding in may occur, depending in part on the policies adopted.

The Legislator should not expect everyone to applaud his attempts to root out the use of incentives that degrade social preferences. Though hard evidence is difficult to come by, incentives that crowd out social preferences are probably fairly common. It would be surprising if those implementing the incentives were entirely unaware of the nonseparability of social preferences and incentives, or of incentives sometimes reducing the joint surplus available in an economic interaction.

Table 7.2. Advice for the Aristotelian Legislator

Advice to the Legislator	Examples, Evidence
When crowding out occurs (unless it is "strong"), a greater use of incentives may be warranted than when crowding out is absent, or abandoning incentives in favor of some other policy (e.g., appeals to social preferences) may be called for.	Less effective incentives may require greater use to attain target levels of effect (chapter III)
Attempts to perfect the conditions necessary for markets to work well in the absence of social preferences (e.g., by making contracts more complete and replacing "missing markets" with well-defined property rights) cannot succeed entirely and may crowd out social preferences and degrade economic performance.	The liberal trilemma; the evolution of trust and cooperation where contracts are incomplete; land reform in the Peruvian highlands; Public Goods games and Trust games pre- and post-incentive
Protect civic-minded citizens from exploitation by the self-interested; minimize worst-case outcomes that may occur for trusting or generous citizens (rule of law, mobility, and insurance).	Third-party punishment of shirkers in a Public Goods game may liberate people to act on their generous motivations.
Avoid moral disengagement. If a policy has a public purpose that would be endorsed by citizens, make sure that the moral message is clear. In advocating a policy, do not assume that self-interest is the only basis of citizens' support.	The Athenian assembly's mobilization of resources for the new Adriatic colony; Irish plastic grocery bag tax; lateness fines in Haifa
Avoid "bad news." Incentives designed to control or take unfair advantage of the target may not work; ensure fairness in the implementation of incentives.	The contrast between the Trust game with fines and Public Goods games with peer punishment; Athenian assembly

Advice to the Legislator	*Examples, Evidence*
Avoid control aversion. Incentives and constraints implemented by peers (especially after deliberation that makes clear their social value) may avoid negative reactions.	Irish plastic bag tax; experimental games with peer deliberation on punishments or controls
In the presence of categorical crowding out, avoid small incentives.	A small fine is the worst of both worlds: incurring the categorical negative effect without the positive marginal incentive effect of the fine (should there be one).
Provide opportunities for people to express their prosociality, both in their own actions and in peer punishment or comments on norm transgressions, especially when these not only mobilize shame but also educate.	Public Goods games with Punishment (including verbal); educative (rather than merely shaming) forms of punishment
For cases in which appeals to social preferences and incentives are substitutes, specialize in one or the other; when they are complements, use both.	Public Goods game with and without "obligations" and fines; Athenian assembly
Where there are no social preferences to crowd out, adopt the standard economic approach to incentives. But the fact that incentives work as predicted for citizens without social preferences does not mean that preferences are absent or that crowding out has not occurred.	Without incentives, experimental subjects act generously in a Public Goods game; with incentives, they behave as the standard model of incentives predicts.

Why, then, do we ever observe pie-shrinking incentives in practice? The pie metaphor gives away the answer. The person deploying the incentives is not interested in the pie, but in his own slice. Even if incentives reduce the total expected surplus associated with an economic interaction, such as taking out a loan or employing a worker, the use of incentives may give the principal a sufficiently larger slice to more than compensate for the smaller pie.

This is what occurred in an experiment by Fehr and Gaechter with Swiss students.[17] The experiment was similar to the Fehr and Rockenbach Trust game; it included both a standard (called "trust") treatment and another treatment in which fines were allowed. The payoffs were such that had subjects responded as if they had entirely self-regarding preferences, the joint surplus (the sum of the payoffs to employer and employee) would have been more than twice as large under the incentive treatment as that under the trust treatment.

But the negative synergy between the incentive and social preferences was so strong that the total surplus was much higher in the trust treatment, that is, without the help of incentives. The counterproductive effect of incentives on the total surplus was true even in those cases in which principals offered exactly the kind of contract that a mechanism designer would recommend when subjects are thought to be entirely self-interested.

But here is why incentives were used anyway. Those employers who used these "optimal" contracts in the incentive treatment received payoffs more than twice as large as the average employer profits in the trust treatment, while the payoffs to employees in the incentive treatment were less than half what they were under conditions of trust. The incentive treatment allowed employers to save enough in wage costs to offset the reductions in work effort and the shrunken surplus. They were better off with a larger share of a smaller pie.

Thus, one of the reasons that constitutive aspirations sometimes lead agents to respond negatively to incentives—namely, that responding to the incentive in the way intended would disproportionately benefit the principal—also explains why these incentives may nonetheless be used by profit-maximizing principals, even when they result in a smaller pie. In this case, simply informing the principals that the result of their actions will be a smaller pie is not effective. If a mutually acceptable division of the pie could be decided on in advance (and enforced afterward), this problem would not arise, because incentives could then be devoted exclusively to increasing the size of the pie rather than being hijacked to enlarge one slice at the expense of the size of the entire pie.

Another challenge for the Legislator arises because populations are made up of individuals with differing mixtures of self-interest and the many forms of social preferences. Can he do better than a "one size fits all" approach? He can, but again he should not expect everyone to applaud.

Suppose, unrealistically, that there are just two types of people, the entirely self-interested and those with a degree of altruism. The Legislator would like to encourage contributions to a public good. A monetary incentive (such as a subsidy for contributing) will encourage contributions from the self-interested, but if incentives and social preferences are substitutes, it may work less well or even backfire among the altruists. The altruists might respond well to hearing about the substantial benefits that the public good will confer on others, but this moral message would be wasted on the self-interested.

An obvious strategy for the Legislator is to separate the two populations, addressing each with the appropriate policy. But this will be difficult because the Legislator does not know each person's type (it is private information), nor will individuals happily sort themselves into the two obvious categories of citizens. But voluntary-separation strategies can sometimes succeed, at least approximately. The modest salaries at a nonprofit public-service organization may deter those unmoved by the organization's mission, while the prospect of serving the mission provides enough additional compensation to attract the committed.[18]

Coordinating social action in a population with mixed motives grows more challenging when we consider the diversity of motives commonly grouped under the heading "social preferences." The Legislator, in designing policies for a population with multiple seemingly prosocial motivations, will quickly find that not all good things go together. Here he confronts the opposite of Adam Smith's invisible hand, which induces self-interested individuals to act in the public interest: instead, in a population with a multiplicity of social preferences—altruism as well as reciprocity, for example—a perverse alchemy can transform good motives into unwanted social outcomes.

Here is how I discovered this. In an experimental Public Goods game, my coauthors and I observed (as expected from figure 7.1) that high levels of cooperation were sustained by peer punishment. We then identified the types of the players: "altruistic," "reciprocal," and neither. "Reciprocals" were those who contributed generously when their group members had done the same in previous rounds, but contributed little otherwise; "altruists" contributed generously irrespective of what the others had done; the rest contributed little under any condition.

We found that while the altruists contributed generously to the public good, they were less likely to inflict peer punishment on free riders. Instead, when it came to sustaining the social norm of contributing, it was the altruists who free rode on other group members' willingness to sacrifice their own payoffs in order to pay to punish low contributors.[19]

Stimulated by this result, Sung-Ha Hwang and I studied the case in detail, wanting to know whether the pattern we had found was just a curiosity or instead might be something the Legislator should worry about. Our resulting paper, "Is Altruism Bad for Co-operation?" showed that under quite plausible conditions, it certainly could be.[20] (When you see a rhetorical question like this in the title of a paper, you can guess the answer.) When individuals are both altruistic and reciprocal in varying degrees, increasing their degree of altruism can reduce the average level of contributions to the public good. The reason is that as those with reciprocal preferences become more altruistic, their willingness to punish free riders diminishes, and this indirect effect of their greater altruism can offset the direct effect of altruism in increasing contributions.

How can the Legislator use this information?

If, like his Athenian antecedents, he planned to engage in moral suasion, he might consider seeking to inculcate either altruism or reciprocity in the citizenry—but not both, at least not in the same individuals. He might also consider segregation if he could do it without incurring the public's wrath at his "moral apartheid." Here is how segregation would help.

He could increase public-goods contributions if he could find a way to segregate the self-interested types and the reciprocators into one subpopulation, and let the altruists have their own group. (I am assuming, probably unwisely, that none of this would affect the long-run distribution of types in the population.) Each group could have its own dedicated policies. But other than the separation itself, no further policies (including incentives) might be required, since the reciprocators' predisposition to punish self-interested free riding might sustain high levels of contribution in that group, as we have seen. Altruists, for their part, might happily contribute.

However off-putting this illustration of the segregation strategy may be to liberal sensibilities (including mine), do not think that separating populations according to their motivations and then designing incentives and punishments accordingly is entirely whimsical. The legal scholar Lynn Stout has proposed that we think along similar lines about the appropriate compensation for injuries due to faulty products:

> Most people have an "internal" incentive, in the form of conscience, to take modest care to avoid harming others. Corporations may lack this incentive. . . .
>   . . . The traditional tort pattern of undercompensating victims . . . [does] not necessarily pose a problem when we are dealing with humans, the vast majority of whom [have consciences]. For natural persons, partial liability may be enough, when added to internal sanction of conscience, to motivate most to take care of harming others.
>   But the same undercompensation pattern may produce too little deterrence when applied to corporations. . . . We may want corporate defendants to pay victims more in damages than human defendants must pay.[21]

Stout's argument is not that the humans who make corporate decisions are less moral than others (remember the Costa Rican CEOs). It is, instead, that when deciding on an appropriate level of care toward others (in the design of children's toys, for example), the responsibility of managers to maximize profits on behalf of shareholders should induce them to take into account the expectation of undercompensation of damages, were these to occur. And this would lead them, if they are faithful in their duty to enhance the wealth of the owners of their corporation, to take insufficient account of the costs that a design flaw might inflict harm on a user of the product, perhaps choosing as a result a design cheaper to produce but more likely to do harm. Stout is merely repeating Milton Friedman's celebrated argument in his essay "The Social Responsibility of Business Is to Increase Its Profits," namely, that "only people can have responsibilities."[22]

Stout might have added, on the basis of the experimental evidence presented earlier, that the diffused responsibility of the decision-making process and the competitive pressure for a firm's survival faced by managers would work in the same direction.[23]

The final challenge for the Legislator follows from the observation that the outcome of his policy interventions will almost never be a simple average of the behaviors characteristic of each personality type in the population. Instead, the outcome will depend on the composition of the population and the social institutions, including informal rules, that determine how the individual's actions add up to aggregate outcomes.

This idea, sometimes summarized a little oversimply as "the whole is not simply the sum of its parts," is not new. It has been around in economics since Adam Smith explained how, by the alchemy of the invisible hand, the self-interest of the brewer, the baker, and the butcher would put someone else's dinner on the table. And it has been around in political philosophy for much longer: the well-ordered society of Machiavelli was an emergent property of an entire system of government, not a simple aggregation of the qualities of the citizens (as we saw in chapter II).

The challenge that Machiavelli's "good governance as an emergent property" approach presents to the Legislator is this. Under some rules—for example, the Public Goods game (without punishment)—the actions of the self-interested induce even the civic-minded to act as if they care only about their own gains. The Legislator's opportunity is that under not very different rules, the reverse occurs.

We have already seen this in the Public Goods with Punishment experiment (figure 7.1). In the absence of the peer-punishment opportunity, even those predisposed to contribute substantial amounts eventually came to act as if they were self-interested. But once the peer punishment of free riders was allowed, the very same population converged on a substantial contribution level, which in the later periods of the game was sustained with very little actual punishment, because egregious free riding had all but disappeared. A combination of the incentive to avoid punishment and the shame of having experienced it apparently led the self-interested to act "as if they were good."

The Legislator's aim in situations like this is to design rules—like the Public Goods with Punishment game—allowing the civic-minded, not the self-interested, to determine the outcome. To see the rudiments of what this requires, imagine that there are just two citizens, who will interact once in a symmetrical Prisoner's Dilemma game (symmetry means that the payoff matrix for the game is identical for each). One of them is known (by both the Legislator and the other player) to wish simply to maximize her payoffs in the game. The other has reciprocal preferences (also known to all): he would prefer to cooperate, but only if the other does.

You already know from what happens in the sequential Prisoner's Dilemma how the Legislator could tweak the rules of this game so that the efficient and equal-sharing outcome—both cooperate—will occur. In the conventional game (when the two make their choices simultaneously), both will defect (the reciprocator knows that the other will defect because it is the dominant strategy for her, so he does too). But the Legislator could change the rules so that the selfish player goes first. She knows that because the reciprocator will move second and, out of reciprocity, will mimic whatever she does, there are now only two possible outcomes of the game: either both cooperate (and both make higher payoffs) or both defect (and they both do less well). By cooperating, the selfish citizen can bring about the former outcome; she does this, and the other reciprocates.

Have we come full circle? Is this, in the end, what Hume had in mind when he imagined that a good constitution would harness the avarice of knaves? It is not, because essential to the happy outcome in the sequential Prisoner's Dilemma, and in the Public Goods game too, is the presence of at least some ethical or other-regarding citizens who, under the proper rules, induce the "wicked" to act as if they were not. That is why, as I say in my subtitle, good incentives are no substitute for good citizens.

The possibility that the right incentives, laws, and other rules of the game can sustainably crowd in social preferences, rather than the opposite, suggests that the Legislator might hope to do better than limiting himself to Rousseau's seemingly prudent injunction with which we began this study (in chapter I) to take "people as they are and laws as they might be." If the Legislator needs a bumper sticker, he might use the subtitle Stout chose for her book on law and morality: Good laws make good people.

Laws as They Might Be for Citizens as They Might Be

Like Besley's "creating better people," Stout's injunction to "make good people" is a jarring expression, but it is hardly a novel idea. Parents try to do this, as do teachers, religious leaders, and others. It is hard to imagine a viable society in which activities aimed at making good people are not widely practiced. Certainly there is no ethnographic or historical record of a successful society indifferent to virtue.

What is novel in the Legislator's plans (at least for a liberal society) is the idea that making good people should be a public policy objective. Compulsory schooling continues to be advocated as a way to teach social norms, which it apparently does with some success. The fact that children rather than adults are involved appears sufficient for many to treat compulsory schooling as consistent with the liberal commitment to neutrality in the question of preferences. But the historical experience of state projects of cultural transformation for entire populations is hardly encouraging.

The German Democratic Republic, like many Communist Party–ruled societies, invested considerable resources directed to the creation of more solidaristic and less selfish citizens. But in a recent experiment, adults born in East Germany cheated for monetary gain twice as frequently as did those born in West Germany, and this was particularly true of those who had reached maturity before the fall of the Berlin Wall.[24]

Nonetheless, the Legislator's amendment of Rousseau's injunction is now being taken up in surprising quarters, and in pursuit of objectives quite different from the "new socialist man."

As the housing bubble burst in 2008 and the financial crisis unfolded, many U.S. homeowners found that their property was worth less than their mortgage obligation to the bank. Some of these "underwater owners" did the math and strategically defaulted on their loans, giving the bank the keys and walking away. Unlike the *New York Times* editorial from two decades earlier ("Ban Greed?

No: Harness It," cited in chapter I), the executive vice president of Freddie Mac, the Federal Home Loan Mortgage Corporation, made a distinctly Aristotelian plea for moral behavior in the economy: "While a personal financial strategy might argue for a strategic default, entire communities and future home buyers can be harmed as a result. And that is why our broader social and policy interests will be best served by discouraging strategic defaults."[25] Rather than trusting that the market, by getting the prices right, would induce people to internalize the external effects of their actions, Freddie Mac urged "borrowers considering a strategic default [to] recognize the damaging impact their actions can have on others." He was hoping, in short, that morals would do the work of prices.

There was no shortage of moral reasoning on the question. In surveys, large majorities held that strategic default was immoral.[26] Most defaults were not strategic at all: they were impelled by job loss or other misfortunes. But Freddie Mac's plea for morality from underwater debtors could not have been very persuasive for those who accused the financial institutions of adhering to a double standard. After pursuing their own interests single-mindedly for decades, they implored homeowners to act otherwise when their own house of cards tumbled. The main determinant of strategic default was economic: how far underwater the property was. But many people condoning the practice gave moral concerns—such as fairness and predatory banking—as prominent reasons.

Freddie Mac–style moral exhortation alone is also likely to be less effective than policies, inspired by Bentham's punishments, that convey a more resonant "moral lesson." Perhaps Bentham had in mind the charivaris of early modern Europe: neighbors, typically women, would surround the home of a philandering husband, a price-gouging baker, or a local dignitary exploiting his status for commercial gain, and then beat pots and pans to express their moral indignation.[27] The tradition lives on: the municipal commissioner of the Indian city of Rajahmundry (in Andhra Pradesh) hired ten drummers and directed them to beat nonstop outside the homes of tax evaders.[28] The drummers said nothing, but the fact that they were accompanied by tax collectors and other officials conveyed a clear message. The policy worked, apparently by evoking the shame of the tax evaders at their transgression of a social norm.

In Bogota, Antanas Mockus, a two-term mayor, recruited hundreds of mimes in white face and clown outfits and sent them into the chaotic city traffic to poke fun at jaywalkers and to lampoon drivers violating the black-and-white pedestrian crosswalks called "zebras." Taxi drivers were particularly notorious for their rude driving.[29] Citizens were invited to nominate a taxi driver for pedestrian-friendly driving, and the first 140 nominated became the founding members of the Knights of the Zebra. At the induction ceremony, Mayor Mockus—a mathematician and philosopher by training—gave each knight a plastic zebra to hang from his or her rearview mirror (yes, there was at least one Lady of the Zebra.)

During his second term (2001–3), he explained that one of the four key ideas of his Civic Culture Program was to "increase the capacity of some citizens to encourage others towards peaceful compliance with rules."[30] To assist in this, he issued hundreds of thousands of thumbs-down cards, which were enthusiastically flashed to drivers transgressing traffic norms, like soccer referees' red cards penalizing players for fouls. There were also thumbs-up cards to recognize acts of traffic kindness. At the same time, the city ordered its police to enforce traffic regulations more strictly.

The year the mayor took office, the incidence of traffic-related deaths exceeded the national average by a considerable amount; when he left, it had fallen to well below the national average. It continued falling, in both relative and absolute terms, after his departure, in a few years reaching just one-third of its former level.)

Equally effective was a campaign to save water when a severe shortage resulted from the collapse of a tunnel that carried water to the city. Appeals from Mockus included a television commercial of the mayor and his wife sharing a shower, the water turned off while soaping. The city awarded prizes to those who led in water saving, and called out water hogs, subjecting them to well-publicized (but modest) penalties. Water consumption fell 14 percent in two months.

Though a causal link to the Civic Culture Program of Mayor Mockus would be impossible to establish, the remarkable result of an unpublished experiment by Sandra Polanía-Reyes could indicate the impact of the mayor's attempt to empower citizens to call out those violating social norms. She implemented a Public Goods with Punishment game identical to that used by Benedikt Herrmann and his coauthors (presented in chapter V; see figures 5.3 and 5.4). Her subjects at the Universidad de los Andes in Bogota had spent a good part of their adolescence with Mockus as their mayor. Unlike the "Arabic speaking," "Southern Europe," and "orthodox / ex-Communist" populations who played this game, but like the students in Boston, Copenhagen, and Seoul, the Bogatanos carefully targeted free riders for punishment, who responded positively, resulting in a level of eventual cooperation on a par with that of the most cooperative of the world's student populations.

Like the tax on plastic grocery bags in Ireland with its surrounding publicity and like drumming back taxes out of evaders in India, the mayor's highly effective campaign to tame Bogota's traffic and to save water attached an unmistakable moral message to formal enforcement and material incentives as well as to more informal peer pressure: driving your car aggressively was not cool. Until the water tunnel was repaired, even cleaning a car raised eyebrows (car washes were prominent among the water hogs). This is what the Athenian assembly did in mounting its Adriatic mission. The objective in all four cases is worthy of the Aristotelian Legislator: to encourage civic action by appealing to both material interests and moral sentiments, framed so that the two work synergistically rather than at cross-purposes. There are limits, of course: not all subsidies can be awarded as prizes, and not all penalties can be flashed like a referee's red cards.

There are more fundamental limits too.

A world hoping for saints might reflect on how the idea of a constitution for knaves came about in the first place, and why it gained such wide acceptance. An important part of this process (as we saw in chapter II) was the realization that saints are not the only alternative to knaves. There are also zealots, for example, those with unbridled intolerance and hatred of those who fall on the wrong side of the us-and-them divide.

Hume and the economists who followed him were confident (unduly so, we have seen) that a good constitution could harness the avarice of knaves to serve the common good. But harnessing the passions of zealots was an entirely different proposition.

When the economist Charles Schultze wrote that "market-like arrangements reduce the need for compassion, patriotism, brotherly love, and cultural solidarity," he considered this a feature, not a bug.[31] One could agree with him, and not only because in an economy of strangers there might not be enough love to make "the world go around," as Alice had feared in her whispered aside in response to the Duchess. One might also worry that a social order requiring, say, patriotism and cultural solidarity for its proper functioning might also provide justification for divisive and intolerant sentiments, just as the arguments in favor of the invisible hand assisted in the social acceptance of a motivation that had previously been counted among the seven deadly sins.

The idea of a constitution for knaves long predated Smith, but his reasoning about the invisible hand led to something important: a mechanism (or more accurately, a set of them), albeit imperfect, for directing self-interest to public ends through a combination of competitive exchanges of privately held property and public policies aimed at getting the prices right where markets failed to do this. Thanks to economists from Smith to Arrow and Debreu and right up to modern mechanism design, we know what a constitution for knaves looks like.

And now that we understand what it takes to make it work, we find it wanting, not only for its inability to implement an efficient use of resources in a liberal society but also for its likely social and cultural effects. Recent evidence that other-regarding and ethical motives are common in most populations greatly enhances the space of feasible policy interventions, which can include, for example, a wise combination of positive incentives and punishments with moral lessons, such as the mix of motivations appealed to by the decree of the Athenian assembly. But while we thus need an alternative to the constitution for knaves, we do not yet have any similar conception of a constitution for a population made up of knaves, saints, and zealots, in which the constitution will influence not only the quality of governance that will emerge as a result, but also the proportion of these types making up the dramatis personae of our social life.

Considered dynamically in this way, and taking account of the dark side of social preferences, the Legislator's challenge is far more difficult than heeding Hume's maxim. Some social preferences may be more difficult than self-interest to channel into socially valued or at least harmless ends. And the positive social preferences of generosity, fair-mindedness, and other civic virtues are a fragile resource for the policy maker, one that may be either empowered by legislation and public policy or irreversibly diminished. This suggests the following extension of Hume's maxim about knaves: good policies and constitutions are those that support socially valued ends not only by harnessing self-interest but also by evoking, cultivating, and empowering public-spirited motives.

It won't work as a bumper sticker. But the need for something along these lines is clear in light of Arrow's point (in chapter I) that social norms facilitate mutually beneficial economic interactions in those cases where contracts cannot cover everything that matters to the parties to the exchange. Examples include the work ethic of the employee, the creativity of the software engineer, or the honesty of the borrower or asset manager. The force of Arrow's argument is likely to increase as the wealth of nations shifts from steel, grain, and other goods readily subject to contract to producing and sharing intangible knowledge, caring for the young and the elderly, and the other forms of wealth characteristic of what is called the "weightless economy."

The same conclusion follows from the fact that many of the greatest challenges now facing the world—epidemics, climate change, personal security, and governing the knowledge-based economy—arise from global and other large-scale human interactions that cannot adequately be governed by channeling entirely self-interested citizens to do the right thing by means of incentives and sanctions, whether provided by private contract or government fiat. With economic inequality increasing in the world's major economies, one may now doubt Dr. Johnson's reassurance that "there are few ways in which a man can be more innocently employed than in getting money." The idea of an economy of knaves now appears to be anything but harmless.

I do not know whether an approach to constitutions, incentives, and sanctions adequate to this challenge can be developed. But we have little choice but to try. The Legislator's mandate is a place to start.

APPENDIX 1

A Taxonomy of Additive Separability and Its Violations

	Indirect effect, Δ^I	*Terminology*
$\Delta^T = \Delta^D$	None	Additive separability; separability, additivity
$\Delta^T > \Delta^D$	Positive	Complementarity, synergy, superadditivity, crowding in
$\Delta^T < \Delta^D$	Negative	Substitutability, negative synergy, subadditivity, crowding out
$\Delta^T < 0$	Negative, more than offsets direct effect	Strong crowding out; incentives are counterproductive

Note: Δ^T, Δ^D, and Δ^I are, respectively, the total, the direct, and the indirect effects of the incentive on the action, and $\Delta^T = \Delta^D + \Delta^I$.

Experimental Games Measuring Social Preferences and the Effects of Incentives

Game	Definition of the game	Real-life example	Predictions with self-regarding players	Experimental regularities	Interpretation of the experimental results
Prisoner's Dilemma	Two players, each of whom can either cooperate or defect. Payoffs are as follows: Cooperate Defect C H, H S, T D T, S L, L $H > L, T > H, L > S,$ $S + T < 2H$	Production of negative externalities (pollution), exchange without binding contracts, status competition	Defect	50% choose to cooperate; communication increases the frequency of cooperation	Reciprocate expected cooperation
Public Goods	N players simultaneously choose their contribution g_i $(0 \le g_i \le y)$, where y is players' endowment; each player i earns $\pi_i = y - g_i + mG$ where G is the sum of all contributions and $m < 1 < mn$.	Team compensation, cooperative production in small-scale societies, overuse of common resources (e.g., water, fishing grounds)	Each player contributes nothing, i.e., $g_i = 0$.	Players contribute 50% of y in the one-shot game. Contributions unravel over time. Majority chooses $g_i = 0$ in final period. Communication strongly increases contribution. Individual punishment opportunities greatly increase contributions.	Reciprocate expected cooperation; when some fail to contribute, reciprocate by contributing less.

	Description	Example	Prediction	Empirical findings	Interpretation
Ultimatum	Division of a fixed sum of money S between a proposer and a responder. Proposer offers x. If responder rejects x, both earn 0; if x is accepted, the proposer earns $S - x$ and the responder earns x.	Monopoly pricing of a perishable good; "eleventh-hour" settlement offers before a deadline; bargaining	Offer $x = \varepsilon$, where ε is the smallest monetary unit. Any $x > 0$ is accepted.	Most offers are between $0.3S$ nd $0.5S$; $x < 0.2S$ is rejected frequently. Competition among proposers has a strong x-increasing effect; competition among responders strongly decreases x.	Responders punish unfair offers; negative reciprocity
Dictator	Like Ultimatum, but the responder cannot reject, i.e., the proposer dictates $(S - x, x)$.	Charitable sharing of a windfall gain (lottery winners giving anonymously to strangers)	No sharing, i.e., $x = 0$.	On average, proposers allocate $x = 0.2S$. There are strong variations across experiments and across individuals. Sensitivity to details of the experimental protocol makes this a noisy measure.	Pure altruism
Trust	Investor has endowment S and makes a transfer y between 0 and S to the trustee. Trustee receives $3y$ and can send back any x between 0 and $3y$. Investor earns $S - y + x$; trustee earns $3y - x$.	Sequential exchange without binding contracts (buying from sellers on eBay)	Trustee repays nothing: $x = 0$. Investor anticipates this and hence invests nothing: $y = 0$.	On average, $y = 0.5S$ and trustees repay slightly less than $0.5S$; x is increasing in y.	Trustees show positive reciprocity.

Game	Definition of the game	Real-life example	Predictions with self-regarding players	Experimental regularities	Interpretation of the experimental results
Gift Exchange	Employer offers a wage w to the worker and announces a desired effort level $\hat{e}$. If worker rejects $(w, \hat{e})$, both earn 0. If worker accepts, he can choose any e between 1 and 10. Then employer earns $10e - w$ and worker earns $w - c(e)$; $c(e)$ is the effort cost, which is strictly increasing in e.	Noncontractibility or non-enforceability of the performance (effort, quality of goods) of workers or sellers.	Worker chooses $e = 1$. Employer pays the minimum wage.	Effort increases with the wage w. Employers pay wages that are far above the minimum. Workers accept offers with low wages but respond with $e = 1$.	Workers reciprocate generous wage offers. Employers appeal to workers' reciprocity by offering generous wages.
Third-Party Punishment	A and B play a Dictator "game." C observes how much of amount S is allocated to B. C can punish A, but the punishment is also costly for C.	Social disapproval of unacceptable treatment of others.	A allocates nothing to B. C never punishes A.	Punishment of A increases as A allocates less to B.	C sanctions violation of a sharing norm even though C's payoffs are not harmed by the violation.

Source for the table: Adapted from Camerer and Fehr (2004)

Sources for the games: Prisoner's Dilemma: Dawes 1980 (survey); Public Goods: Ledyard 1995 (survey); Ultimatum: Güth, Schmitberger, and Schwarze 1982 (introduced the game), Camerer 2003 (survey); Dictator: Kahneman, Knetsch, and Thaler 1986 (introduced the game), Camerer 2003 (survey); Trust: Berg, Dickhaut, and McCabe 1995 (introduced the game), Camerer 2003 (survey); Gift Exchange: Fehr and Fishbacher 2001 (introduced the game); Third-Party Punishment: Fehr, Kirchsteiger, and Riedl 1993 (introduced the game).

APPENDIX 3

Total, Direct, and Indirect Effects of the Subsidy in the Irlenbusch and Ruchala (2008) Experiment

Type of effect	Method of calculation	Bonus of 60	Bonus of 12
Direct	Subsidy times slope of separability line	$25 (= 60 \times 0.417)$	$5 (= 12 \times 0.417)$
Indirect categorical	Change in contribution with ε bonus	$-2.48 (= 34.56 - 37.04)$	$-2.48 (= 34.56 - 37.04)$
Indirect marginal	Change in slope times subsidy	$-6.54 (= [0.308 - 0.417]60)$	$-1.31 (= [0.308 - 0.417]12)$
Sum of indirect effects		-9.02	-3.79
Total effect		15.98	1.21

APPENDIX 4

Trust and the Liberal Rule of Law

This is a model of the relationship between the liberal state and trust, illustrating part of the argument at the end of chapter V.

Consider a population composed of a large number of people who interact in randomly selected pairs to engage in an exchange in which they may either behave opportunistically (for example, steal each other's goods) or exchange goods to their mutual benefit. Call these strategies "defect" and "cooperate," with payoffs describing a coordination game (also called an assurance game), as in the top payoff matrix in figure A.4. The structure of the game is such that if a player knows that the other will cooperate, then the payoff-maximizing strategy is also to cooperate (both then receive 4). But if the other is known to be a defector, then payoffs are maximized by also defecting (both then receive 2). The two equilibria are thus mutual defect and mutual cooperate (shaded cells in the payoff table, boxed payoffs in the right panel).

Expected payoffs for cooperators and defectors, which depend on the player's subjective probability (p) that the other will cooperate, are labeled π_C and π_D in the right-hand panel. They are both increasing in (p). A player wishing to maximize her expected payoff will cooperate if she believes that the other will cooperate with at least some probability p^*. This so-called critical value is determined by the intersection of the two payoff functions (to the right of p^*, expected payoffs are higher if one cooperates). Because in the absence of the rule of law (thick lines in the figure), the critical value, p^*,

233

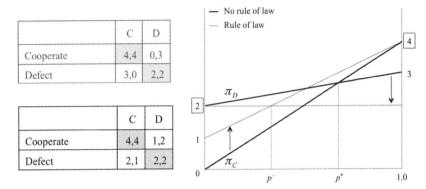

Figure A.4. The rule of law and cooperative norms Left panel:
*Payoffs in the exchange game (upper without the rule of law, lower with
the rule of law); the payoffs of the row player are the first entry in each
cell.* Right panel: *Expected payoffs based on the type of one's partner
(heavy lines without the rule of law, thin lines with the rule of law).*

exceeds one-half, defection is termed the risk-dominant strategy, that is, it
maximizes the expected payoffs of an individual who believes that his or her
partner is equally likely to cooperate or defect. The rule of law (thin lines)
reduces the gains of defecting on a cooperator and also reduces the cost to
a cooperator if her partner defects. This lowers the critical value from p^* to
p^-. By requiring a smaller probability that the other will cooperate in order
to motivate the player to cooperate, these changes make cooperation the
risk-dominant strategy, and thus make cooperating easier to sustain.

Notes

I. The Problem with *Homo economicus*

1. Rousseau 1984.
2. Gneezy and Rustichini 2000.
3. Gasiorowska, Zaleskiewicz, and Wygrab 2012.
4. Warneken and Tomasello 2008, 1787.
5. Sandel 2012; 2013, 121.
6. Satz 2010.
7. Horace 2004, 199.
8. Kahneman and Tversky 2000; Kahneman 1994; Thaler and Sunstein 2008.
9. Kahneman 1994.

II. A Constitution for Knaves

1. Belkin 2002.
2. Greenberger 2003.
3. Similar ground has been beautifully covered (though in quite different ways from the story I will recount) in the studies by Dumont (1977) and Hirschman (1977).
4. Aristotle 1962, 103.
5. Confucius 2007, 20.
6. Hayek 1948, 12.
7. *New York Times* 1988.
8. Buchanan 1975, 71.
9. Holmes 1897.
10. Hayek 1948, 11.
11. Machiavelli 1984, 69–70.
12. Strauss 1988, 49.

13. Machiavelli 1984, 109.
14. Ibid., 71.
15. Quoted in Benner 2009.
16. Machiavelli 1984, 174, 180.
17. Mandeville 1924, 24.
18. Mandeville 1988a, 366.
19. Ibid., 369.
20. Smith 1976a, bk. 4, ch. 2.
21. Ibid., bk. 1, ch. 2.
22. Hume 1964, 117–18.
23. Bentham 1962, 380.
24. Smith 1976b, 3.
25. Holmes 1897.
26. Machiavelli 1984, 103, 121; Benner 2009.
27. Aristotle 2006, 1382b7–9.
28. Bloomfield 1952, 95.
29. Boswell 1980, 597.
30. Hobbes 2005, 104 (ch. 13).
31. Machiavelli 1900, 92.
32. Spinoza 1958, 261.
33. Mandeville 1988b, 407.
34. Smith 1976a, bk. 4, ch. 9.
35. Mandeville 1924, 37.
36. Mill 1844, 97.
37. Edgeworth 1881, 104.
38. Arrow 1972, 351.
39. Wrzesniewski et al. 2014.
40. Carroll 2000, 92.
41. Smith 1976a, bk. 1, ch. 10.
42. Gauthier 1986, 84, 96. For the point he is making, he should have added "assuming that all contracts are complete," which, he assured me, he had intended.
43. Durkheim 1967, 189.
44. Bowles 2004.
45. Arrow and Hahn 1971, vi–vii.
46. Durkheim 1967, 189.

47. Arrow 1971, 22.

48. Schumpeter 1950, 448.

III. Moral Sentiments and Material Interests

1. Laffont and Matoussi 1995; Lazear 2000. The same is true in many experiments, for example, the public-goods experiment in the study by Falkinger et al. (2000).

2. Angrist and Lavy 2009.

3. Fryer 2011.

4. Holmas et al. 2010.

5. Besley, Bevan, and Burchardi 2008.

6. Ginges et al. 2007.

7. Frey and Jegen 2001.

8. Wilkinson-Ryan 2010.

9. Fehr and Fischbacher 2002, C16.

10. I address some challenges of inferring individuals' social preferences from these behavioral experiments at the beginning of the next chapter. A good survey of the use of experimental games to measure social preferences is the study by Camerer and Fehr (2004). A brief review of the main results of experiments on social behavior is in chapter 3 of Bowles and Gintis (2011).

11. Fehr and Gaechter 2000b; Camerer 2003.

12. Loewenstein, Thompson and Bazerman 1989, 433.

13. Andreoni 1990. Experimental evidence on the nature and extent of social preferences is surveyed in the study by Bowles and Gintis (2011).

14. Cardenas, Stranlund, and Willis 2000.

15. Irlenbusch and Ruchala 2008.

16. Bowles and Polanía-Reyes 2012.

17. Heyman and Ariely 2004.

18. Cardenas 2004.

19. Hwang and Bowles 2014; Bowles and Hwang 2008. Related studies addressing similar problems of incentives when people are motivated by social preferences are those by Benabou and Tirole (2006), Seabright (2009), Bar-Gill and Fershtman (2005), Bar-Gill and Fershtman (2004), and Heifetz, Segev, and Talley (2007).

20. Sung-Ha Hwang and I explore conditions under which the underuse of an incentive by a naïve legislator will occur (depending on the nature of the crowding-

out problem) in three papers: Hwang and Bowles 2014, Bowles and Hwang 2008, Hwang and Bowles 2015.

21. Falk and Heckman 2009; Levitt and List 2007.
22. Benz and Meier 2008.
23. Baran, Sapienza, and Zingales 2010.
24. Carpenter and Seki 2011.
25. Gneezy, Leibbrandt, and List 2015.
26. Fehr and Leibbrandt 2011.
27. Rustagi, Engel, and Kosfeld 2010.
28. Further evidence on the external validity of the behavioral experiments presented here is in Bowles and Gintis (2011).
29. Fehr and List 2004.

IV. Incentives as Information

1. Packard 1995, 135.
2. Bowles and Polanía-Reyes 2012.
3. Andreoni and Miller 2002.
4. Our data set includes all the economic experiments we were able to locate that allow for this or some other test of the separability assumption.
5. Hayek 1945, 1937.
6. Ross and Nisbett 1991; Tversky and Kahneman 1981.
7. Healy 2006.
8. Lepper et al. 1982, 51; lowercase roman numerals added.
9. Benabou and Tirole 2003; Fehr and Rockenbach 2003.
10. Fehr and Rockenbach 2003.
11. Similar cases of crowding out due to the "bad news" conveyed by the incentive are at work in experiments among student subject pools in Switzerland, the United States, Italy, France, and Costa Rica (as well as Germany), and in a diverse set of games, including Gift Exchange, Public Goods, and a charity-giving setting similar to Dictator. Costa Rican businessmen also responded negatively to the bad news that incentives conveyed.
12. Bandura 1991; Shu, Gino, and Bazerman 2011, 31.
13. Zhong, Bohns, and Gino 2010.
14. Kaminski, Pitsch, and Tomasello 2013.
15. Fiske 1991, 1992.

16. Falk and Szech 2013a.
17. Hoffman et al. 1994.
18. Ellingsen et al. 2012.
19. Schotter, Weiss, and Zapater 1996, 38.
20. Barr and Wallace 2009; Henrich et al. 2010.
21. Grant 2012.
22. Lepper and Greene 1978; Deci and Ryan 1985; Deci, Koestner, and Ryan 1999.
23. Deci 1975.
24. Lepper, Greene, and Nisbett 1973, 7
25. Warneken and Tomasello 2008, 1788.
26. Lepper, Greene, and Nisbett 1973.
27. Lepper et al. 1982, 62.
28. Falk and Kosfeld 2006.
29. Burdin, Halliday, and Landini 2015.
30. Li et al. 2009.
31. Greene 2014.
32. Greene et al. 2001; Loewenstein, O'Donoghue, and Sudeep 2015; Sanfey et al. 2006.
33. Sanfey et al. 2006; the earlier study was by Sanfey et al. (2003).
34. Camerer, Loewenstein, and Prelec 2005.
35. Small, Loewenstein, and Slovic 2007.
36. Skitka et al. 2002.
37. Loewenstein and O'Donoghue 2015.
38. Bowles and Gintis 2011.
39. Cohen 2005.
40. Loewenstein and O'Donoghue 2015.
41. I model and explain how this vicious cycle of cultural decline might occur and suggest reasons why it has not been the fate of liberal societies; see Bowles 2011.

V. A Liberal Civic Culture

1. Marx 1956, 32.
2. Fisman and Miguel 2007.
3. Burke 1955, 86.
4. Montesquieu 1961, 81.
5. Some of it is surveyed in the study by Bowles (1998).

6. Kohn 1969; Kohn and Schooler 1983; Kohn 1990.

7. Kohn et al. 1990, 967.

8. Ibid.

9. Kohn 1990, 59.

10. Barry, Child, and Bacon 1959.

11. Ibid.

12. Sung-Ha Hwang and I have developed this explanation in more detail (Hwang and Bowles 2015).

13. Bowles 2004; Cavalli-Sforza and Feldman 1981; Boyd and Richerson 1985.

14. Zajonc 1968.

15. Lepper et al. 1982.

16. It is of course possible that the incentive induces large numbers of self-interested people to act as if they were generous, leading to an offsetting perception error by observers.

17. Falkinger et al. 2000.

18. Gaechter, Kessler, and Konigstein 2011.

19. Frohlich and Oppenheimer 2003.

20. Ibid., 290.

21. Arrow 1972, 3.

22. Frohlich and Oppenheimer 2003, 290.

23. Henrich et al. 2005.

24. Henrich et al. 2006; Henrich et al. 2010.

25. Woodburn 1982.

26. Herrmann, Thoni and Gaechter 2008a.

27. Fehr and Gaechter 2000a.

28. These statistics and those below are calculated from data reported by Herrmann, Thoni, and Gaechter (2008b).

29. Mahdi 1986; Wiessner 2005.

30. Ertan, Page, and Putterman 2009.

31. Mahdi 1986; Boehm 1984.

32. Gellner 1988, 144–45.

33. Voltaire 1961, 18.

34. Smith 2010, 254–55.

35. Bowles 2004, 232–49.

36. D'Antoni and Pagano 2002; Bowles and Pagano 2006; Bowles 2011.

37. Elias 2000.

38. Rawls 1971, 336.

39. Shinada and Yamagishi 2007.

40. Bohnet et al. 2008.

41. Yamagishi, Cook, and Watabe 1998; Yamagishi and Yamagishi 1994; Ermisch and Gambetta 2010.

42. Tabellini 2008.

43. Alesina and Giuliano 2011.

44. Greif 1994.

45. Gellner 1983.

VI. The Legislator's Dilemma

1. The careful reader of the article will know that he actually said, "The superiority of the liberal economy is incontestable and can be demonstrated mathematically" (Debreu 1984; my translation).

2. Titmuss 1971; Arrow 1972; Solow 1971; Bliss 1972.

3. A Cornell University dissertation two years later (Upton 1974) suggested that monetary incentives substantially reduced highly motivated potential donors' likelihood of giving blood; but the work was never published and little read.

4. Lucas 1976, 41–42.

5. Hirschman 1985, 10.

6. Taylor 1987.

7. My first paper in this project (Bowles 1989) was well received when I presented it at a seminar held at the University College London Department of Philosophy in 1989, but the main claims that I advanced there lacked empirical support (experimental economics was in its infancy), so I set it aside.

8. Aaron 1994.

9. Frey 1997.

10. Ostrom 2000.

11. Mellstrom and Johannesson 2008. Other economists turned to problems of law and public policy in cases in which social preferences and incentives were not separable: Bar-Gill and Fershtman 2004, 2005; Aghion, Algan, and Cahuc 2011; Cervellati, Esteban, and Kranich 2010.

12. Laffont 2000; Maskin 1985; Hurwicz, Schmeidler, and Sonnenschein 1985.

13. Gibbard 1973; Hurwicz 1972, 1974.

14. Dworkin 1985, 191; see also Goodin and Reeve 1989.

15. Jones 1989, 9.

16. Machiavelli 1984, 69–70.

17. Becker 1974, 1080.

18. Bergstrom 1989.

19. Royal Swedish Academy of Sciences 2007, 9.

20. Gibbard 1973; Laffont and Maskin 1979.

21. Chatterjee 1982.

22. Chatterjee's results apply to the double auction a similar result demonstrated by d'Aspremont and Gerard-Varet (1979) in the case of the revelation of preferences for a public good. Under their mechanism, truthful revelation is incentive compatible, but the mechanism requires that participation be mandatory.

23. Hwang and Bowles (2016) explain the reason.

24. Machiavelli 1984, 111.

25. Royal Swedish Academy of Sciences 2007, 6.

26. Besley 2013, 492.

27. Lipsey and Lancaster 1956–57.

28. Weber 1978, 636.

29. Parsons 1967, 507.

30. Ouchi 1980; Sahlins 1974; Durkheim 1967; Tonnies 1963.

31. Loewenstein and Small 2007.

32. Kollock 1994, 341.

33. Brown, Falk, and Fehr 2004.

34. This was studied by Axelrod and Hamilton (1981), who refined and extended the earlier insights of Shubik (1959), Trivers (1971), and Taylor (1976).

35. Ostrom 1990.

36. My account is based on Braaten 2014.

37. Mallon 1983.

38. In the village Palanpur (in Uttar Pradesh, India), the extension of the labor market (and the resulting increased geographic mobility) appears to have reduced the costs of exit and, hence, the value of one's reputation, thereby undermining the informal enforcement of lending contracts (Lanjouw and Stern 1998, 570). Similar cases in which the greater mobility and, hence, anonymity of traders, induced and facilitated by market incentives, undermined the ethical and other-regarding social norms that underpinned the preexisting norm of contractual enforcement come

from long-distance traders in early modern Europe (Greif 1994, 2002) and shoe manufacturers in Brazil and Mexico (Woodruff 1998; Schmitz 1999).

VII. A Mandate for Aristotle's Legislator

1. This account is based on work by Ober (2008, 124–34) and Christ (1990).

2. Cooley 1902; Yeung and Martin 2011.

3. Akerlof and Kranton 2010.

4. Bowles 2012; Fong 2001.

5. I have this from Chelsey Evans, who coordinated the drive.

6. Fehr and Rockenbach 2003.

7. Interpretations other than this "unfair intent" explanation are possible, however, because the larger the desired back-transfer, the more costly the compliance. Thus, for larger demands, simply returning nothing and paying the fine (as many of the subjects did) might have been attractive to self-interested subjects, who, had they been faced with a lower demand, would have maximized payoffs by complying. It seems from this and similar experiments that fines may have negative effects even when imposed to implement a fair outcome and even when the decision to use the fine is made not by the investor, but rather by chance (Fehr and List 2004; Houser et al. 2008). In these cases, the fine appears to have compromised the trustee's sense of autonomy. But the experiments also are consistent with the idea that threats deployed in self-interested ways can backfire. When they do, it is probably because accepting unfair treatment is inconsistent with an individual's project to constitute herself as person who is not easily taken advantage of.

8. Carpenter et al. 2009.

9. Barr 2001; Masclet et al. 2003.

10. Schnedler and Vadovic 2011. A large number of other experiments have found positive effects for incentives imposed by the decision of the targets of the incentives rather than by the experimenter or by a principal in the role of employer or investor; see the work by Kocher et al. (2008); Cardenas, Stranlund, and Willis (2005); Tyran and Feld (2006); Ertan, Page, and Putterman (2009); Mellizo, Carpenter, and Matthews (2014).

11. Bentham 1970, 26.

12. Garvey 1998.

13. *Times* (London) 2014.

14. Loewenstein and Small 2007.

15. Rosenthal 2008.

16. Galbiati and Vertova 2014. In my taxonomy, their result is a case of categorical crowding; see also Galbiati and Vertova 2008.

17. Reported in Fehr and Falk 2002.

18. Besley and Ghatak 2005.

19. Carpenter et al. 2009.

20. Hwang and Bowles 2012.

21. Stout 2011, 171–72.

22. Friedman 1970.

23. Schotter, Weiss, and Zapater 1996; Falk and Szech 2013b.

24. Ariely et al. 2015.

25. Bisenius 2001.

26. This account is based on the studies by Guiso, Sapienza and Zingales (2013) and White (2010).

27. Tilly 1981.

28. Farooq 2005.

29. This account is based on the following studies: World Bank 2015, 176–77; Martin and Ceballos 2004; Mockus 2002; Humphrey 2014; Riano 2011.

30. Mockus 2002, 24.

31. Schultze 1977.

Works Cited

Aaron, Henry. 1994. "Public Policy, Values, and Consciousness." *Journal of Economic Perspectives* 8, no. 2: 3–21.

Aghion, Philippe, Yann Algan, and Pierre Cahuc. 2011. "Civil Society and the State: The Interplay between Cooperation and Minimum Wage Regulation." *Journal of the European Economic Association* 9, no. 1: 3–42.

Akerlof, George A., and Rachel Kranton. 2010. *Identity Economics: How Our Identities Shape Our Work, Wages, and Well-Being.* Princeton, N.J.: Princeton University Press.

Alesina, A., and Paola Giuliano. 2011. "Family Ties and Political Participation." *Journal of the European Economic Association* 9, no. 5: 817–39.

Andreoni, James. 1990. "Impure Altruism and Donations to Public Goods: A Theory of Warm-Glow Giving." *Economic Journal* 100:464–77.

Andreoni, James, and John Miller. 2002. "Giving according to GARP: An Experimental Test of the Consistency of Preferences for Altruism." *Econometrica* 70, no. 2: 737–53.

Angrist, Joshua, and Victor Lavy. 2009. "The Effects of High Stakes High School Achievement Rewards: Evidence from a Randomized Trial." *American Economic Review* 99, no. 4: 1384–414.

Ariely, Dan, Ximena Garcia-Rada, Lars Hornuf, and Heather Mann. 2015. "The (True) Legacy of Two Really Existing Economic Systems." Munich Discussion Paper No. 2014–26. Available at SSRN: http://dx.doi .org/10.2139/ssrn.2457000.

Aristotle. 1962. *Nicomachean Ethics.* Translated by Martin Ostwald. Indianapolis: Bobbs-Merrill.

———. 2006. *On Rhetoric: A Theory of Civic Discourse.* Translated by George A. Kennedy. Oxford: Oxford University Press.

Arrow, Kenneth J. 1971. "Political and Economic Evaluation of Social Effects and Externalities." In *Frontiers of Quantitative Economics,* edited by M. D. Intriligator, 3–23. Amsterdam: North Holland.

———. 1972. "Gifts and Exchanges." *Philosophy and Public Affairs* 1, no. 4: 343–62.

Arrow, Kenneth J., and Frank H. Hahn. 1971. *General Competitive Analysis.* Advanced Textbooks in Economics 12, San Francisco: Holden-Day.

Axelrod, Robert, and William D. Hamilton. 1981. "The Evolution of Cooperation." *Science* 211:1390–96.

Bandura, Albert. 1991. "Social Cognitive Theory of Moral Thought and Action." In *Handbook of Moral Behavior and Development,* vol. 1, *Theory,* edited by William Kurtines and Jacob Gewirtz, 45–103. Hillsdale, N.J.: Erlbaum.

Bar-Gill, Oren, and Chaim Fershtman. 2004. "Law and Preferences." *Journal of Law, Economics, and Organization* 20, no. 2: 331–53.

———. 2005. "Public Policy with Endogenous Preferences." *Journal of Public Economic Theory* 7, no. 5: 841–57.

Baran, Nicole M., Paola Sapienza, and Luigi Zingales. 2010. "Can We Infer Social Preferences from the Lab? Evidence from the Trust Game." Chicago Booth Research Paper No. 10–02. Available at SSRN: http://dx.doi.org/10.2139/ssrn.1540137.

Barr, Abigail. 2001. "Social Dilemmas, Shame-Based Sanctions, and Shamelessness: Experimental Results from Rural Zimbabwe." Working Paper WPS/2001.11, Centre for the Study of African Economies, Oxford University.

Barr, Abigail, and Chris Wallace. 2009. "Homo Aequalis: A Cross-Society Experimental Analysis of Three Bargaining Games." Economics Series Working Paper no. 422, Department of Economics, University of Oxford. Available at EconPapers: http://econpapers.repec.org/ repec:oxf:wpaper:422.

Barry, Herbert III, Irvin L. Child, and Margaret K. Bacon. 1959. "Relation of Child Training to Subsistence Economy." *American Anthropologist* 61:51–63.

Becker, Gary. 1974. "A Theory of Social Interactions." *Journal of Political Economy* 82:1063–93.

Belkin, Douglas. 2002. "Boston Firefighters Sick—or Tired of Working." *Boston Globe,* January 18.

Benabou, Roland, and Jean Tirole. 2003. "Intrinsic and Extrinsic Motivation." *Review of Economic Studies* 70:489–520.

———. 2006. "Incentives and Prosocial Behavior." *American Economic Review* 96, no. 5: 1652–78.

Benner, Erica. 2009. *Machiavelli's Ethics.* Princeton, N.J.: Princeton University Press.

Bentham, Jeremy. 1962. *The Works of Jeremy Bentham,* vol. 8. Edited by John Bowring. New York: Russell and Russell.

———. 1970. *An Introduction to the Principles of Morals and Legislation.* Edited by J. H. Burns and H. L. A. Hart. London: Athlone. Orig. pub. 1789.

Benz, Matthias, and Stephan Meier. 2008. "Do People Behave in Experiments as in the Field? Evidence from Donations." *Experimental Economics* 11, no. 3: 268–81.

Berg, Joyce, John Dickhaut, and Kevin McCabe. 1995. "Trust, Reciprocity, and Social History." *Games and Economic Behavior* 10:122–42.

Bergstrom, Theodore C. 1989. "A Fresh Look at the Rotten Kid Theorem—and Other Household Mysteries." *Journal of Political Economy* 97:1138–59.

Besley, Timothy. 2013. "What's the Good of the Market: An Essay on Michael Sandel's *What Money Can't Buy.*" *Journal of Economic Literature* 1:478–93.

Besley, Timothy, Gwyn Bevan, and Konrad Burchardi. 2008. "Accountability and Incentives: The Impacts of Different Regimes on Hospital

Waiting Times in England and Wales." London School of Economics, http://econ.lse.ac.uk/staff/tbesley/papers/nhs.pdf.

Besley, Timothy, and Maitreesh Ghatak. 2005. "Competition and Incentives with Motivated Agents." *American Economic Review* 95:616–36.

Bisenius, Don. 2010. "A Perspective on Strategic Defaults." Available at: www .freddiemac.com/news/featuredperspectives/20100503_bisenius.html.

Bliss, Christopher J. 1972. "Review of R.M. Titmuss, *The Gift Relationship: From Human Blood to Social Policy.*" *Journal of Public Economics* 1:162–65.

Bloomfield, Morton. 1952. *The Seven Deadly Sins.* East Lansing: Michigan State University Press.

Boehm, Christopher. 1984. *Blood Revenge: The Enactment and Management of Conflict in Montenegro and Other Tribal Societies.* Lawrence: University Press of Kansas.

Bohnet, Iris, Fiona Greig, Benedikt Herrmann, and Richard Zeckhauser. 2008. "Betrayal Aversion: Evidence from Brazil, China, Oman, Switzerland, Turkey, and the United States." *American Economic Review* 98, no. 1: 294–310.

Boswell, James. 1980. *Life of Johnson.* Edited by R. W. Chapman Oxford: Oxford University Press. Orig. pub. 1791.

Bowles, Samuel. 1989. "Mandeville's Mistake: Markets and the Evolution of Cooperation." Paper presented to the September Seminar meeting of the Department of Philosophy, University College London.

———. 1998. "Endogenous Preferences: The Cultural Consequences of Markets and Other Economic Institutions." *Journal of Economic Literature* 36, no. 1: 75–111.

———. 2004. *Microeconomics: Behavior, Institutions, and Evolution.* Princeton, N.J.: Princeton University Press.

———. 2011. "Is Liberal Society a Parasite on Tradition?" *Philosophy and Public Affairs* 39, no. 1: 47–81.

———. 2012. *The New Economics of Inequality and Redistribution.* Cambridge: Cambridge University Press.

Bowles, Samuel, and Herbert Gintis. 2011. *A Cooperative Species: Human Reciprocity and Its Evolution.* Princeton, N.J.: Princeton University Press.

Bowles, Samuel, and Sung-Ha Hwang. 2008. "Social Preferences and Public Economics: Mechanism Design When Preferences Depend on Incentives." *Journal of Public Economics* 92, no. 8–9: 1811–20.

Bowles, Samuel, and Ugo Pagano. 2006. "Economic Integration, Cultural Standardization, and the Politics of Social Insurance." In *Globalization and Egalitarian Redistribution,* edited by Samuel Bowles, Pranab Bardhan, and Michael Wallerstein, 239–305. Princeton, N.J.: Princeton University Press.

Bowles, Samuel, and Sandra Polanía-Reyes. 2012. "Economic Incentives and Social Preferences: Substitutes or Complements?" *Journal of Economic Literature* 50, no. 2: 368–425.

Boyd, Robert, and Peter J. Richerson. 1985. *Culture and the Evolutionary Process.* Chicago: University of Chicago Press.

Braaten, Ragnhild Haugli. 2014. "Land Rights and Community Cooperation: Public Goods Experiments from Peru." *World Development* 61:127–41.

Brown, Martin, Armin Falk, and Ernst Fehr. 2004. "Relational Contracts and the Nature of Market Interactions." *Econometrica* 72, no. 3: 747–80.

Buchanan, James. 1975. *The Limits of Liberty.* Chicago: University of Chicago Press.

Burdin, Gabriel, Simon Halliday, and Fabio Landini. 2015. "Third-Party vs. Second-Party Control: Disentangling the Role of Autonomy and Reciprocity." Institute for the Study of Labor (IZA) Discussion Paper No. 9251. Available from SSRN: http://papers.ssrn.com/sol3/papers.cfm?abstract_id=2655291.

Burke, Edmund. 1955. *Reflections on the Revolution in France.* Chicago: Gateway Editions. Orig. pub. 1790.

Camerer, Colin. 2003. *Behavioral Game Theory: Experimental Studies of Strategic Interaction.* Princeton, N.J.: Princeton University Press.

Camerer, Colin, and Ernst Fehr. 2004. "Measuring Social Norms and Preferences Using Experimental Games: A Guide for Social Scientists." In *Foundations of Human Sociality: Economic Experiments and Ethnographic Evidence from Fifteen Small-Scale Societies,* edited by Joe

Henrich, Samuel Bowles, Robert Boyd, Colin Camerer, Ernst Fehr, and Herbert Gintis, 55–96. Oxford: Oxford University Press.

Camerer, Colin, George Loewenstein, and Drazen Prelec. 2005. "Neuroeconomics." *Journal of Economic Literature* 43, no. 1: 9–64.

Cardenas, Juan Camilo. 2004. "Norms from Outside and Inside: An Experimental Analysis on the Governance of Local Ecosystems." *Forest Policy and Economics* 6:229–41.

Cardenas, Juan Camilo, John K. Stranlund, and Cleve E. Willis. 2000. "Local Environmental Control and Institutional Crowding-Out." *World Development* 28, no. 10: 1719–33.

———. 2005. "Groups, Commons, and Regulations: Experiments with Villagers and Students in Colombia." In *Psychology, Rationality, and Economic Behavior: Challenging the Standard Assumptions,* edited by Bina Agarwal and Alessandro Vercelli, 242–70. London: Macmillan.

Carpenter, Jeffrey, Samuel Bowles, Herbert Gintis, and Sung-Ha Hwang. 2009. "Strong Reciprocity and Team Production: Theory and Evidence." *Journal of Economic Behavior and Organization* 71, no. 2: 221–32.

Carpenter, Jeffrey, and Erika Seki. 2011. "Do Social Preferences Increase Productivity? Field Experimental Evidence from Fishermen in Toyama Bay." *Economic Inquiry* 49, no. 2: 612–30.

Carroll, Lewis. 2000. *The Annotated Alice: The Definitive Edition of "Alice's Adventures in Wonderland" and "Through the Looking-Glass" by Lewis Carroll.* New York: Norton.

Cavalli-Sforza, L. L., and Marcus W. Feldman. 1981. *Cultural Transmission and Evolution: A Quantitative Approach.* Monographs in Population Biology 16. Princeton, N.J.: Princeton University Press.

Cervellati, Matteo, Joan Esteban, and Laurence Kranich. 2010. "Work Values, Endogenous Sentiments, and Redistribution." *Journal of Public Economics* 94, nos. 9–10: 612–27.

Chatterjee, Kalyan. 1982. "Incentive Compatibility in Bargaining under Uncertainty." *Quarterly Journal of Economics* 97, no. 1: 717–26.

Christ, Matthew. 1990. "Liturgy Avoidance and Antidosis in Classical Athens." *Transactions of the American Philosophical Association* 10:147–69.

Cohen, Jonathan. 2005. "The Vulcanization of the Human Brain: A Neural Perspective on Interactions between Cognition and Emotion." *Journal of Economic Perspectives* 19, no. 4: 3–24.

Confucius. 2007. *The Analects of Confucius.* Translated by Burton Watson. New York: Columbia University Press.

Cooley, Charles Horton. 1902. *Human Nature and the Social Order.* New York: Scribner's Sons.

D'Antoni, M, and Ugo Pagano. 2002. "National Cultures and Social Protection as Alternative Insurance Devices." *Structural Change and Economic Dynamics* 13:367–86.

d'Aspremont, Claude, and Louis-Andre Gerard-Varet. 1979. "On Bayesian Incentive Compatible Mechanisms." In *Aggregation and Revelation of Preferences,* edited by Jean Jacques Laffont, 269–88. Amsterdam: North Holland.

Dawes, Robyn M. 1980. "Social Dilemmas." *Annual Review of Psychology* 31:169–93.

Debreu, Gerard. 1984. "La Supériorité du Libéralisme Est Mathématiquement Démontrée." *Le Figaro,* March 10.

Deci, Edward L. 1975. *Intrinsic Motivation.* New York: Plenum.

Deci, Edward L., Richard Koestner, and Richard M. Ryan. 1999. "A Meta-Analytic Review of Experiments Examining the Effects of Extrinsic Rewards on Intrinsic Motivation." *Psychological Bulletin* 125, no. 6: 627–68.

Deci, Edward L., and Richard M. Ryan. 1985. *Intrinsic Motivation and Self-Determination in Human Behavior.* New York: Plenum.

Dumont, Louis. 1977. *From Mandeville to Marx: The Genesis and Triumph of Economic Ideology.* Chicago: University of Chicago Press.

Durkheim, Emile. 1967. *De la Division du Travail Social.* Bibliothèque De Philosophie Contemporaine. Paris: Presses universitaires de France. Orig. pub. 1902.

Dworkin, Ronald. 1985. *A Matter of Principle.* Cambridge, Mass.: Harvard University Press.

Edgeworth, F. Y. 1881. *Mathematical Psychics: An Essay on the Application of Mathematics to the Moral Sciences.* London: Kegan Paul.

Elias, Norbert. 2000. *The Civilizing Process.* Oxford: Blackwell. Orig. pub. Basel, 1939.

Ellingsen, Tore, Magnus Johannesson, Johanna Mollerstrom, and Sara Munkhammar. 2012. "Social Framing Effects: Preferences or Beliefs?" *Games and Economic Behavior* 76, no. 1: 117–30.

Ermisch, John, and Diego Gambetta. 2010. "Do Strong Family Ties Inhibit Trust?" *Journal of Economic Behavior and Organization* 75, no. 3: 365–76.

Ertan, Arhan, Talbot Page, and Louis Putterman. 2009. "Who to Punish? Individual Decisions and Majority Rule in Mitigating the Free-Rider Problem." *European Economic Review* 3:495–511.

Falk, Armin, and James Heckman. 2009. "Lab Experiments Are a Major Source of Knowledge in the Social Sciences." *Science* 326, no. 5952: 535–38.

Falk, Armin, and Michael Kosfeld. 2006. "The Hidden Costs of Control." *American Economic Review* 96, no. 5: 1611–30.

Falk, Armin, and Nora Szech. 2013a. "Morals and Markets." *Science* 340, no. 6133: 707–11.

———. 2013b. "Organizations, Diffused Pivotality, and Immoral Outcomes." University of Bonn Discussion Papers 15S, http://www.econ2.uni -bonn.de/members-of-the-chair/szech/pivotality_falk_szech_dp.pdf.

Falkinger, Josef, Ernst Fehr, Simon Gaechter, and Rudolf Winter-Ebmer. 2000. "A Simple Mechanism for the Efficient Provision of Public Goods." *American Economic Review* 90, no. 1: 247–64.

Farooq, Omer. 2005. "Drumming Tax Sense into Evaders." BBC News, March 11. http://news.bbc.co.uk/go/pr/fr/-/2/hi/south_asia/4340497 .stm.

Fehr, Ernst, and Armin Falk. 2002. "Psychological Foundations of Incentives." *European Economic Review* 46, nos. 4–5: 687–724.

Fehr, Ernst, and Urs Fischbacher. 2001. "Third Party Norm Enforcement." Working Paper no. 6. Institute for Empirical Research in Economics, University of Zurich.

———. 2002. "Why Social Preferences Matter." *Economic Journal* 112, no. 478: C1–C33.

Fehr, Ernst, and Simon Gaechter. 2000a. "Cooperation and Punishment in Public Goods Experiments." *American Economic Review* 90, no. 4: 980–94.

———. 2000b. "Fairness and Retaliation: The Economics of Reciprocity." *Journal of Economic Perspectives* 14, no. 3: 159–81.

Fehr, Ernst, Georg Kirchsteiger, and Arno Riedl. 1993. "Does Fairness Prevent Market Clearing? An Experimental Investigation." *Quarterly Journal of Economics* 114:817–68.

Fehr, Ernst, and Andreas Leibbrandt. 2011. "A Field Study on Cooperativeness and Impatience in the Tragedy of the Commons." Journal of Public Economics 95, nos. 9–10: 1144–55.

Fehr, Ernst, and John List. 2004. "The Hidden Costs and Returns of Incentives: Trust and Trustworthiness among CEOs." *Journal of the European Economic Association* 2, no. 5: 743–71.

Fehr, Ernst, and Bettina Rockenbach. 2003. "Detrimental Effects of Sanctions on Human Altruism." *Nature* 422, no. 13 March: 137–40.

Fiske, Alan Page. 1991. *Structures of Social Life: The Four Elementary Forms of Human Relations.* New York: Free Press.

———. 1992. "The Four Elementary Forms of Sociality: Framework for a Unified Theory of Social Relations." *Psychological Review* 99, no. 4: 689–723.

Fisman, Raymond, and Edward Miguel. 2007. "Corruption, Norms, and Legal Enforcement: Evidence from Diplomatic Parking Tickets." *Journal of Political Economy* 115, no. 6: 1020–48.

Fong, Christina. 2001. "Social Preferences, Self-Interest and the Demand for Redistribution." *Journal of Public Economics* 82, no. 2: 225–46.

Frey, Bruno. 1997. "A Constitution for Knaves Crowds Out Civic Virtues." *Economic Journal* 107, no. 443: 1043–53.

Frey, Bruno, and Reto Jegen. 2001. "Motivation Crowding Theory: A Survey of Empirical Evidence." *Journal of Economic Surveys* 15, no. 5: 589–611.

Friedman, Milton. 1970. "The Social Responsibility of Business Is to Increase Its Profits." *New York Times Magazine,* September 13.

Frohlich, Norman, and Joe A. Oppenheimer. 2003. "Optimal Policies and Socially Oriented Behavior: Some Problematic Effects of an Incentive Compatible Device." *Public Choice* 117:273–93.

Fryer, Roland. 2011. "Financial Incentives and Student Achievement: Evidence from Randomized Trials." *Quarterly Journal of Economics* 126, no. 4: 1755–98.

Gaechter, Simon, Benedikt Herrmann, and Christian Thoni. 2010. "Culture and Cooperation." *Philosophical Transactions of the Royal Society B* 365:2651–61.

Gaechter, Simon, Esther Kessler, and Manfred Koenigstein. 2011. "The Roles of Incentives and Voluntary Cooperation for Contractual Compliance." Discussion Paper 2011–06. Centre for Decision Research and Experimental Economics, School of Economics, University of Nottingham, https://www.nottingham.ac.uk/cedex/news/papers/2011–06.aspx.

Galbiati, Roberto, and Pietro Vertova 2008. "Obligations and Cooperative Behavior in Public Good Games." *Games and Economic Behavior* 64, no. 1: 146–70.

———. 2014. "How Laws Affect Behaviour: Obligations, Incentives and Cooperative Behavior." *International Review of Law and Economics* 38: 48–57.

Garvey, Stephen P. 1998. "Can Shaming Punishments Educate?" *University of Chicago Law Review* 65:733–94.

Gasiorowska, Agata, Tomasz Zaleskiewicz, and Sandra Wygrab. 2012. "Would You Do Something for Me? The Effects of Money Activation on Social Preferences and Social Behavior in Young Children." *Journal of Economic Psychology* 33, no. 3: 603–8.

Gauthier, David. 1986. *Morals by Agreement.* Oxford: Clarendon.

Gellner, Ernest. 1983. *Nations and Nationalism.* New Perspectives on the Past. Ithaca, N.Y.: Cornell University Press.

———. 1988. "Trust, Cohesion, and the Social Order." In *Trust: Making and Breaking Cooperative Relations,* edited by Diego Gambetta, 142–57. Oxford: Basil Blackwell.

Gibbard, Allan. 1973. "Manipulation of Voting Schemes: A General Result." *Journal of Economic Theory* 41, no. 4: 587–601.

Ginges, Jeremy, Scott Atran, Douglas Medin, and Khalil Shikaki. 2007. "Sacred Bounds on Rational Resolution of Violent Political Conflict." *Proceedings of the National Academy of Science* 104, no. 18: 7357–60.

Gneezy, Uri, Andreas Leibbrandt, and John List. 2015. "Ode to the Sea: Workplace Organizations and Norms of Cooperation" *Economic Journal*. doi: 10.1111/ecoj.12209.

Gneezy, Uri, and Aldo Rustichini. 2000. "Pay Enough or Don't Pay at All." *Quarterly Journal of Economics* 115, no. 2: 791–810.

Goodin, Robert E., and Andrew Reeve, eds. 1989. *Liberal Neutrality.* London: Routledge.

Grant, Ruth. 2012. *Strings Attached: Untangling the Ethics of Incentives.* Princeton, N.J.: Princeton University Press.

Greenberger, Scott. 2003. "Sick Day Abuses Focus of Fire Talks." *Boston Globe,* September 17.

Greene, Joshua. 2014. "Moral Tribes: Emotion, Reason, and the Gap between Us and Them." London: Penguin.

Greene, Joshua, R. Brian Sommerville, Leigh E. Nystrom, John M. Darley, and Jonathon D. Cohen. 2001. "An fMRI Investigation of Emotional Engagement in Moral Judgement." *Science* 293:2105–8.

Greif, Avner. 1994. "Cultural Beliefs and the Organization of Society: An Historical and Theoretical Reflection on Collectivist and Individualist Societies." *Journal of Political Economy* 102, no. 5: 912–50.

———. 2002. "Institutions and Impersonal Exchange: From Communal to Individual Responsibility." *Journal of Institutional and Theoretical Economics* 158, no. 1: 168–204.

Guiso, Luigi, Paola Sapienza, and Luigi Zingales. 2013. "The Determinants of Attitudes toward Strategic Default on Mortgages." *Journal of Finance* 67:1473–515.

Güth, Werner, Rolf Schmittberger, and Bernd Schwarze. 1982. "An Experimental Analysis of Ultimatum Bargaining." *Journal of Economic Behavior and Organization,* 3:367–88.

Hayek, Friedrich A. 1937. "Economics and Knowledge." *Economica* 4, no. 13: 33–54.

———. 1945. "The Use of Knowledge in Society." *American Economic Review* 35, no. 4: 519–30.

———. 1948. *Individualism and Economic Order.* Chicago: University of Chicago Press, 1948.

Healy, Kieran. 2006. *Best Last Gifts.* Chicago: University of Chicago Press.

Heifetz, A., E. Segev, and E. Talley. 2007. "Market Design with Endogenous Preferences." *Games and Economic Behavior* 58: 121–53.

Henrich, Joseph, Robert Boyd, Samuel Bowles, Colin Camerer, Ernst Fehr, Herbert Gintis, Richard McElreath, Michael Alvard, Abigail Barr, Jean Ensminger, et al. 2005. "'Economic Man' in Cross-Cultural Perspective: Behavioral Experiments in 15 Small-Scale Societies." *Behavioral and Brain Sciences* 28: 795–855.

Henrich, Joseph, Jean Ensminger, Richard McElreath, Abigail Barr, Clark Barrett, Alexander Bolyanatz, Juan Camilo Cardenas, Michael Gurven, Edwins Gwako, Natalie Henrich, et al. 2010. "Markets, Religion, Community Size and the Evolution of Fairness and Punishment." *Science* 327: 1480–84.

Henrich, Joseph, Richard McElreath, Abigail Barr, Jean Ensminger, Clark Barrett, Alexander Bolyanatz, Juan Camilo Cardenas, Michael Gurven, Edwins Gwako, Natalie Henrich, et al. 2006. "Costly Punishment across Human Societies." *Science* 312: 1767–70.

Herrmann, Benedikt, Christian Thoni, and Simon Gaechter. 2008a. "Antisocial Punishment across Societies." *Science* 319, no. 7: 1362–67.

———. 2008b. "Supporting Online Material for 'Antisocial Punishment across Societies.'" *Science* 319, no. 7: 1362–67.

Heyman, James, and Dan Ariely. 2004. "Effort for Payment: A Tale of Two Markets." *Psychological Science* 15, no. 11: 787–93.

Hirschman, Albert O. 1977. *The Passions and the Interests: Political Arguments for Capitalism before Its Triumph.* Princeton, N.J.: Princeton University Press.

————. 1985. "Against Parsimony: Three Ways of Complicating Some Categories of Economic Discourse." *Economics and Philosophy* 1, no. 1: 7–21.

Hobbes, Thomas. 2005. *Leviathan.* Edited by G. A. J. Rogers and Karl Schuhmann. 2 vols. London: Continuum. Orig. pub. 1651.

Hoffman, Elizabeth, Kevin McCabe, Keith Shachat, and Vernon L. Smith. 1994. "Preferences, Property Rights, and Anonymity in Bargaining Games." *Games and Economic Behavior* 7, no. 3: 346–80.

Holmas, Tor Helge, Egil Kjerstad, Hilde Luras, and Odd Rune Straume. 2010. "Does Monetary Punishment Crowd Out Pro-Social Motivation? A Natural Experiment on Hospital Length of Stay." *Journal of Economic Behavior and Organization* 75, no. 2: 261–67.

Holmes, Oliver Wendell, Jr. 1897. "The Path of the Law." *Harvard Law Review* 10, no. 457: 457–78.

Horace. 2004. *Odes and Epodes.* Edited and translated by Niall Rudd. Cambridge, Mass.: Harvard University Press.

Houser, Daniel, Erte Xiao, Kevin McCabe, and Vernon Smith. 2008. "When Punishment Fails: Research on Sanctions, Intentions, and Non-Cooperation." *Games and Economic Behavior* 62:509–32.

Hume, David. 1964. *David Hume: The Philosophical Works.* Edited by Thomas Hill Green and Thomas Hodge Grose. 4 vols. Darmstadt: Scientia Verlag Aalen. Reprint of the 1882 London ed.

Humphrey, Michael. 2014. "Violence and Urban Governance in Neoliberal Cities in Latin America." *Arena Journal* 41–42:236–59.

Hurwicz, Leonid. 1972. "On Informationally Decentralized Systems." In *Decision and Organization,* edited by Roy Radner and B. McGuire, 297–336. Amsterdam: North-Holland Press.

————. 1974. "The Design of Mechanisms for Resource Allocation." In *Frontiers of Quantitative Economics,* vol. 2, edited by M. D. Intrilligator and D. A. Kendrick, 3–42. Amsterdam: North Holland Press.

Hurwicz, Leonid, David Schmeidler, and Hugo Sonnenschein, eds. 1985. *Social Goals and Social Organization: Essays in Memory of Elisha Pazner.* Cambridge: Cambridge University Press.

Hwang, Sung-Ha, and Samuel Bowles. 2012. "Is Altruism Bad for Cooperation?" *Journal of Economic Behavior and Organization* 83:340–41.

———. 2014. "Optimal Incentives with State-Dependent Preferences." *Journal of Public Economic Theory* 16, no. 5: 681–705.

———. 2016. "Incentives, Socialization, and Civic Preferences." Working paper, Santa Fe Institute.

Irlenbusch, Bernd, and G. K. Ruchala. 2008. "Relative Rewards within Team-Based Compensation." *Labour Economics* 15: 141–67.

Jones, Peter. 1989. "The Neutral State." In *Liberal Neutrality,* edited by Robert Goodin and Andrew Reeve, 9–38. London: Routledge.

Kahneman, Daniel. 1994. "New Challenges to the Rationality Assumption." *Journal of Institutional and Theoretical Economics* 150, no. 1: 18–36.

Kahneman, Daniel, Jack L. Knetsch, and Richard Thaler. 1986. "Fairness as a Constraint on Profit Seeking: Entitlements in the Market." *American Economic Review* 76:728–41.

Kahneman, Daniel, and Amos Tversky. 2000. *Choices, Values, and Frames.* Princeton, N.J.: Princeton University Press.

Kaminski, Juliane, Andrea Pitsch, and Michael Tomasello. 2013. "Dogs Steal in the Dark." *Animal Cognition* 16: 385–94.

Kocher, Martin, Todd Cherry, Stephan Kroll, Robert Netzer, and Matthias Sutter. 2008. "Conditional Cooperation on Three Continents." *Economic Letters* 101:175–78.

Kohn, Melvin L. 1969. *Class and Conformity.* Homewood, Ill.: Dorsey.

———. 1990. "Unresolved Issues in the Relationship between Work and Personality." In *The Nature of Work: Sociological Perspectives,* edited by Kai Erikson and Steven Peter Vallas, 36–68. New Haven, Conn.: Yale University Press.

Kohn, Melvin L., Atsushi Naoi, Carrie Schoenbach, Carmi Schooler, and Kazimierz Slomczynski. 1990. "Position in the Class Structure and Psychological Functioning in the U.S., Japan, and Poland." *American Journal of Sociology* 95, no. 4: 964–1008.

Kohn, Melvin L., and Carmi Schooler. 1983. *Work and Personality: An Inquiry into the Impact of Social Stratification.* Norwood, N.J.: Ablex.

Kollock, Peter. 1994. "The Emergence of Exchange Structures: An Experimental Study of Uncertainty, Commitment, and Trust." *American Journal of Sociology* 100, no. 2: 313–45.

Laffont, Jean Jacques. 2000. *Incentives and Political Economy.* Oxford: Oxford University Press.

Laffont, Jean Jacques, and Eric Maskin. 1979. "A Differentiable Approach to Expected Utility-Maximizing Mechanisms." In *Aggregation and Revelation of Preferences,* edited by Jean Jacques Laffont, 289–308. Amsterdam: North Holland.

Laffont, Jean Jacques, and Mohamed Salah Matoussi. 1995. "Moral Hazard, Financial Constraints, and Share Cropping in El Oulja." *Review of Economic Studies* 62, no. 3: 381–99.

Lanjouw, Peter, and Nicholas Stern, eds. 1998. *Economic Development in Palanpur over Five Decades.* Delhi: Oxford University Press.

Lazear, Edward. "Performance Pay and Productivity." 2000. *American Economic Review* 90, no. 5: 1346–61.

Ledyard, J. O. "Public Goods: A Survey of Experimental Research." In *The Handbook of Experimental Economics,* edited by A. E. Roth and J. Kagel, 111–94. Princeton, N.J.: Princeton University Press, 1995.

Lepper, Mark R., and David Greene. 1978. *The Hidden Costs of Reward: New Perspectives on the Psychology of Human Motivation.* Hillsdale, N.J.: Erlbaum.

Lepper, Mark R., David Greene, and Richard E. Nisbett. 1973. "Undermining Children's Intrinsic Interest with Extrinsic Reward: A Test of the 'Overjustification' Hypothesis." *Journal of Personality and Social Psychology* 28, no. 1: 129–37.

Lepper, Mark R., Gerald Sagotsky, Janet Defoe, and David Greene. 1982. "Consequences of Superfluous Social Constraints: Effects on Young Children's Social Inferences and Subsequent Intrinsic Interest." *Journal of Personality and Social Psychology* 42, no. 1: 51–65.

Levitt, Steven D., and John List. 2007. "What Do Laboratory Experiments Measuring Social Preferences Reveal about the Real Word." *Journal of Economic Perspectives* 21, no. 1: 153–74.

Li, Jian, Erte Xiao, Daniel Houser, and P. Read Montague. 2009. "Neural Responses to Sanction Threats in Two-Party Economic Exchanges." *Proceedings of the National Academy of Science* 106, no. 39: 16835–40.

Lipsey, Richard, and Kelvin Lancaster. 1956–57. "The General Theory of the Second Best." *Review of Economic Studies* 24, no. 1: 11–32.

Loewenstein, George, Ted O'Donoghue, and Bhatia Sudeep. 2015. "Modeling Interplay between Affect and Deliberation." *Decision* 2, no. 2: 55–81.

Loewenstein, George, and Deborah Small. 2007. "The Scarecrow and the Tin Man: The Vicissitudes of Human Suffering and Caring." *Review of General Psychology* 11, no. 2: 112–26.

Loewenstein, George, Leigh Thompson, and Max H. Bazerman. 1989. "Social Utility and Decision Making in Interpersonal Contexts." *Journal of Personality and Social Psychology* 57, no. 3: 426–41.

Lucas, Robert E., Jr. 1976. "Econometric Policy Evaluation: A Critique." *Carnegie-Rochester Conference Series on Public Policy* 1:19–46.

Machiavelli, Niccolò. 1984. *Discorsi sopra la Prema Deca Di Tito Livio.* Milan: Rizzoli. Orig. pub. 1513–17. Translations from this work are by the present author.

———. 1900. *Il Principe.* Edited by Giuseppe Lisio. Florence: Sansoni. Orig. circulated 1513. Translations from this work are by the present author.

Mahdi, Niloufer Qasim. 1986. "Pukhutunwali: Ostracism and Honor among Pathan Hill Tribes." *Ethology and Sociobiology* 7, no. 3–4: 295–304.

Mallon, Florencia E. 1983. *The Defense of Community in Peru's Central Highlands: Peasant Struggle and Capitalist Transition, 1860–1940.* Princeton, N.J.: Princeton University Press, 1983.

Mandeville, Bernard. 1924. *The Fable of the Bees, or Private Vices, Publick Benefits.* Oxford: Clarendon.

———. 1988a. "A Search into the Nature of Society." In *The Fable of the Bees,* edited by F. B Kaye, 323–70. Indianapolis: Liberty Fund.

———. 1988b. "A Vindication of the Book, from the Aspersions Contain'd in a Presentment of the Grand Jury of Middlesex." In *The Fable of the Bees,* edited by F. B Kaye, 381–412. Indianapolis: Liberty Fund.

Martin, Gerard, and Miguel Ceballos. 2004. *Bogota: Anatomia de una Transformacion: Politicas de Seguridad Ciudadana, 1995–2003.* Bogota: Editorial Pontificia Universidad Javeriana.

Marx, Karl. 1956. *The Poverty of Philosophy.* Moscow: Foreign Language Publishing House. Orig. pub. 1847.

Masclet, David, Charles Noussair, Steven Tucker, and Marie-Claire Villeval. 2003. "Monetary and Non-Monetary Punishment in the Voluntary Contributions Mechanism." *American Economic Review* 93, no. 1: 366–80.

Maskin, Eric. 1985. "The Theory of Implementation in Nash Equilibrium: A Survey." In *Social Goals and Social Organization: Essays in Memory of Elisha Pazner,* edited by Leonid Hurwicz, David Schmeidler and Hugo Sonnenschein, 173–341. Cambridge: Cambridge University Press.

Mellizo, Philip, Jeffrey Carpenter, and Peter Hans Matthews. 2014. "Workplace Democracy in the Lab." *Industrial Relations Journal* 45, no. 4: 313–28.

Mellstrom, Carl, and Magnus Johannesson. 2008. "Crowding Out in Blood Donation: Was Titmuss Right?" *Journal of the European Economic Association* 6, no. 4: 845–63.

Mill, John Stuart. 1844. *Essays on Some Unsettled Questions of Political Economy.* London: Parker.

Mockus, Antanas. 2002. "Coexistence as Harmonization of Law, Morality, and Culture." *Prospects* 32, no. 1: 19–37.

Montesquieu, Charles-Louis de Secondat, baron de. 1961. *L'esprit des Lois.* Paris: Garnier. Orig. pub. 1748.

New York Times. 1988. "Ban Greed? No: Harness It." Editorial. January 20.

Ober, Josiah. 2008. *Democracy and Knowledge: Innovation and Learning in Classical Athens.* Princeton, N.J.: Princeton University Press.

Ostrom, Elinor. 2000. "Crowding Out Citizenship." *Scandinavian Political Studies* 23, no. 1: 3–16.

———. 1990. *Governing the Commons: The Evolution of Institutions for Collective Action.* Cambridge: Cambridge University Press.

Ouchi, William. 1980. "Markets, Bureaucracies, and Clans." *Administrative Science Quarterly* 25:129–41.

Packard, David. 1995. *The HP Way: How Bill Hewlett and I Built Our Company*. New York: Collins.

Parsons, Talcott. 1967. *Sociological Theory and Modern Society*. New York: Free Press.

Rawls, John. 1971. *A Theory of Justice*. Cambridge: Harvard University Press.

Riano, Yvonne. 2011. "Addressing Urban Fear and Violence in Bogota through the Culture of Citizenship." In *Ethnicities: Metropolitan Cultures and Ethnic Identities in the Americas*, edited by Martin Butler, Jens Martin Gurr and Olaf Kaltmeier, 209–25. Tempe, Ariz.: Bilingual Review Press.

Rosenthal, Elisabeth. 2008. "Motivated by a Tax, Irish Spurn Plastic Bags." *New York Times*, February 2.

Ross, Lee, and Richard E. Nisbett. 1991. *The Person and the Situation: Perspectives of Social Psychology*. Philadelphia: Temple University Press.

Rousseau, Jean-Jacques. 1984. *"Of the Social Contract" and "Discourse on Political Economy."* Translated by Charles M. Sherover. New York: Harper and Row. Orig. pub. 1762.

Royal Swedish Academy of Sciences. 2007. "Mechanism Design Theory." Stockholm: Royal Swedish Academy of Sciences. Available at www.nobelprize.org/nobel_prizes/economic-sciences/laureates/2007/advanced-economicsciences2007.pdf.

Rustagi, Devesh, Stefanie Engel, and Michael Kosfeld. 2010. "Conditional Cooperation and Costly Monitoring Explain Success in Forest Commons Management." *Science* 330:961–65.

Sahlins, Marshall. 1974. *Stone Age Economics*. Chicago: Aldine.

Sandel, Michael. 2012. *What Money Can't Buy: The Moral Limits of Markets*. New York: Farrar, Straus and Giroux.

———. 2013. "Market Reasoning as Moral Reasoning: Why Economists Should Re-Engage with Political Philosophy." *Journal of Economic Perspectives* 27:121–40.

Sanfey, Alan, George Loewenstein, Samuel McClure, and Jonathan Cohen. 2006. "Neuroeconomics: Cross-Currents in Research on Decision-Making." *TRENDS in Cognitive Sciences* 10, no. 3: 108–16.

Sanfey, Alan, James Rilling, Jessica Aronson, Leigh Nystrom, and Jonathan Cohen. 2003. "The Neural Basis of Economic Decision-Making in the Ultimatum Game." *Science* 300:1755–58.

Satz, Debra. 2010. *Why Some Things Should Not Be for Sale: The Limits of Markets.* Oxford: Oxford University Press.

Schmitz, Hubert. 1999. "From Ascribed to Earned Trust in Exporting Clusters." *Journal of International Economics* 48:138–50.

Schnedler, Wendelin, and Radovan Vadovic. 2011. "Legitimacy of Control." *Journal of Economics and Management Strategy* 20, no. 4: 985–1009.

Schotter, Andrew, Avi Weiss, and Inigo Zapater. 1996. "Fairness and Survival in Ultimatum and Dictatorship Games." *Journal of Economic Behavior and Organization* 31, no. 1: 37–56.

Schultze, Charles L. 1977. *The Public Use of Private Interest.* Washington, D.C: Brookings Institution.

Schumpeter, Joseph. 1950. "The March into Socialism." *American Economic Review* 40, no. 2: 446–56.

Seabright, Paul. 2009. "Continuous Preferences and Discontinuous Choices: How Altruists Respond to Incentives." *BE Journal of Theoretical Economics* 9, article 14.

Shinada, Mizuhu, and Toshio Yamagishi. 2007. "Punishing Free Riders: Direct and Indirect Promotion of Cooperation." *Evolution and Human Behavior* 28:330–39.

Shu, Lisa, Francesca Gino, and Max H. Bazerman. 2011. "Dishonest Deed, Clear Conscience: Self-Preservation through Moral Disengagement and Motivated Forgetting." *Personality and Social Psychology Bulletin* 37, no. 3: 330–49.

Shubik, Martin. 1959. *Strategy and Market Structure: Competition, Oligopoly, and the Theory of Games.* New York: Wiley.

Skitka, Linda, Elizabeth Mullen, Thomas Griffin, Susan Hutchinson, and Brian Chamberlin. 2002. "Dispositions, Scripts, or Motivated Correction? Understanding Ideological Differences in Explanations for Social Problems." *Journal of Personality and Social Psychology* 83:470–87.

Small, Deborah, George Loewenstein, and Paul Slovic. 2007. "Sympathy and Callousness: The Impact of Deliberative Thought on Donations to Identifiable and Statistical Victims." *Organizational Behavior and Human Decision Processes* 102:143–53.

Smith, Adam. 1976a. *An Inquiry into the Nature and Causes of the Wealth of Nations.* Edited by R. H. Campbell and A. S. Skinner Oxford: Clarendon. Orig. pub. 1776.

———. 1976b. *Theory of Moral Sentiments.* Edited by D. D. Raphael and A. L. Macfie Oxford: Clarendon. Orig. pub. 1759.

———. 2010. *Lectures on Justice, Police, Revenue, and Arms.* Edited by Edwin Cannan Whitefish. Montana: Kessinger. Orig. pub. 1896.

Solow, Robert. 1971. "Blood and Thunder." *Yale Law Journal* 80, no. 8: 1696–711.

Spinoza, Benedict de. 1958. *The Political Works.* Edited and translated by A. G. Wernham Oxford: Clarendon.

Stout, Lynn. 2011. *Cultivating Conscience: How Good Laws Make Good People.* Princeton, N.J.: Princeton University Press.

Strauss, Leo. 1988. *What Is Political Philosophy?* Chicago: University of Chicago Press.

Tabellini, Guido. 2008. "Institutions and Culture." *Journal of the European Economic Association* 6, no. 2: 255–94.

Taylor, Michael. 1976. *Anarchy and Cooperation.* London: Wiley.

———. 1987. *The Possibility of Cooperation.* New York: Cambridge University Press.

Thaler, Richard, and Cass Sunstein. 2008. *Nudge: Improving Decisions about Health, Wealth, and Happiness.* New Haven, Conn.: Yale University Press.

Tilly, Charles. 1981. "Charivaris, Repertoires, and Urban Politics." In *French Cities in the Nineteenth Century,* edited by John M. Merriman, 73–91. New York: Holmes and Meier.

Times [London]. 2014. "Doctors Who Miss Cancer to Be Named." June 30.

Titmuss, Richard. 1971. *The Gift Relationship: From Human Blood to Social Policy.* New York: Pantheon.

Tonnies, Ferdinand. 1963. *Community and Society.* New York: Harper and Row.

Trivers, R. L. 1971. "The Evolution of Reciprocal Altruism." *Quarterly Review of Biology* 46:35–57.

Tversky, Amos, and Daniel Kahneman. 1981. "The Framing of Decisions and the Psychology of Choice." *Science* 211, no. 4481: 453–58.

Tyran, Jean-Robert, and Lars Feld. 2006. "Achieving Compliance When Legal Sanctions Are Non-Deterrent." *Scandinavian Journal of Economics* 108, no. 1: 135–56.

Upton, William Edward, III. 1974. "Altruism, Attribution, and Intrinsic Motivation in the Recruitment of Blood Donors." *Dissertation Abstracts International* 34, no. 12: 6260-B.

Voltaire. 1961. "Sur Les Presbyteriens." In *Melanges,* edited by Jacques van den Heuvel, 16–18. Paris: Gallimard, 1961.

Warneken, Felix, and Michael Tomasello. 2008. "Extrinsic Rewards Undermine Altruistic Tendencies in 20-Month-Olds." *Developmental Psychology* 44, no. 6: 1785–88.

Weber, Max. 1978. *Economy and Society: An Outline of Interpretive Sociology.* Berkeley: University of California Press. Orig. pub. 1922.

White, Brent. 2010. "Take This House and Shove It: The Emotional Drivers of Strategic Default." *SMU Law Review* 63: 1279–1318.

Wiessner, Polly. 2005. "Norm Enforcement among the Ju/'Hoansi Bushmen: A Case of Strong Reciprocity?" *Human Nature* 16, no. 2: 115–45.

Wilkinson-Ryan, Tess. 2010. "Do Liquidated Damages Encourage Efficient Breach: A Psychological Experiment." *Michigan Law Review* 108:1–43.

Woodburn, James. 1982. "Egalitarian Societies." *Man* 17:431–51.

Woodruff, Christopher. 1998. "Contract Enforcement and Trade Liberalization in Mexico's Footwear Industry." *World Development* 26, no. 6: 979–91.

World Bank. 2015. *The World Development Report: Mind, Society, and Behavior.* Washington D.C.: World Bank.

Wrzesniewski, Amy, Barry Schwartz, Xiangyu Cong, Michael Kane, Audrey Omar, and Thomas Kolditz. 2014. "Multiple Types of Motives Don't Multiply the Motivation of West Point Cadets." *Proceedings of the National Academy of Sciences of the United States of America* 111, no. 30, 10990–95.

Yamagishi, Toshio, Karen S. Cook, and Motoki Watabe. 1998. "Uncertainty, Trust, and Commitment Formation in the U.S. and Japan." *American Journal of Sociology* 104:165–94.

Yamagishi, Toshio, and Midori Yamagishi. 1994. "Trust and Commitment in the United States and Japan." *Motivation and Emotion* 18:9–66.

Yeung, King-To, and John Levi Martin. 2011. "The Looking Glass Self: An Empirical Test and Elaboration." *Social Forces* 93, no. 3: 843–79.

Zajonc, Robert B. 1968. "Attitudinal Effects of Mere Exposure." *Journal of Personality and Social Psychology Monograph Supplement* 9, no. 2, pt. 2: 1–27.

Zhong, Chen-Bo, Vanessa Bohns, and Francesca Gino. 2010. "Good Lamps Are the Best Police: Darkness Increases Dishonesty and Self-Interested Behavior." *Psychological Science* 21, no. 3: 311–14.

Index

Noah
walter